T. Ryle D

GW00734125

Charlie

The Political Biography of Charles J. Haughey

Gill and Macmillan

To Gina and Pat

Published in Ireland by
Gill and Macmillan Ltd
Goldenbridge
Dublin 8
with associated companies in
Auckland, Dallas, Delhi, Hong Kong,
Johannesburg, Lagos, London, Manzini,
Melbourne, Nairobi, New York, Singapore,
Tokyo, Washington
© T. Ryle Dwyer 1987
5   4   3   2   1
0   7171   1449   X
Print origination in Ireland by Wellset
Printed in Great Britain by
Richard Clay Ltd, Bungay, Suffolk

Other books by T. Ryle Dwyer
Irish Neutrality and the USA, 1939-47
Eamon de Valera (Gill's Irish Lives)
Michael Collins and the Treaty
De Valera's Darkest Hour: In Search of National Independence, 1917-1932
De Valera's Finest Hour: In Search of National Independence, 1932-1959

Contents

Preface

Preface

After completing my preliminary research on this book I made a conscious decision not to conduct any interviews but to base the study almost exclusively on material already on the public record. Throughout his thirty years in politics Charlie Haughey has cultivated a very high public profile and has been the subject of millions of words in print. What has not been printed is probably not worth writing, or else potentially so libellous that no publisher would dare handle it.

Haughey has given reporters his own version of the various events in which he has been involved. He testified on oath on two separate occasions about matters relating to the famous Arms Crisis. Since then he has refused to answer any further questions on the matter. It would be naive to expect that he would now say anything different about those events. Hence any interviews would not only be pointless but also potentially inhibiting because it would probably make it more difficult to achieve a detached sense of impartiality if one were indebted to him for giving up the necessary time for an interview. The same consideration also militated against seeking interviews with his opponents. They have undoubtedly said all they are about to say on the record for the time being, and it would be particularly unfair for a writer to allow himself to be influenced by anything derogatory they might have to say without being prepared to stand over their accusations.

As Haughey is still active in politics, this book is of necessity an interim look at his political career. My aim has been to examine the available evidence as fairly and dispassionately as possible and then to present a balanced, objective account so that readers can formulate their own interim assessment of the man's contribution to Irish political life.

I would like to thank Dick Spring for the loan of over one hundred volumes of the *Dáil Debates*. I would also like to gratefully acknowledge the help of the staff of the Kerry County Library, especially Michael Costello, as well as the staffs of the National Library of Ireland, Trinity College Library and Cork City Public Library. I would also like to express my appreciation to the cartoonists who have consented to allow their material to be reproduced, to my mother for reading the proofs, and finally I wish to thank Fergal Tobin for his editorial guidance and help.

TRD
Tralee

1
A Man with Real Charisma

The Background of a Politician

Irish Press, 31 January 1983

DURING a session of the New Ireland Forum in 1983 Charles J. Haughey was accused of having leaked details of the deliberations to the press. He was obviously stunned by the accusation. Having suffered so much at the hands of the press, he indignantly asked how anyone could believe that he, of all people, would do such a thing. Then, as members of the forum looked on in amazement, he burst into tears and began sobbing uncontrolledly.

Some months earlier he had been battling for his political life in the midst of a controversy in which the media had been whipped into a frenzy about irregularities concerning official taps placed on the telephones of two journalists and the supposed bugging of a conversation between a former minister and the Tánaiste (Deputy Prime Minister) of his short-lived government in 1982. Haughey denounced the taps and called for a judicial enquiry, but his call was ignored as his leadership became the focus of intense criticism. In response he accused the media of conspiring with his enemies to destroy him.

It was not the first time a Fianna Fáil leader accused the press of such bias. The party's founder, Eamon de Valera, felt so mistreated back in the 1920s and 1930s that he set up his own daily newspaper, the *Irish Press*. There can be little doubt that he had a legitimate grievance, especially during the civil war and its bitter aftermath when he was accused of being primarily responsible for causing the civil strife.

'We have arrested the man who called up anarchy and crime, and who did more damage than anyone could have conceived', the Minister for Justice, Kevin O'Higgins, charged following de Valera's arrest in August 1923. The government decided to bring charges against him 'with the least possible delay'.

De Valera would have welcomed a chance to clear his name in court but he was never given the opportunity, because the Attorney-General found that the only hard evidence of any purported misconduct was an inflammatory letter which de Valera wrote to the secretary of Cumann na mBan during the civil war. Having accused him of so much, the government would have become a laughing stock if it only charged him with inciting Cumann na mBan — of all organisations! Consequently no formal charges were ever preferred, but de Valera was still held without trial for the next eleven months.

In the following years de Valera challenged his political opponents to agree to an impartial historical commission to investigate the causes of the civil war, but the challenge was contemptuously ignored. Had the press bothered to examine the available evidence impartially, it would have realised that the more serious charges being made against de Valera were not being substantiated.

Like his predecessor, Haughey also suffered at the hands of his political opponents. All too often his critics have given no specific reasons for their hostility towards him; they just base their criticism on a vague evaluation of his whole career, as Garret FitzGerald did in his infamous 'flawed pedigree' speech in 1979. In view of the unfortunate historical precedent set in de Valera's case, there is a need to examine Haughey's political career in depth.

Charles James Haughey was born in Castlebar, Co. Mayo, on 16 September 1925, the third child of Commandant Johnny Haughey. Both his father and mother, the former Sarah McWilliams, were from Swartragh, Co. Derry in what had become Northern Ireland. The two of them were active in the republican movement during the war of independence.

Although a staunch republican, Johnny Haughey followed Michael Collins and served in the Free State army during the civil war of 1922-23. Over the years it would be conveniently forgotten by many people that the Treaty split which divided the independence movement and led to the civil war had little to do with the partition issue. Eamon de Valera, the republican leader, basically accepted the Treaty's partition clauses.

'We will take the same things as agreed on there [in the treaty],' he told a secret session of Dáil Éireann on 15 December 1921. 'Let us accept that, but put in a declaratory phrase which will safeguard our right.' In short, he was prepared to accept the *de facto* existence of partition but wished to assert a *de jure* claim to sovereignty over the whole island.

Michael Collins and his colleagues had signed the Treaty on behalf of all of Ireland, though they recognised the right of the people of the six northeastern counties to secede from the Irish Free State and retain the powers conferred by the Government of Ireland Act of 1920. However, if the Unionists chose to withdraw, a Boundary Commission was to be set up to redraw the border in line with the wishes of the inhabitants. In theory this could mean the transfer to Northern Ireland of unionist areas in counties Donegal, Cavan or Monaghan, but Collins was confident this would not happen because those areas were just pockets in a nationalist hinterland. What he confidently expected was the transfer to the Irish Free State of counties Fermanagh and Tyrone with their nationalist majorities, as well as the contiguous nationalist areas in counties Armagh, Down and Derry. This would have included the city of Derry and the southern halves of counties Armagh and Down. Northern Ireland then have been so mutilated that it would be unable to survive as an economic entity.

The British had resorted to partition rather than confront the armed minority concentrated in the Six Counties, and Collins was prepared to emulate the Unionists by arming northern nationalists. He hoped that Westminster would agree to re-partition rather than confront an armed minority in Northern Ireland. As the forces under Collins were furnished with British weapons, he secretly sent their existing weapons to republicans in the Six Counties. He also sent some 400 British rifles to Donegal with instructions for General Joseph Sweeney to hold the weapons for an emissary who turned out to be Johnny Haughey, who then brought the guns over the border.

Those who followed Collins were convinced he was determined to end partition, but he was killed in August 1922 and his successors lacked his militant determination. With the country discredited in international eyes by an idiotic civil war, the government felt unable to resist in 1925 when the Boundary Commission decided against transferring nationalist areas because, as Collins had argued, this would undermine partition. Thus the spirit of the 1921 Treaty was flagrantly violated and the rights of Northern nationalists ignored as they were compelled to live under a system they despised. Had Collins lived, would things have been different?

Followers of Collins who placed a high priority on ending partition became disillusioned as his successors virtually ignored the question following his death. Johnny Haughey quit the army in 1928 and moved to Sutton, Co. Dublin, before buying a farm in the vacinity of Dunshaughlin, Co. Meath, where Charlie, or Cathal as he was known to his family, began school.

While farming, however, Johnny developed multiple sclerosis. Unable to manage the farm properly, he sold it and the family moved to Belton Park Road, Dublin, in the early 1930s. With him sick and the family dependent on his army pension, supplemented by a small IRA pension awarded to his wife, things could not have been easy for the large family. Charlie had three brothers, Seán, Eoghan, and Pádraig, and three sisters, Maureen, Peggy, and Sheila.

After moving to Dublin, Charlie attended Schoil Mhuire

National School in Marino, where he demonstrated a high scholastic and athletic ability. He played on the school's football and hurling teams and finished in first place in the Dublin Corporation's scholarship examination. His memory of those early years were of playing football and hurling, collecting birds' eggs, and going to movies when he had the money.

'Cowboy films were the big deal,' he recalled. 'People like Gene Autry and things like that.' He spent 'a lot of his summer holidays' with his grandmother in Northern Ireland. 'It was a small farm and I got a very good insight there of life on a small farm and of the social life and economics of small farming,' he explained. 'And I also got a very clear impression of the community situation in Northern Ireland — how the Catholic small farmers viewed their Protestant neighbours and how they lived with them.'

From Scoil Mhuire he went on to St Joseph's Christian Brothers School, Fairview, where he was again a brilliant student and outstanding athlete. He mastered subjects with apparent ease and was usually first in his class in every subject. His classmates included Harry Boland, with whom he later went into business, and George Colley, with whom he would eventually develop a bitter political rivalry. In his final year at St Joseph's he not only won a County Council Scholarship to University College, Dublin (UCD), but also achieved the distinction of being selected to represent the Leinster colleges in both football and hurling. As a result his memories of his years with the Irish Christian Brothers were not as painful as those of some of his contemporaries.

'I liked school,' he recalled. 'By and large the games at school made up for the less attractive side of it. If you did something awful or outrageous, you got the leather, but it certainly left no scars on me.'

Haughey's teenage years spanned a particularly turbulent period on the international scene. The Second World War erupted the month before his thirteenth birthday and did not end until the month before his twentieth. 'When I was a teenager, the war was on, so the whole environment was totally different', he remembered. 'The whole country was down to subsistence level.' There was extensive rationing and private motor cars virtually vanished from the roads, with the result

5

that movement was severely restricted and opportunities for foreign travel practically eliminated. 'The big thing,' he noted, 'was the number of one's friends that went off to join the British army because there was no work. You either joined the Irish army or the British army.'

Haughey never had any interest in the British army, which was hardly surprising in view of his family background, especially when one of his uncles, Pat McWilliams, was interned in Northern Ireland for the duration of the war. Then, towards the end of his first year at UCD, Haughey was involved in an incident which received international publicity.

The incident occurred on 7 May 1945 following the announcement that Germany would formally surrender next day. Celebrating the news, a group of students at Trinity College, which was still widely identified as an anglophile institution, began flying the allied flags from the flagpole on the roof of the entrance to the college in the heart of the city. When people on the street took exception to the Irish tricolour being flown beneath the other flags, the Trinity students responded by taking down the Irish flag and trying to burn it.

On hearing what had happened a group of UCD students organised a counter-demonstration. With some demonstrators carrying Nazi flags they marched on Trinity College. Outside the entrance, the scene of the earlier incident, Haughey produced a Union Jack and he and a colleague proceeded to burn it. What had started out in fairly good humour turned very ugly and a riot ensued as the police baton-charged the gathering. Some of the crowd broke away and later stoned the residence of the British representative and the offices of the United States Consul-General.

During his time at UCD Haughey took an active part in student affairs and the social life of the college. Among the girls he dated was Maureen Lemass, whom he married in 1951, and also Joan O'Farrell, who later married a fellow student, Garret FitzGerald. The two young men knew each other in college but were never friends.

Professor Paddy McGilligan later contended that young Haughey was involved in Fine Gael circles, which would hardly have been surprising in view of his father's service during the civil war. But Haughey vehemently denied that he was 'at any

6

time a member, supporter or admirer of, or in any way associated with either Cumann na nGaedheal or Fine Gael.' At the time two of Haughey's closer friends were Harry Boland and George Colley, both sons of Fianna Fáil deputies. He was apparently attracted to the party, but did not join until 1948, the year following his father's death.

After receiving a Bachelor of Commerce degree Haughey went to work for the accounting firm of Boland, Burke and Company, along with Harry Boland, who was a brother of one of the principals of the firm. Both did their accounting examinations, and Haughey got through at the first try. He also studied for the Bar at King's Inns, but apparently his primary interests were elsewhere because, while he did get called to the Bar in 1949, he came at the tail end of his class and never practised. Instead he formed a partnership with Harry Boland in 1951 and they set up their own accounting business, Haughey, Boland and Company Ltd.

Haughey kept irregular hours at the office as he concentrated on drumming up business for the firm with some free spending socialising. He was particularly active in the Gaelic Athletic Association. Standing little over five feet six inches in height, he normally played in the half-forward line, where he was noted for his tenacious play and quick temper. On one occasion he was suspended for a year after striking a linesman. He won a county championship football medal with Parnells, while his brother Pádraig (Jock) was a member of the famous Dublin football team of the 1950s. Charlie was also very active as an officer in the FCA, a kind of Home Guard, where he first made friends with Des Francis and Pat O'Connor.

By then he had already shown a keen interest in politics. He first became involved with Fianna Fáil in helping with postering for the Boland and Colley families in the general election of 1948. He formally joined the party that year and was elected secretary of a Fairview cumann. In 1951 he received a Fianna Fáil nomination to run for the Dáil in that year's general election but, even though he was shortly to marry the daughter of Seán Lemass, the heir apparent to the Fianna Fáil leadership, he fared dismally at the polls, finishing last of his party four candidates with only 1,629 first-preference votes.

At the age of twenty-seven he was co-opted to fill a Fianna

Fáil vacancy on Dublin Corporation, but he again failed miserably and lost his deposit for the second time when he ran for the Dáil in the general election of 1954. He again finished last of his party's four candidates with only a slight improvement in his vote. In the aftermath of the Fianna Fáil defeat in this election, Lemass was charged with reorganising the party and he picked Haughey and a number of active young men like George Colley, Brian Lenihan, and Eoin Ryan to help travel to party cumainn throughout the country.

Then, although Eugene Timmons — the party's other unsuccessful candidate in Dublin North East — had finished ahead of Haughey in the previous two general elections, Haughey nevertheless got the party's nomination for the by-election in 1956 to fill a vacancy caused by the death of the colourful independent, Alfie Byrne. This time he lost out to Byrne's son, but as his party's only standard bearer he made a credible showing and finally managed to win election to the Dáil at his fourth try in the general election of 1957, when Fianna Fáil had a landslide victory.

Following his election Haughey promptly adopted a professional approach towards the communications media. He tried to employ the gossip columnist Terry O'Sullivan as a personal public relations officer, but O'Sullivan declined, so he hired Tony Grey of the *Irish Times*. In his early years in politics therefore he projected a high public profile and enjoyed a good press. But he was quiet about his own private life and especially his business dealings. He quickly amassed a considerable fortune at a time when politics was not a particularly well paid profession. In 1960 he bought Grangemore, a large Victorian mansion on a 45-acre site in Raheny in north Dublin. He reportedly paid around £50,000 and sold it before the end of the decade for over four times that amount after planning permission had been granted to build houses on the land. In the meantime he managed to buy a farm in Ashbourne, Co. Meath, purchased a chicken hatchery, some race horses, and bought Innishvicillaun — one of the Blasket Islands, some ten miles off the coast of Kerry.

In 1969 Haughey bought Abbeyville in Kinsealy, Co. Dublin. This fine eighteenth-century mansion had served as a summer home for several lord lieutenants of Ireland prior to the government's acquisition of the Viceregal Lodge (now Aras an Uachtaráin). Abbeyville was designed by the renowned architect, James Gandon, whose more famous works included the Custom House and Four Courts in Dublin. Haughey, his wife, and four children, Eimear, Conor, Ciarán and Seán, who were all born between 1955 and 1961, moved into the house. The 250-acre estate contained some of the finest gardens in the Dublin area, and Haughey sought to develop part of the property into a wildlife preserve and set up a stud farm on the grounds.

By then Haughey's political career had taken off. In 1959 Seán Lemass took over as Taoiseach and Haughey, as his son-in-law, was quickly singled out as a likely successor. He promptly became the victim of what one admirer would later describe as 'the Fine Gael Rumour Machine.' An endless stream of unflattering rumours began to flow about Haughey's private life and business dealings.

'Now to be a wealthy politician was the sin of the day — and Charlie Haughey was indecently wealthy,' according to that admirer, the columnist John Healy. 'If a pub changed hands, Haughey was the secret buyer.' At one point he supposedly owned about five public houses on the north and south sides of Dublin. His amorous activities, both real and imagined, were also the subject of much public speculation. 'There were enough rumours about him to form a legend of sorts,' according to Conor Cruise O'Brien.

Haughey would later state that his own great regret in life was that he was born too early for permissive era. 'To my dying day,' he said, 'I'll regret that I was too late for the free society! We missed out on that! It came too late for my generation!'

Looking back he felt there was too much authority both in the home and on the streets during his younger days. 'My mother knew what was best for me, and told me what to do, and what not to do, and insisted that I did or didn't do it,' he explained. Likewise on the streets he noted that people were afraid of the police. 'In my day,' he said, 'if a guard said to you "fuck off", you fucked off as quick as you could!'

It was not really that he did that much out of the way. 'We only saw a policeman when he came to stop us playing football on the road,' he noted. 'Of course we robbed orchards and things like that'. He also admitted that he 'always had a hidden desire to do something like 'knocking off' an expensive car, but there were almost no cars on the roads when he was a teenager.

As a parent he adopted a less authoritarian approach with his own children. 'I think we were much more understanding and sympathetic to our children than our parents were to us', he said. 'We certainly trusted them far more.'

Eimear grew up to take charge of his stud, while the oldest son Conor qualified as a mining engineer. Ciarán took over the Celtic Helicopter firm, while the youngest, Seán, has entered politics. Although most prominent Irish politicians seemed to leave the country during their summer vacations, Haughey remained in Ireland and took his holidays on Innishvicillaun, where he could be closer to his family and get away from the hussle and bussle of politics and city life.

'The main attraction of the island, apart from its natural beauty, and the wildness of it, is that we're more of a family down there,' he explained. 'Fortunately, the kids and the wife like it as much as I do. It's as much their place as mine. I really got to know my kids better down there; in Dublin we're always coming and going. We meet tangentially, coming in and going out in the hall. But down there we're together, and we share experiences together.'

Over the years Haughey has assiduously patronised the arts, both by introducing legislation to help writers and artists and by adorning his home and grounds with sculptures and paintings by Irish artists. 'He was an aristocrat in the proper sense of the word; not a nobleman or even a gentleman, but one who believed in the right of the best people to rule, and that he himself was the best of the best people', Cruise O'Brien wrote in 1972 at a particularly low point in Haughey's political career. The writer's use of the past tense betrayed a rather premature tendency to write off politically the man from Kinsealy. 'People liked him', Cruise O'Brien continued, 'not for the possession of any of the more obviously likeable qualities, but for lending some colour to life in a particularly drab period.'

Opponents often charged Haughey with arrogance and even with incompetence, but nobody ever accused him of being dull. By the end of the sixties he was unquestionably one of the most influential politicians in the country, but then things turned sour in 1970. He was dismissed from the government and subsequently charged with conspiring to import arms illegally for the use of the IRA in Northern Ireland. Although he beat the charges in court, he had an uphill struggle to regain his political standing. In the circumstances it was an achievement for Haughey just to survive politically but he did much more. By 1977 he was back in government as Minister for Health and Social Welfare. In that year the polls indicated he was deeply distrusted by the Irish public. Indeed, of the front bench members of his his party, he was rated as the one that most people would least like to see as Taoiseach, yet before the decade was over, he was Taoiseach.

'Coming to terms with Charlie Haughey is like making your confirmation or losing your virginity,' according to Anne Harris, who described him as 'the acceptable face of fantasy'. Over the years he has provided inspiration for Irish people wishing to fantasise about money, power and the good life. As such he fulfils much the same role as the royal family in Britain, with the result that he is a particular favourite with women.

'Haughey is all things to all women without necessarily having to do anything to any of them,' Harris continued. 'He has a way with women. Young women and matrons alike ache for him.' She compared him to Alexis, the character played by Joan Collins in the popular soap-opera, *Dynasty*. 'They both share a taste for champagne, a passion for power. And they both command a compelling awe.'

He is a man with *charisma* in the true sense. This much abused word has often been confused with charm or popularity by political commentators. Nevertheless a politician with charisma in the proper sense of the word must possess more than popularity and charm. One of the essential dimensions of charismatic political leadership is that followers must believe 'their leader to have superhuman qualities'. Probably only three Irish politicians in twentieth century could therefore be described as possessing real charisma — Eamon de Valera, Michael Collins, and Charlie Haughey. In the latter's case the elusive superhuman quality has been manifested in his extraordinary ability to survive.

Before his election to the Dáil in 1957 he had to survive not only two dismal showings in general elections, failure to retain the seat to which he was co-opted on Dublin Corporation, as

11

well as a by-election defeat. While Minister for Justice he overcame a near mutiny within the police in 1961, survived a virtual revolt by farmers as Minister for Agriculture in 1966, and overcame his dismissal as Minister for Finance and the subsequent gun-running charges to stage a dramatic recovery and be elected Taoiseach during the 1970s. Then in the early 1980s he had to survive three different challenges to his leadership of Fianna Fáil. On the third occasion he was written off by virtually the whole media. The *Irish Press* took the extraordinary step of publishing what amounted to his political obituary, and bookmakers made the mistake of offering odds on the selection of his successor without taking the possibility of his survival into account. Yet he again survived. Afterwards one writer noted that his critics would probably wait for three days after Haughey's death before reporting the event — just in case!

Haughey admitted to being fascinated by politics and being lured into political life by two different considerations. There was his wish to get things done and what he said in sporting terms has been called 'the roar of the crowd.'

'I think it's only worthwhile and can only justify all the disadvantages and the unpleasantness if you can positively achieve things and have a say, a real say in the world around you', he contended. 'What politics should be about is making the world a better place for those you serve.' In short he wanted to do things for people because he enjoys the acclamation of the crowd.

'One of the absolute things that can be said about Charles Haughey is this,' the *Irish Times* noted in a 1969 profile: 'he is a man who wants power. He has everything else.' But he pursued his ambition with such a singlemindedness that many people found his quest for power disconcerting. 'Ambition,' the *Irish Times* continued, 'is a trait we admire in people. Yet when we isolate it in a politician and recognise it, we tend to resent it as an indecency.'

Haughey candidly admitted that he sought election to the Dáil because the power to shape things was to be found there. The primary duty of deputies is to legislate, and in this area he has excelled. He has enjoyed the cut and thrust of debate, together with the tactics and diplomacy required to steer bills through the Oireachtas (Parliament). But above all, as he said himself, he has relished 'the intricacies that are involved in providing good, sound legislation.' Piloting legislation requires enormous patience and extraordinary attention to detail because bills are meticulously examined, often by opposition deputies whose only aim is to embarrass the minister responsible for the legislation. As Minister for Justice, in particular, Haughey introduced a phenomenal amount of legislation as he sought to update the country's legal system. Covering this period even in a cursory way tends to make tedious reading but it gives an insight into the great patience of a man who is better known for his short temper.

This is only one of the many apparent contradictions in the character of this extraordinary individual who is held up by some as the prototype of the uncaring capitalist, yet who can and does point to evidence he had demonstrated of social concern in the various departments in which he has served. He contends that he was particularly concerned in each department 'to make sure that whatever progress was achieved was distributed to the greatest possible extent and as fairly as possible to those who needed it.' Having grown up in a family that was dependent on his father's pension, he has introduced some imaginative schemes to help pensioners, such as the free travel, free electricity and free telephones.

Tending to dismiss such measures as gimmicks to curry popularity, some critics have charged that he would do almost anything to win votes. 'No one will dispute,' the playwright Hugh Leonard once wrote, 'that to catch a vote Mr Haughey would unhesitatingly roller-skate backwards into a nunnery, naked from the waist down and singing *Kevin Barry* in Swahili.' Yet for Haughey, pleasing the people is the very essence of representative democracy.

He has been prepared to help people and be generous even when there was no political advantage to be gained. For instance, after learning that a German crew had spent some days on Innishvicillaun following the crash of their bomber off the island in November 1940 he traced the five airmen and invited them to the island. In fact, he gave them his house and the run of Innishvicillaun for a fortnight in the summer of 1980. There was certainly no political advantage to be gained from this because none of the men had votes in Ireland and, in any event, their visit was never publicised.

This side of Haughey's character has not generally been recognised, except by those who know him. It helps to explain his enormous popularity among his own constituents. Despite his early difficulties in getting elected to the Dáil he has been returned at the head of the poll in every general election since then.

'I have a perfectly good relationship with my people, my constituency,' he explained to one interviewer. 'They know me. I know they trust me and I think they like me. They don't think I'm a bad person or am out to do anything detrimental to them or their interests. And *that's* what matters. That is the compensation for when you read something in the paper that you know is unfair — grossly unfair — and wrong. And when that happens you're inclined to get outraged and angry and upset about it.

'I could instance a load of fuckers whose throats I'd cut and push over the nearest cliff', he told the interviewer. In particular he singled out the smug, knowall commentators who pontificate. 'They'll say something today and they're totally wrong about it — completely wrong — and they're shown to be wrong about it. Then the next day they're back, pontificating the same as ever', he said. 'I suppose if anything annoys me, that annoys me.'

Those people that Haughey likes get sworn at ribaldly with no expletives deleted. He is intensely loyal to his friends, even to a point of leaving himself wide open to the charge of violating the public trust in appointing people to offices for which they are unsuited. Indeed, he seemed to admit that he may have carried his loyalty too far. 'I am perhaps a little sentimental or romantic in my loyalties to people,' he acknowledged. But in return he has demanded an unwavering personal loyalty and has tended to regard any questioning of his motives or actions as a betrayal.

At times Haughey seems almost paranoid in his suspicions of the media and as a result grants comparatively few interviews. On occasions on which he has been surprised by reporters coming up to him unexpectedly he has made some unguarded comments which he would probably not have made if he had realised he was going to be quoted in the press. In the autumn of 1982, for example, a reporter approached him and identified himself as being attached to the *Irish Times*. Haughey promptly betrayed his apparent annoyance at some recent editorials.

'Who writes the *Irish Times* editorials, anyway?' he asked. 'They read like they have been done by an old woman sitting in a bath with the water getting cold around her fanny!'

Normally before an interview his aide, P. J. Mara, warns the interviewer not to ask 'the Boss' questions about his private business affairs or the arms crisis. As Mara so graphically put it to one interviewer: 'No oul' Arms Trial shite now!'

This then is the story of the political career of Charles J. Haughey, 'Arms Trial shite' and all.

2
The Young Lochinvar

Backbencher and Parliamentary Secretary
1957-61

Dublin Opinion, July 1961

WHEN Haughey entered the Dáil the leadership of Fianna Fáil
was still heavily dominated by the old guard of the party. The
Taoiseach, Eamon de Valera, and eight of his eleven ministers
had been founding members thirty years earlier. The exceptions
were Jack Lynch, Neil Blaney and Kevin Boland. It was a party
where bright young men were soon going to get their opportunities. The old guard could not last for ever.

There were a number of extremely bright and able young
men beginning to make reputations for themselves in the party.
Brian Lenihan, Patrick Hillery, Donogh O'Malley and George
Colley were all contemporaries of Haughey.

Clearly in a hurry to make his mark in politics, Haughey waited less than two months to deliver his maiden speech in the Dáil during the debate on the budget. He suggested the new government should follow the example of Northern Ireland in constructing factory buildings for lease to industrialists. This plan, which would help both to promote the establishment of new factories, and to assist the recovery of the heavily depressed building industry, foreshadowed the practice later adopted by the Industrial Development Authority.

Haughey was unambiguously capitalist in his approach. Profit motivation formed the central theme of his economic philosophy. 'The trouble with this country is that too many people are making insufficient profits,' he told the Dáil in his maiden address. 'It would be well for this country from every point of view and particularly from the point of view of the weaker sections of the community if our industrialists were put in a position where they could make adequate profits which would ensure their continuation in business and their being able to finance further expansion.' His message was simple. He argued that enhanced profits would give industry the incentive to expand, thereby providing employment for the less well off in society.

'Once and for all, let us get rid of this cant that there is something illegal, immoral or wrong in profits,' he declared. He suggested research and development could be encouraged by exempting from income tax the royalties earned by inventors. Complaining that the Finance Bill of 1959 only allowed inventors to spread their earnings over six years, he called for a total exemption. 'In spite of our economy, one of the things we need today is to encourage productivity in every possible way,' he explained. 'We should be trying to encourage inventors, people who have technical skill and know-how, to bring forth inventions which will help our industry.' Arguing that the amount of money involved would be insubstantial and 'not be of any significance' in relation to the overall revenue needed by the government,' he called on the Minister for Finance to adopt his suggestion. His comments foreshadowed his own conduct as Minister for Finance in the following decade.

Pro-capitalist he certainly was, but he was no monetarist, content to leave everything to market forces. He believed in state involvement and state investment, especially to modernise native industries like agriculture and fisheries. In only his second address to the Dáil, for example, Haughey complained the state was making 'a very pathetic investment' in fisheries, which he believed were 'capable of giving such a tremendous return.' He advocated that *An Bord Iascaigh Mhara* should expand its involvement to research, education and training. He contended that virtually everything needed for this could be provided within the country, with the exception of engines. There was a plentiful supply of fish off the coast while modernisation of the fishing industry would provide employment in boat building, harbour reconstruction, and fish processing. Consequently he called for the formulation of a 'long term plan to contemplate a far greater volume of investment in the industry'.

He admitted to knowing 'very little about agriculture,' but this did not stop him speaking on the subject. In the debate on the bill to establish the Agricultural Institute, for instance, he talked forcefully about the need for agricultural research, which he said should 'be broadened to include market research on a world wide scale for Irish agriculture. Possibly the biggest problem facing Irish agriculture and our national economy,' he contended, 'is not so much the necessity for an increase in agricultural production as the means to sell that production when it is produced.' Once again, his main point was that a proper profit incentive did not exist. 'It has always been clear to me that if the Irish farmer is given a price for his products, he will embarrass you with his production.'

Young, highly educated and enthusiastic, Haughey attracted attention as a man of the future. By repeatedly calling for more research and development, he was basically advocating change and modernisation, and this marked him off from the conservative orthodoxy of his party elders.

He spoke in the Dáil with all the confidence and brashness of youth as he took on opposition spokesmen and even dared to advise ministers from his own party. But from his earliest days in the Dáil, he exhibited a characteristic which did not diminish with age: a habit of becoming personal when challenged. On one occasion he queried figures cited by the Fine Gael leader, James Dillon, whom he accused of being a better orator than mathemathican. When Dillon referred to his long years of experience in the Dáil, Haughey retorted: 'It is not for me to suggest that the deputy may have gone a little senile.' Although an inexperienced backbencher, he was not afraid to debate with Dillon, who was one of the greatest orators ever to sit in Dáil Éireann. He not only took on Dillon, but he sometimes got the better of him and won the respect of the Fine Gael leader, at least for a time.

During a debate in June 1957, for instance, Dillon admitted that as Minister for Agriculture and Fisheries a few years earlier, he had been advised to scrap some boats. Even though he knew this would be the best course, he decided against it because Fianna Fáil would make political capital out of his decision.

'It was a lack of moral courage on your part,' Haughey interjected. Not many people ever got away with accusing James Dillon of a lack of moral courage.

At times, he could become quite waspish with opponents. His sarcastic sense of humour often provoked a bitter response from across the floor and, in turn, exposed not only his own inability to accept criticism gracefully but also his viperish ability to counter-attack.

One of the earliest such incidents involved veiled aspersions from the Fine Gael benches about his character and friends. It occurred in April 1959 during a debate on estimates for the Department of Justice. The Fine Gael deputy, Oliver J. Flanagan, was complaining about some unsolved murders that had been committed in his constituency.

'Maybe you did them yourself,' Haughey chipped in sarcastically.

'I will leave that to Deputy Haughey's friends,' Flanagan replied. 'He does not have to go outside a very wide circle.'

There followed some exchanges when Flanagan tried to argue that 'political crime is one thing; cold-blooded murder and robbery is another.' Haughey contended that this implied condoning political murder, and the two deputies accused each other of advocating 'mob rule.'

'I should be glad,' Flanagan said, 'if Deputy Haughey would get up and let us hear the speech he would make in favour of the robbers, thieves and plunderers.'

'And perjurers,' Haughey interjected pointedly.

'I hope,' Flanagan continued, seething with indignation, 'I

19

have got a sense of humour, but sometimes my sense of humour is inclined to explode. I know Deputy Haughey and members of his family maybe a little too well to say the things I might be provoked to say but, if I say them in the course of the debate, no matter how hurtful they may be, I hope Deputy Haughey will accept them in the spirit in which I accept the ugly remarks he made now. I shall show the Deputy; if he opens his mouth again, I shall tell him something he and his family will not like to hear.'

The acting speaker, who had already called Haughey to order a number of times during this slanging-match, now intervened again, this time to point out that Haughey's family had nothing to do with the business of the house and the whole unseemly business was mercifully concluded.

Behind Haughey's brash youthful confidence there was a competence which belied his parliamentary inexperience as he took on opposition spokesmen and even dared to advise his own ministers. When it came to some new measures for income tax relief in the budget of 1959, for instance, Finance Minister Jim Ryan admitted Haughey had a 'better grip of it' than himself. It was not long therefore before he was being considered for higher office. The fact that his father-in-law — Seán Lemass — succeeded de Valera as Taoiseach in 1959 certainly did not hurt Haughey's political prospects.

With Oscar Traynor, the Minister for Justice, ailing and no longer able to keep up with the full workload of his department, Lemass suggested that a Parliamentary Secretary be appointed to assist him. Traynor submitted a list of four potential candidates suggested by his Department. The first of those refused the job and the other three were rejected by the Taoiseach. Haughey was nominated instead.

There is confusion over who actually suggested Haughey. According to some accounts it was Lemass, but others contend it came from within the cabinet and that the Taoiseach only reluctantly agreed to offer the post to his son-in-law. In any case Traynor was bitterly opposed to the appointment. He and Haughey were from the same constituency and their election rivalry had clearly cut deeply. Traynor told Peter Berry, then Assistant Secretary of the Department for Justice, that the Taoiseach had predicted Haughey would probably reject the post because it would interfere with his efforts to build up his expanding practice as a chartered accountant. According to Haughey, Lemass actually advised him not to take the post.

'As Taoiseach,' Lemass said to him, 'it is my duty to offer you the post of Parliamentary Secretary and as your father-in-law I am advising you not to take it.'

'I was an accountant at the time and doing fairly well and I think he was sounding a warning,' Haughey recalled. 'Look,' he thought the Taoiseach was trying to tell him, 'politics is a most uncertain career and if you want to look after my daughter the way she should be looked after, you'd better stick to your accountancy.'

But there was no doubt in Haughey's mind about what he should do. 'I never had any hesitation about taking the job,' he explained. 'I think I told him I'd think it over, but I came back next day and said I'd take it.'

Ever since entering politics he had been determined to make a career of it, so he was not about to turn down an opportunity of advancement. He admitted 'a Parliamentary Secretary in those days was not a very important office,' but he did not care about the trappings of office, he wanted power and this was a step closer to the real thing.

Traynor was particularly unhappy about the appointment. 'If he had the remotest idea that he would be saddled with Deputy Haughey he would have turned down the offer in the first instance,' according to Berry. But there seemed to be no legitimate grounds for opposing the selection of Haughey. 'I knew from mutual acquaintances,' Berry wrote, 'that he was regarded as a first-class intelligence with initiative, application and tenacity.'

The Minister for Justice was unable to refer to a specific reason why Haughey should not be appointed, but he clearly harboured deep reservations about the appointee's suitability for higher office. Such reservations, which were shared by others at the time, would be expressed repeatedly throughout Haughey's career, but no specific reasons would ever be given, except for murky insinuations about his character or friends.

'Mr Traynor told me,' Berry wrote, 'that his misgivings were shared by my former Minister, Mr Gerald Boland, and other senior Ministers.' Gerry Boland, whose son, Harry, was still in partnership with Haughey in the accounting firm, expressed his personal disapproval to Berry 'more than once in earlier years'.

Lemass announced Haughey's appointment in the Dáil on 9 May 1960. It would undoubtedly have been the subject of debate had not the standing rules of the house precluded discussion on the appointment of Parliamentary Secretaries. The Fine Gael leader meekly accepted the decision when the speaker ruled out any debate. Thus, Haughey's initial elevation to office passed without Dáil comment.

During his tenure as Parliamentary Secretary, he sought work which he could process without referring to Traynor, who was reluctant to hand over such responsibility. This led to some friction.

'Throughout 1961,' Berry recalled, 'the Minister expressed uneasiness about his working arrangements with the Parliamentary Secretary whom he felt was undermining him both in his constituency and in the parliamentary party.' Basically Haughey took over Traynor's duties piloting legislation through the Dáil, while the Minister concentrated on administrative matters connected with the Department of Justice.

In accordance with Oireachtas procedure, the first stage in the enactment of legislation consisted of securing permission to introduce a bill, which would then be published without debate. The second stage comprised a general debate on the bill. Haughey would outline the measure in a general way, emphasising its important features. Other deputies would then have the chance to comment on it, and he would wind up the discussion, usually by responding to some of the general points made by the other deputies. The third step, or committee stage, involved a detailed examination in which Haughey would take the house through every aspect of the bill piece by piece. At this stage deputies could make specific suggestions to improve the bill. Frequently their suggestions would just be verbal changes which Haughey could accept without resorting to a formal vote of the house. Other suggestions might be taken under advisement. The Dáil would then await any Senate amendments, which would be taken up at the fourth, or report stage. Unless the bill had to be referred to the Senate again, it would clear the house with the completion of the report stage, and it would be deemed an Act once signed into law by the President.

At the time of Haughey's appointment some bills had already been introduced and had had their first reading, but Traynor had been unable to take them any further. Thus the new parliamentary Secretary piloted five different bills from the second stage right through to their enactment. Those were the Solicitors (Amendment) Bill, 1960; Charities Bill, 1957; Rent Restrictions Bill, 1960: Civil Liability Bill, 1960; and the Defamation Bill, 1961.

Some of these were very complicated pieces of legislation, while others were fairly straightforward and uncontentious. For instance, the Defamation Bill, the second stage of which was only moved on 3 May 1961, was passed into law before the summer recess. It was largely a composite bill in which various old acts of the Westminster parliament — such as the Libel Acts of 1843 and 1845, the Law of Libel Amendment Act of 1889, and the Slander of Women Act of 1891 — were all re-enacted in a single Irish statute with only very slight modifications. John A. Costello, the former Taoiseach, voiced his 'complete approval' of the bill, so it had an easy passage through the Oireachtas, as did the Solicitors (Amendment) Bill. But the Rent Restrictions Bill was highly technical and very complicated. One deputy noted that only lawyers participated in its debate 'because no one else could understand it.'

The most important feature of the bill was a provision allowing landlords to increase controlled rents by 12.5 per cent. Having remained static since 1926, these rents were seen as a disincentive to providing rented accomodation. By allowing rent increases Haughey hoped the profit incentive would encourage landlords to make flats in old houses and thereby provide much needed rental accomodation. The legislation, which he emphasised was designed 'to procure the maximum amount of decontrol, consistent with the avoidance of any hardship to tenants', contributed to Haughey's growing reputation as a friend of the property developers.

When Declan Costello tried to have houses of less than a certain valuation exempted from the increase in order to protect the poor, Haughey rejected the move by contending it would be better to cope with this under social legislation, such as by increasing the old age pension. He also rejected a Fine Gael suggestion calling for fair rent courts, which he contended would simply create a lawyers' paradise.

Although a qualified lawyer himself, Haughey could never be

...mplicating the legal system for the benefit of the
...ead, he worked to simplify the system both for the
... legal practitioners, especially after he became
...ustice in 1961. But this desire for simplification was
...e he was still a Parliamentary Secretary.

...l Liability Bill, for instance, was another piece of
...d legislation which was largely aimed at simplifying
legal p... edures in order to cut down on the amount of litigation
by ensuring that 'all matters of liability' arising out of a particular case would be heard in one action, except in very unusual
cases. The Charities Bill, 1957 was another complicated piece of
legislation. First drafted back in 1954, it ran into difficulty over
its definition of 'charitable purposes.' A new bill was drafted
omitting any definition of 'charitable purposes', and it was
introduced in the Dáil in July 1957 but lay dormant until
rescued by Haughey, who moved its second stage in November
1960. From the political standpoint the bill was not very con-
tentious because it had basically been drafted during the life of
the previous coalition government. Thus the opposition was
largely responsible for it and could hardly be very critical of its
own work. Nevertheless, James Dillon and Haughey did argue
over the retention of the existing practice of allowing a member
of the Commissioners of Charitable Donations and Bequests to
sit on the bench. After all, Haughey noted, this practice had
been followed for 100 years.

'Is that not a lovely comment from a young Lochinvar come
out of the West?' Dillon asked. 'It lasted for a hundred years.'

'Without complaint,' interjected Haughey.

'Without complaint,' Dillon exclaimed sarcastically. 'Sin
has existed since the world began but the world is not better off
for its survival. If it is wrong now, the fact that it has been wrong
for a hundred years does not make it any better.'

In the course of his legislative duties the Parliamentary Secretary would clash with Dillon on a number of occasions, but the
Fine Gael leader developed a real regard for Haughey's industry
and legislative skill. For instance, when the Dáil continued to sit
into August 1961, it was obvious that the backlog of legislation
was being cleared in order to facilitate an early general election.
Dillon complained that the legislation was being rushed, but he
was at pains to exonerate Haughey.

'I do not blame the Parliamentary Secretary,' the Fine Gael leader explained. 'On the contrary I compliment him on the skill with which he has had recourse to his brief. He has read out to the House learned discourses on various aspects of this legislation which, I have no doubt, will be quoted from the Official Reports hereafter as evidence of his exceptional and outstanding ability.' Referring to Haughey's 'carefully-prepared briefs' as a testimony of 'his extraordinary erudition', Dillon hoped to be as well briefed himself when his own party came to power. 'Indeed,' he continued, 'I hope I shall make half as good use of the brief.' This was an extraordinary tribute from the leader of another party just before an election — and all the more extraordinary when compared to later remarks by Fine Gael leaders, including Dillon himself.

In the ensuing election Traynor decided to retire. Haughey was presented with the relatively easy task of retaining his seat. In fact, he more than doubled his vote to head the poll with 8,566 votes. In the process he helped Fianna Fáil to gain an extra seat in the constituency by taking three of the five seats. His two successful colleagues were his friend and future critic, George Colley, and Eugene Timmons who finally made it to the Dáil on his third attempt. The increase was particularly remarkable in that the party's vote dropped nationally and it lost its overall majority in the Dáil. Charlie Haughey had become a political force to be reckoned with.

3
Fingered by Time

Minister for Justice
1961-64

Mr Haughey: 'Here's one facade nobody'll mind being pulled down.'
Dublin Opinion, February 1962

ALTHOUGH Fianna Fáil was five seats short of an overall majority, Seán Lemass was again proposed as Taoiseach when the Dáil reconvened on 11 October 1961. Two of the independent deputies stated they would be supporting the nomination of Lemass on the grounds that he had a better chance of forming a stable government, and another independent deputy indicated he would be abstaining, so Lemass was assured of victory. But before the voting began he made it clear that he had made no deals with any of those people for their support.

'I have not asked any deputy in this House, outside the members of my own party, to support the motion, either by their vote or by their abstention', he said. 'If I should be elected Taoiseach, it would be my intention to implement the programme of my party in all respects.'

Following his re-election, Lemass renominated twelve of his outgoing cabinet — the one change in personnel being necessitated by the retirement of Oscar Traynor. Most ministers retained their old posts. The last man nominated and the only new appointment to the cabinet was Haughey as Minister for Justice. He had clearly earned his promotion by doing an effective job as Parliamentary Secretary. Now he took over full responsibility for the department.

Fine Gael deputies were strongly critical of the Lemass team, but only two deputies mentioned Haughey's appointment, and both of them actually spoke of it in favourable terms. For instance, Michael J. O'Higgins was quite caustic about the 'dull, unenterprising and unimaginative' cabinet being appointed, but he singled out Haughey as an exception. 'I sincerely congratulate the Taoiseach', he said, 'on the new appointment he has proposed, the appointment of Deputy Haughey as Minister. I have no doubt it will improve the team which the Taoiseach is suggesting to the House.'

Thus the opposition comments upon Haughey's appointment were favourable. Although such treatment was not unprecedented for a new minister, it was the last time Haughey was appointed to any ministerial portfolio without being subjected to severe criticism, especially from the Fine Gael benches.

His new duties were wide-ranging. The Department of Justice was responsible for the conditions under which the country's courts functioned, matters relating to the police force, the administration of the prison service, the Land Registry Office, the Registry of Deeds Office, and the Public Records Office, as well as the interpretation of a large number of statutes connected with the control of aliens, the granting of citizenship, and the adoption of children. In addition, the censorship of books and films were conducted under the aegis of his department, which was also responsible for drafting a wide range of legislation. In fact, on the first day of the new Dáil two pieces of legislation, the Coroners Bill and the Gárda Siochána Bill — for which Haughey would have responsibility — were introduced. The Dáil then adjourned until 15 November 1961.

During the recess the need for gárda reform became particularly apparent when there was a near mutiny within the force, which had become demoralised as a result of low pay, poor promotional prospects, and a feeling that its leadership were out of touch with the problems of the rank and file. When a request from the Gárda Representative Body for a pay increase was turned down, some discontented elements began holding meetings in Dublin stations. These were banned by the commissioner under the force's disciplinary code, so a meeting was called for the Macushla Ballroom in Dublin in early November 1961. Gardaí were forbidden to attend this meeting and some senior officers were stationed outside to take the names of the several hundred members who showed up. The 'Macushla Revolt', as the incident became known, took on added significance when the young guards decided on a 'go slow' campaign.

Dublin traffic was thrown into near chaos as gárdaí stopped directing traffic and refused to give out parking tickets. On 8 November the commissioner responded by asking that Haughey summarily dismiss eleven of the ring leaders. The minister duly complied but at the same time issued a statement emphasising his willingness to enquire into gárda grievances 'on receiving an assurance from the commissioner that discipline had been fully restored throughout the force'. A crisis within the force seemed imminent until the Catholic Archbishop of Dublin, John Charles McQuaid, intervened with an assurance that discipline would be restored if gárda grievances were investigated by the Department of Justice.

On 13 November Haughey announced the requested review would be undertaken. 'The fact that the guarantee has been given by the archbishop is good enough for me,' he said. 'I am satisfied that full discipline has now been restored to the force and the commissioner agrees with me.'

The eleven dismissed men were reinstated and proceedings were dropped against others for attending secret meetings contrary to gárda regulations. Haughey also assured the Dáil that there would be no victimisation of those who had taken part in the whole affair. In the end the whole thing turned out to be little more than a storm in a tea cup. 'But it had a vital significance for the development of the force over the next decade', according to gárda historian Conor Brady. The authorities were 'thoroughly shaken by the realisation that the force could not be relied upon unquestioningly'. This led to a tightening in discipline which was to have some repercussions, but at the same time the standing and influence of the Gárda Representative Body (which was broken up into three separate units representing superintendants and chief superintendants, sergeants and inspectors, and ordinary gárdaí was considerably strengthened.

Haughey got on well with his staff at the Department of Justice. Peter Berry, who had taken over as permanent secretary of the department in February 1961, had a good though sometimes stormy working relationship with the new minister.

'Haughey was a dynamic minister,' Berry recalled years later. 'He was a joy to work with and the longer he stayed the better he got.' He was quick to master the bureaucratic mystique of the department and the method by which policies were formulated and implemented. Berry, who had served in the Department of Justice under fourteen different ministers beginning with Kevin O'Higgins back in the 1920s, noted that 'Haughey learned fast and was in complete control of his department from the outset.' In fact, he rated him 'the ablest' of all those ministers. 'He did not interfere in minor details,' Berry explained, 'but where political kudos or political disadvantage might arise he was sharp as a razor.'

In his first month in office Haughey drew up a ten-point programme that he wished implemented. His first goal was to crush the IRA's border campaign, which had been going on since 1956.

The IRA had clearly lost most of the sympathy it had enjoyed at the start of the campaign. Back in 1957 Sinn Féin had won four seats in the Dáil but now, four years later, the party had just fared dismally. None of the twenty-one candidates fielded in 1961 were successful. Fourteen actually lost their deposits as the party secured only 3 per cent of the first-preference vote. It was an obvious disaster for them and was recognised as such even by the republicans themselves.

'The all too public denial of support of the polls had badly damaged morale,' according to historian J. Bowyer Bell. 'There had been no spectacular operation in the North. Public and private pressure to call off the campaign was growing. The

Army Council agreed that a big effort must be made to rectify the situation but that they might have to quit.'

On 12 November the IRA ambushed an RUC patrol near Jonesboro, Co. Armagh, killing one of the constables. He was the sixth policeman to be killed in the campaign. The ambush was a last gasp effort on the part of the IRA.

The Dublin government responded decisively. On 22 November Haughey announced the reactivation of the Special Criminal Court, which had been dormant since the end of the Second World War. It quickly began handing down severe sentences. For instance, men found guilty of the possession of fire arms were being sentenced to six months in jail in the District Courts, while those convicted in the Special Criminal Court were sentenced to an average of five years each. One man who had been sentenced to six months in 1959 following an abortive ambush was now sentenced to eight years in jail. In the following weeks thirty-one people were sentenced to stiff prison terms.

While implementing this policy of the stick Haughey also began holding forth a carrot in early February when he offered an amnesty to those who surrendered their weapons. Of course, by then he knew that the IRA leadership had already secretly decided to quit because the campaign had run aground on the rocks of public hostility and indifference. The amnesty offer should therefore be seen both as a means of facilitating the IRA's desire to end hostilities and as a ploy to score political points for the government in general and the Minister for Justice in particular.

'I offered an arms amnesty, with good results,' Haughey explained. The facts seemed to support him, because the IRA publicly announced it was calling off the campaign within a month. 'Because of the effective action we took,' he contended, 'they actually called it off publicly. I think it's about the only time in history the IRA publicly renounced a campaign.'

The suspension of previous IRA campaigns had been followed by public agitation to free republican prisoners, but this time Haughey moved quickly to prevent the question becoming a major political issue. During March he announced the government was again disbanding the Special Criminal Court and all those held in custody under the Offences Against the State Act were released.

The border campaign was over. In comparison with the troubles of the following decade the five-year campaign, which claimed a total of nineteen lives, seemed like little more than a series of skirmishes. Haughey only arrived on the scene when the proverbial writing was already on the wall, but he deserves credit for turning the screw at the right psychological moment. He thereby helped to end the campaign and clear up its loose ends with competence and despatch.

'I know,' he told the Dáil, 'that it is the wish of every right-thinking person that we are finished, finally, with this kind of unlawful activity and that all those who have supported it will realise that they have been out of touch with the realities of our time.'

Reviewing the events of his first year of office Haughey named the ending of the border campaign as his department's 'most important single achievement, from the point of view of law and order'. He was also able to point to a modest drop in the overall crime rate as well as an increase in detection rates, though violent crimes and house breakings had increased. While the investigation of crimes came under the aegis of the Department of Justice, the Attorney-General, Andreas O'Keefe, was responsible for the actual prosecution of those charged with offences. Hence Haughey distanced himself from involvement in the débâcle surrounding the prosecution of Paul Singer of Shanahan Stamps Limited. Arrested in 1959, Singer was convicted of fraud involving more than £700,000 almost two years later, but the conviction was overturned and a new trial ordered after it was disclosed that the foreman of the convicting jury was an investor in the company. The second trial, which began on 3 November 1961 and continued until 24 January 1962, was the longest in the country's history. Much to the embarrassment of the government, the proceedings culminated in the judge directing the jury to find Singer not guilty. He was therefore freed and promptly vanished, leaving hundreds of thousands of pounds unaccounted for, with the result that the whole judicial system came in for criticism.

There was further criticism some weeks later after a member of the government was prosecuted for drunken driving. In the past, charges against prominent politicians or their friends would be 'yanked' and never get to court, but Haughey adopted a different approach. He refused to square cases but he would make arrangements to have them heard outside the normal court hours so that there would be no press around. In this way Haughey felt the needs of justice were being served without subjecting the politician to damaging publicity. Later, if he was accused of 'yanking' the charges, he could refute the accusation by producing the court record.

One of the cases heard quietly in this manner involved a conviction for drunken driving against Donogh O'Malley, then Parliamentary Secretary to the Minister for Finance. The case had an unseemly sequel shortly afterwards when the gárda who arrested O'Malley was assigned to new duties. Contending that his assignment amounted to victimisation, the gárda — a six year member of the force — refused to carry out his orders and he was then given the option of resigning voluntarily or being dismissed from the gárdaí. He therefore resigned.

As a result questions were asked in the Dáil. Richie Ryan accused the government of conducting ' a reign of terror' within the Gárda Siochána and the Department of Justice. In reply Haughey suggested that members of the opposition were just scavenging politically. Irritated by the charge, Gerard Sweetman, the deputy leader of Fine Gael, threatened to ask embarrassing questions about 'an amazing coincidence' concerning another gárda who had also been asked to resign recently.

'There are some "quare" files in my office too,' Haughey warned. There was no mistaking his naked threat to reveal information that would be embarrassing to Fine Gael deputies. 'Let us not be pushed too far,' James Dillon blustered, but he and his colleagues did not dare pursue the gárda's case any further.

During 1961 juvenile crime reached its highest level since the foundation of the state. Haughey responded by having a special crime unit set up, and he introduced a Juvenile Liaison Scheme that had been operating with some success in Britain.

'The task of this gárda unit,' he explained, 'will be, with the co-operation of parents, teachers, clergy, youth leaders and other persons and organisations interested in youth welfare, to guide young boys into channels of activity leading to good citizenship.' Under the scheme, juvenile offenders could be placed under police supervision without being committed to any penal institution. 'It was an idea which if developed could have revolutionised the whole concept of policing in Ireland', according to Conor Brady. 'Unfortunately its potential was not realised either by subsequent commissioners or ministers.'

Haughey also demonstrated an enlightened outlook towards penal reform. 'Prison is not, and is not intended to be, a home from home and prison will always be a place of punishment,' he believed, 'but it seems to me that our prisons nowadays must to an increasing extent become places of rehabilitation as well.'

On retiring as Governor of Mountjoy Jail in 1970, Seán Kavanagh credited Haughey (then ironically facing a possible prison sentence himself) with reforming the prison service. 'Since 1962,' Kavanagh explained, 'some excellent schemes for the reform and rehabilitation of prisoners have been initiated notably by Mr Charles J. Haughey while Minister for Justice.' Those reforms included the establishment of a corrective training unit as well as the building of a hostel to accomodate prisoners who would be granted daily release to outside employment obtained for them through a new prison welfare service. A full-time welfare officer was appointed to Mountjoy in order to assist in the work of rehabilitation and to help prisoners with personal problems. Such schemes had been in operation as part of modern prison treatment in England, Sweden, and other countries for several years. 'But before 1962,' Kavanagh noted, 'little or no interest in them was taken in our Department of Justice, especially where the extra cost of putting them into effect became obvious.'

The Department of Justice had often been frustrated in its schemes by lack of money until Haughey's appointment. 'At the time of his becoming Minister for Justice,' Berry recalled, 'the Department had been bogged down for quite some time, primarily through lack of adequate finance. Successive Ministers for Justice had failed to get the necessary monies from the Department of Finance but Mr Haughey proved very adroit at extracting the necessary financial support.' He was a good man to cut through red tape.

Haughey worked long hours, on average a ten-hour day, and he prided himself on efficiency and getting things done. He could be a good listener, but he became irritable when people became long-winded. He sought to emulate the capacity of his father-in-law to be make quick, considered decisions without agonising interminably over the pros and cons, as had been the practice in de Valera's government. Haughey's telephone conversations were short and to the point, and his notes to civil servants working under him were characteristically brief — often consisting of no more than the word 'OK' written in the margin of their memoranda to him.

The secretary of the department had been keenly interested in prison reform, so the two of them had a good, if occassionally stormy, working relationship. 'Berry was a very, very dedicated, devoted civil servant,' according to Haughey, but there were a few problems between them because the secretary tended to be rather set in some of his ideas. 'He needed to be under the control, guidance and direction of a minister who could take a much broader view of things', Haughey contended.

Berry recalled two incidents in which he clashed with Haughey. The first took place shortly after the new minister took office. As Parliamentary Secretary he had promised a minor appointment with a small capitation grant to someone, unaware that Traynor had already made the appointment. On becoming minister, Haughey could have removed his predecessor's appointee but this would have been resented by the deputies who had approached Traynor in the first place, so he decided to let Traynor's appointment stand while at the same time appointing his own man as well. This would have required a second grant, which Berry, as the department's accounting officer, refused to sanction.

'I told Mr Haughey,' Berry wrote, 'that I couldn't make payment and when he insisted I said that, of course, I would obey his direction but that I was requested under the Rules to report the matter to the Minister for Finance and to the Committee of Public Accounts.' With that the matter was dropped. And Berry, who was about to go on vacation, made sure it could not be revived in his absence. He informed the assistant secretary of the department of the details of the matter.

'On my return,' Berry continued, 'the assistant secretary told me that he had received a ministerial directive to appoint the second man to the post, that he had informed the minister that he was aware of the accounting officer's refusal earlier and that

34

the minister would be liable to personal surcharge. He said that the minister was furious with me, not alone for my refusal but for forewarning the assistant secretary, thus causing the minister to lose face.'

The second incident occurred over Haughey's desire to have a certain individual appointed immigration officer at Cork Airport. He explained to Berry that Jack Lynch had made representations on behalf of a man already based in Cork. The gárda commissioner, who was charged with the responsibility of making recommendations, set up a board, which ranked the individual being backed by Lynch and Haughey only fourth in the order of merit.

Having been appointed by the government, Berry had no intention of acting 'as a rubber stamp for the minister in official matters'. He believed he had duty to advise the minister, whether or not the minister wanted that advice. Hence Berry objected to the appointment and warned Haughey that he would be 'open to grave criticism' if he disregarded the advice of the commissioner and the board. 'And', Berry added, 'I could not lend my support to it.'

Haughey was furious. 'Well,' he said, 'I have appointed No. 4.' He then threw the file at Berry, who walked out leaving the papers strewn on the floor.

'It would make for chaos in administration and would not serve government or parliament if senior civil servants were not free to brief their ministers and government according to conscience and their specialised knowledge and judgments,' the secretary later argued. 'There were occasions in the years to come where I and my colleagues were subjected to this kind of pressure but I always encouraged my colleagues by word and example to record their true arguments without in any way questioning the minister's authority to make the final decisions.'

The second incident was undoubtedly complicated by Haughey's inability to accept criticism gracefully — a difficulty already noted and one which would surface again and again throughout his political career. Berry had a valid point when he contended that departmental secretaries should advise their ministers, but the latter should be free to disregard that advice without being lectured about their responsibilities, no matter how experienced the secretary. Quite often recommendations from people on the ground turn out to be much better than those from departmental heads and interview boards. Haughey was charged with making the appointment and the ultimate responsibility was his. From the tone of Berry's own account of the incident, it would appear that he not only lectured Haughey on his ministerial duties, but also went beyond the bounds of propriety by asking the gárda commissioner to 'spread the word that I was not a party to the minister's decision'.

Haughey's greatest impact as Minister for Justice was in the field of legislation. He managed to pilot an enormous number of bills through the Oireachtas. On occasions he had as many as five different bills going through the Dáil together. Those necessitated a tremendous amount of his time as the house made its tortuous way through every section of every bill. Listing the bills gives some idea of the amount of work involved, expecially when one realises that Dáil and Seanad Reports provide only a limited perspective on the amount of work involved. 'Parliamentary bills are like icebergs in that less than one-fifth of the work put into their structure appears above the surface', Haughey explained. 'A great deal of consultation goes on between the promoting department and the various interests involved, with experts on points of law at issue, and then the minister and government in turn have to immerse themselves in the intricacies and decide on policy and major issues.'

In preparing the legislation the new minister worked closely with Roger Hayes, whom he found 'passionately committed to law reform. For the first time ever,' Haughey said, 'he found, in me, somebody who could give expression to his desire for law reform.' In January 1962 the department published a white paper outlining the measures he hoped to introduce.

By then Haughey had already introduced the Coronors Bill, Gárda Siochána Bill, Criminal Justice (Legal Aid) Bill, and the Short Titles Bill. In the next two and a half years he introduced the Official Secrets Bill, Courts (Supplemental Provisions Amendment) Bill, Street and House to House Collections Bill, Intoxicating Liquor Bill, Statute Law Revision (Pre-Union Irish Statutes) Bill, Hotel Proprietors Bill, Adoption Bill, Fire Arms Bill, Criminal Justice (Abolition of Capital Punishment) Bill, Registration of Titles Bill, Funds of Suitors Bill, Courts Bill (1963), Guardianship of Infants Bill, Pawnbrokers Bill,

Extradition Bill, Civil Liability (Amendment) Bill, and the Succession Bill.

Those bills covered a very wide area of legislation, extending from family law to international law. Some were essentially new measures, while others amended or simply re-enacted laws dating as far back as the fourteenth century. According to Haughey, for instance, the Statute Law Revision (Pre-Union Irish Statutes) Bill, which dealt with legislation passed before 1800, was introduced to remove from the statute book a 'great mass of obsolete legislation' so that an updated index could be produced 'to the whole of statute law in force in the state'.

While the state was only forty years old, all laws in force at the time of independence remained on the statute books, unless formally repealed or amended since then. As a result some of the legislation was totally obsolete. For instance, the Act of Union of 1800 had been effectively repealed by the Constitution of 1937 but it still remained on the Statute Book because it had never been formally repealed. Thus what the new Minister for Justice was basically trying to do, was to start modernising the country's whole legal system. 'It is desirable,' he contended, 'that so far as possible our law should be contained in modern statutes passed by the Oireachtas and it should be our ultimate aim to get ourselves into a position where that would apply to all our statute law.'

The Criminal Justice Bill 1963 sought to abolish the death penalty for all but certain specified crimes like treason, and the murder of a gárda or an ambassador. 'Very shortly after becoming Minister for Justice,' Haughey later recalled, 'I went up to Mountjoy to see the condemned cell and I was so revolted by the whole atmosphere that I resolved to do away with the death penalty.' Afterwards he was sorry he had not abolished capital punishment completely, but at the time the remaining capital crimes 'seemed to be so remote and academic that they were of no practical importance'.

Some of the more minor bills were to cause as much trouble as complicated ones, especially in the uncertain political climate prevailing in which the government was unable to depend on majority support in the Dáil. There were vociferous objections to the Intoxicating Liquor Bill, 1962, which only extended opening hours in some minor respects — the most notable being slightly earlier opening and later closing times on Sundays. The Courts (Supplemental Provisions Amendment) Bill, also came in for strong criticism because it contained substantial salary increases for members of the judiciary. Haughey contended the measure was necessary to ensure the best and most capable people were on the bench.

'Do we not all know that a man's work or value is judged by what he earns?' he asked on introducing that bill. 'It is a human and natural thing and it is something which is very common here — to look down on a man who does not earn as much as you do. I think it applies to all levels of our society.' While that kind of thinking may have been fundamental to Haughey's philosophy it had no appeal whatever to a socialist like Noel Browne, who argued that people like the Little Sisters of the Poor or the Carmelite fathers earned very little, but this did not mean that society placed more value on the services of a brothel keeper just because he was paid more money. He had a valid point, but Haughey was unwilling to concede this gracefully. Instead he flippantly remarked that Browne would know more about whore masters than himself. It was a coarse example of Haughey at his least attractive.

Although he was acquiring a growing reputation as a friend of the rich and influential, Haughey never lost his populist edge. The Criminal Justice (Legal Aid) Act provided for free legal aid, although this was confined to cases in which the court thought it 'Essential in the interest of justice'. Haughey admitted the measure was rather restrictive; he would have liked to make free legal aid as widely available as possible, but the measure was new and experimental.

Of course, legislation relating to welfare matters had practically nothing to do with the Department of Justice. Presumably Haughey was so busy with his own enormous workload that he did not have time to concern himself with other matters. In the Dáil he generally confined himself to questions relating to his own department. When he did digress it was usually to speak on financial issues, like the budget. Here his remarks foreshadowed the compassionate approach he would later adopt as Minister for Finance. For instance, he strongly supported the introduction of the controversial turnover tax in the budget of 1963 by arguing that it would afford the government the enhanced financial viability necessary to increase children's allowances and social welfare benefits.

'We are not political fools,' Haughey explained on deputising for the Minister for Finance during the committee stage of the Finance Bill. 'We do not do unpopular things for the fun of it. We made up our minds on the improvements which had to be brought about in our social welfare arrangements, health services, and so on, and we satisfied ourselves beyond any shadow of doubt that the money required could not be provided by any of the conventional methods.' Hence the government decided to introduce this sales tax as 'the fairest, the most effective, and the cheapest way of raising the money required for our plans.'

Noel Browne objected that the new tax would hurt the poor more than the rich because both would have to pay it equally. His criticism led to some rather unseemly exchanges in which Haughey charged that Browne had 'difficulty proving he is not a communist'.

A few days later *Time* magazine went on sale describing Haughey as 'the shrewed, hard-knuckled Minister for Justice, who is tipped as potential Prime Minister'. And he seemed to confirm the hard-knuckled aspect by promptly getting involved in another unsavoury row with Browne, whom he accused of being arrogant, dictatorial, and possessing 'the communist mentality'. Browne, in reply, accused him of behaving like a fascist. 'That,' said Haughey, 'rubs off me much more lightly.'

By squabbling with Browne, a recognised champion of the poor and underprivileged, Haughey was inevitably seen as a friend of the rich, and his ostentatious lifestyle exacerbated the impression. Fianna Fáil had always been proud that it represented the men with cloth caps and open-necked shirts, but the Minister for Justice was representative of a new breed in the party. A wealthy businessman who owned racehorses and rode to hounds, he came to be classified as one of the men in the mohair suits. He enjoyed his prosperity and flaunted it, with the result that in no time at all he became the subject of lurid gossip and colourful rumours.

The *Sunday Independent* provoked his wrath by publishing a cartoon depicting him in the midst of a group of drunken people in evening dress being off-loaded from a paddy wagon outside a gárda station, as a gárda was saying: 'Come on out, you tallyhoing, hunt-balling pack . . . Oh sorry Mr Minister, I didn't see you in there.' Although this was mild in comparison to some later cartoons, Haughey threatened legal action and the *Sunday Independent* settled by making a contribution to a charity of his choice.

Some of the bills introduced by the Minister for Justice were designed to protect children. The Fire Arms Act regulated the use of air guns, while the Adoption Act extended the age at which children could be adopted from seven to nine years old, and dropped the stipulation that the adopting parents had to be Irish citizens. The Guardianship of Infants Act consolidated previous legislation and amended it to the extent that henceforth the child's welfare would be the first and paramount consideration. The act also strengthened the rights of the mother by stipulating for the first time that each of the parents had equal rights to guardianship and custody.

Just before the summer recess in 1964 Haughey introduced the Succession Bill, a fairly novel piece of legislation which sought to ensure that testators provided adequately for their dependents in their wills. One of the main aims of the bill was to prevent a man leaving his family destitute while all his money was left for something like masses for the repose of his soul. The bill was an extremely complicated piece of legislation which had some serious defects, but before the Dáil could discuss them, Haughey was moved from the Department of Justice.

In early October Paddy Smith, the Minister for Agriculture, resigned in protest over aspects of the government's economic policies. This placed Lemass in a tricky situation because the resignation could easily lead to a political crisis and bring down the minority government. Hence he had to move fast, but he could not appoint a replacement from outside the cabinet without the approval of the Dáil. He therefore took over the Justice portfolio himself and appointed Haughey Minister for Agriculture.

'Lemass was a great politician', Haughey later argued. 'He had a great capacity to anticipate things, to be ahead of the developments, not having to react to them. On that occasion he had the new appointment made before the general public were aware of the resignation. He didn't allow any atmosphere to build up. It was all over and done with before most people knew what was happening.'

40

Haughey's new appointment was clearly a promotion, which might well have led to charges of nepotism under different circumstances, because at first glance he seemed one of the most unlikely ministers for agriculture.

'Dublin was agog last night with speculation about Mr Haughey's chances of making a go of Agriculture,' one *Irish Times* reporter noted following the announcement. The newspaper itself noted in an editorial that the new minister's aptitude for agriculture was an unknown quantity. 'His urban and urbane background, his knowledge of law and accountancy, and even horses and horsemanship, do not seem at first glance to fit him for the post', the leader contended. 'We can only wait and see whether he can sufficiently adopt his considerable talents to a new and challenging position.'

4

The Minister and the Cowboys

Minister for Agriculture and Fisheries
1964-66

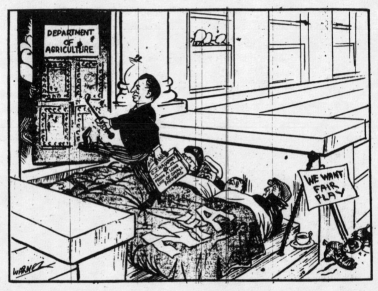

Doormat

Sunday Independent, 23 October 1966

THE appointment of Haughey as Minister for Agriculture raised many eyebrows. Some farmers had already been complaining that the government was out of touch with the problems of the agricultural community and the Taoiseach's son-in-law could only have increased that image. After all, Haughey, who was generally seen as the prototype of the modern urban politician, had already told the Dáil that he knew nothing about agriculture.

He had generally been tight-lipped about his business dealings but following his new appointment he disclosed that he owned a farm in Co. Meath and had already gone in for farming in a modern, progressive way. Hitherto, for instance, Irish egg production had been largely a sideline in which the wives of farmers kept free range hens as a means of earning extra income, but now the market was being flooded with cheap eggs following the advent of the battery hen. When Michael Pat Murphy of the Labour Party complained in the Dáil that prices had fallen so drastically that nobody could make money keeping chickens, Haughey announced he owned a profitable poultry farm.

'I have 2,000 hens,' he said, 'and I made £874 net profit out of them in twelve months. I can show the deputy audited accounts to prove it.'

Haughey's motives in making the disclosure were transparent. He was obviously trying to dispel the notion of those who 'felt that the minister knew nothing about agriculture,' according to Murphy.

Haughey's duties in the Department of Agriculture were largely administrative, in marked contrast to his period at Justice where he was involved in piloting so much legislation through the Oireachtas. Now his Dáil functions were mainly restricted to answering questions about the administrative functions of the Department for Agriculture, or justifying the necessary legislation to finance its activities.

One of his earliest acts was to introduce a supplementary estimate to cover cost overruns due largely to his predecessor's failure to guage the likely response to the calved-heifer scheme which had been introduced in January in an attempt to build up the national herd by giving a grant for every heifer-in-calf. The scheme was so successful that cattle numbers reached their targeted figure for 1968 by the end of the first year. As a result costs soared and the first year cost was more than seven times the £405,000 originally estimated.

Haughey was taking over the agricultural portfolio at a challenging time. Ireland was moving towards membership of the EEC and he realised that all aspects of the economy needed to be modernised. 'We know that free trade is coming,' he told the Dáil in 1963, 'and we must prepare the country for conditions of free trade and keener competition that will arise in those conditions. We must gear the economy to meet the challenge.' The economy of the country had been gradually coming out of the recession of the 1950s. The recovery was most apparent in the industrial sector which had been seriously

43

depressed, while the improvement in agriculture was less dramatic and more gradual. But in 1964 and 1965 there was a dramatic advance.

'All indications are that 1964 was one of the best years ever for Irish agriculture,' Haughey told the Dáil in his review of the year. He noted that cattle exports were up. There was an 11 per cent increase in store cattle exports and a 66.6 per cent increase for fat cattle. Cattle exports to the continent almost quadrupled in value from £3.3 millions to £12.7 millions. As a result the average farm income rose by a phenomenal 20 per cent.

In keeping with his modern, progressive image, Haughey enthusiastically supported a wide range of modernisation and incentive schemes. Given the success of the calved-heifer scheme, he introduced a farrow-sow scheme to build up pig numbers, and a hogget-ewe scheme to do the same for the sheep population. He was also enthusiastic about the promotion of disease eradication as he announced plans for veterinary laboratories at Cork, Limerick, Athlone and Sligo to supplement the one already at Abbotstown, Co. Dublin.

Survey teams were set up to examine the different facets of agriculture, like horse breeding and the glasshouse industry, with a view to suggesting measures of adjustment for adaptation to international trade in the event of the country joining the EEC. Haughey also established a committee to consider and recommend desirable ways of improving the quality, handling and marketing of Irish wool.

By the time of his second annual review of the agricultural scene on 11 May 1966 he was still painting an optimistic picture. 'I am convinced,' he said, 'that the prospects for the agricultural industry were never better.'

But he realised that increased production did not guarantee an increased income for farmers. In 1965 they received an average rise in income of about 5 per cent, which he contended was slightly higher than the average rise in industrial wages, but he did not mention that this was partly the result of a drift from the land which meant that agricultural earnings were being distributed among fewer people. From 1964 to 1966, for instance, the number of those employed in the agricultural sector dropped by 45,000 people.

There were already some ominous implications as 'food surpluses were appearing everywhere,' according to Haughey. On becoming Minister for Agriculture, he later explained, he was struck by the fact that 'we were planning for major increases in our agricultural production and exports, while the markets in which we could dispose of them were becoming more and more restricted.' In particular, the highly protective nature of the Common Agricultural Policy of the EEC was rapidly curtailing the opportunities for Irish expansion and even the countries of the European Free Trade Association had been 'steadily pursuing their own protectionist agricultural policies.' Hence he enthusiastically welcomed the agricultural aspects of the Anglo-Irish Free Trade Agreement, which were due to come into effect in June 1966

'It is,' he said, 'impossible to exaggerate the importance of the breakthrough represented by the fact that the agreement provides for the extension of the British agricultural support price system to our finished products — 25,000 tons of carcass beef and 5,550 tons of carcass lamb.' One of the most important aspects of the agreement, as far as he was concerned, was the fact that it provided a safeguard for Irish produce in the event of restrictions in the British market. 'It is true that it is difficult to estimate in accounting terms the value of the agreement to Irish agriculture and fisheries. In the long term, the value will be enormous if we make full use of the opportunities now available.' He estimated it would be worth £10 millions a year at the outset.

The accord was 'an agreement of opportunity', according to Haughey. 'It will be the aim of my department, with the assistance of the advisory services, the Agricultural Institute, the co-operative movement, the colleges and universities, to help the farmer in every way to meet this great new challenging opportunity,' he explained. 'If we work together, united and agreed on the objective to be achieved, then this agreement will surely mark the beginning of a period of development and progress to Irish agriculture unparalleled in our history.'

This optimistic agricultural projection would begin to haunt the minister even before the end of the month as he ran into difficulties with the main farming organisations, the Irish Creamery Milk Suppliers' Association (ICMSA) and National Farmers' Association (NFA).

In the late spring the ICMSA became quite militant in demanding higher milk prices as it advocated the introduction of a new two-tier price system in accordance with which all farmers would receive an extra 4 pence per gallon for the first 7,000 gallons of milk they produced annually and 2 pence per gallon for any milk above that quota. Since the average milk delivery was only around 3,600 gallons per year, it meant that almost all dairy farmers would enjoy the full benefits of such an increase. Only the very largest farmers, who were more likely to be members of the rival NFA, would exceed the quota.

Under the leadership of its president, John Feely, the ICMSA placed a picket outside Leinster House on 27 April 1966. The government responded rather high-handedly by having the twenty-eight picketers arrested under the Offences Against the State Act, but Feely defiantly announced the picket would remain until his organisation's demands were met. Seventy-eight farmers were arrested while picketing next day and a further eighty the following day as the dispute escalated.

At the outset Haughey seemed to adopt a firmer approach to the ICMSA protest than his more flexible response to the Macushla Revolt within the Gárda Síochána in his previous ministry. As with the earlier controversy involving the gárdaí, he refused to talk while the protesters were acting illegally, but this time he made it clear that he would not concede to the protesters' demands in any event. He said he would like to help farmers by conceding the price increase being sought, but the government simply could not afford to do so because it would cost £6 million, which amounted to more than 15 per cent of the annual agricultural budget at the time. While the minister closed the question of a milk price increase, he nevertheless offered to discuss 'other ways in which the income of the dairy farmer can be increased'.

The ICMSA removed its picket for a time so that discussions could be held between its leaders and the minister on 4 May, but there was no progress. 'They gave me to understand clearly that they were only interested and would accept nothing less than their original two-tier price system', Haughey later told the Dáil. He had strong objections to this two-tier system, from both philosophical and administrative standpoints. For one thing, the reduced price for milk above the quota would be 'a disincentive to increased production' and would thus stunt progress. 'It would be bad economics,' he said, 'to discourage more efficient and more large-scale production'. Moreover it would be an administrative nightmare because it would be impossible to prevent abuses by farmers producing more than the quota. They would simply have their surpluses delivered in the name of a friend or another member of the family.

Prompted by his own capitalist instincts Haughey also had serious reservations about granting any price increase under the circumstances for fear it would lead to socialised agriculture. 'There is a danger that agitation directed only to getting higher prices may develop a kind of dole mentality which would eventually make agriculture subservient to the state,' he contended. 'What I want to achieve is a self-reliant, independent and progressive agriculture, fully backed by, but not utterly dependent on, the state.'

Before the end of the month, however, Haughey was sounding a more sombre note from the exuberant optimism of April. 'The task which confronts me, indeed any Minister for Agriculture,' he told the Dáil on 26 May 1966, 'is of such vast proportions and the problems are so intractable that I do not think it is possible ever to be enthusiastic about the progress which is being achieved at any given moment compared with what still remains to be done.' He then proceeded to back down on the milk price issue by announcing an immediate increase of 2 pence per gallon with a further penny per gallon for quality milk after 1 April 1967. Counting the one penny per gallon previously given for quality milk, this meant that farmers not producing milk with a high enough cream content would actually get the requested 4 pence per gallon extra within twelve months, if they got their milk up to the desired quality.

In view of the strong, reasoned stand taken by Haughey against any increase only weeks earlier, questions must be asked about his eventual surrender. Why did he virtually capitulate on the issue?

There was no doubt in the minds of many people, especially in opposition circles, that the concessions were related to the presidential election campaign being conducted at the time. The Fine Gael candidate, T. F. O'Higgins, was running very well in Dublin and other urban areas, so President de Valera

47

needed his party's traditional rural support if he was going to win a second term. This support would obviously be endangered if the Fianna Fáil government was still at odds with farmers over the price of milk. Hence Haughey, who was de Valera's national director of elections, pulled a political stroke and shored up the President's rural support by conceding the milk price increase. In view of the narrowness of de Valera's subsequent victory, the price concessions quite conceivably made the difference between victory and defeat. It appeared that Haughey had backed down for political reasons under ICMSA pressure and he would pay for this dearly before the year was out.

Figuratively speaking Haughey was flying high at this time and it was the start of a particularly crucial period because Seán Lemass indicated his intention to retire as Taoiseach within the next twelve months. His son-in-law, who had never made any secret of his aspirations for the office, was clearly in an advantageous position to succeed him. As Minister for Agriculture, Haughey was in one of the most influential posts in the government and his comparative youth was a decided advantage because, on his next birthday, he would be the same age as John F. Kennedy when the latter became the youngest President ever to be elected in the United States. Kennedy had made a profound impression on the Irish people, and Haughey never seemed averse to being compared with the late President. And those comparisons extended beyond the political arena.

Much of Haughey's success was due to his own ability to sell himself. Now he was trying to convince people he was a success as Minister for Agriculture. If he could do this and thereby secure a rural base, then he would be the next Taoiseach without much doubt because — notwithstanding his short temper and vindictive reputation — he was already widely seen as the prototype of the young, suave, highly educated, articulate, urban politician.

Having talked so favourably about the prospects for Irish agriculture and having boasted about the success of the calf-heifer scheme in building up the national herd, Haughey came in for particular criticism when things began to go wrong as the bottom virtually fell out of the cattle market during the summer. The problems, which were the result of a series of external factors, were really beyond his control. On average about 80 per cent of Irish cattle and beef were exported, so there was little the Department of Agriculture could do about controlling those markets.

In April 1966 the EEC virtually closed its doors to Irish cattle by introducing a prohibitive tariff on all beef imports from outside the community. Irish farmers therefore had to turn to the British market to sell their surplus cattle, and they ran into serious difficulties here too. A seaman's strike initially blocked imports and then when it was settled a glut developed as the backlog was dumped on the market. This was then complicated by a credit squeeze which impaired the ability of British importers to keep Irish cattle for the two months necessary to claim their government's subsidy. Hence the demand for Irish cattle dropped.

As prices tumbled Haughey came in for criticism. In as much as the events were beyond his control, the criticism was unfair, but he had left himself wide open to censure by his failure to prepare farmers for the slump, which became inevitable following the closing of EEC markets in April. Of course, apprising the farmers at that stage would have meant giving them bad news just before the presidential election and that was not Haughey's way of doing things. Instead, having already said it was 'impossible to exaggerate' the importance of British subsidies for Irish cattle under the Anglo-Irish Free Trade Agreement which was due to come into force in June, he proceeded to say that the prospects for Irish agriculture were 'never better'.

At the annual general meeting of the NFA in August Rickard Deasy, the organisation's president, criticised the minister's handling of events. Always highly sensitive to criticism at the best of times, Haughey responded by cancelling a planned meeting with NFA leaders.

On 29 September, as cattle prices continued to fall, he told the Dáil that farmers should hold on to their animals to await better prices, but the NFA responded by advising them to sell as soon as possible because prices would continue to drop. That night RTE reported the minister's statement followed by the NFA's contradictory advice on its nightly television news. Haughey immediately telephoned the news department to protest.

'I felt compelled in the public interest to protest that the NFA statement should be carried immediately after mine,' Haughey explained. 'I gave specific advice to farmers in reply to questions from deputies in the Dáil as the responsible minister, and I felt that to have my advice followed by [a] contradiction from an organisation could only lead to confusion and damage the industry.'

The deputy news editor telephoned the head of news at his home and the item was dropped from further broadcasts, but the *Sunday Independent* broke the story. As a result questions were asked in the Dáil, and Haughey came across rather arrogantly as he argued that RTE had been wrong to air advice that contradicted him as minister. 'I think it was a very unwise thing to say the least of it, for Radio Telefís Éireann to follow that solemn advice of mine given as Minister for Agriculture with a contradiction by one organisation,' he said, 'I pointed this out to the news room of Telefís Éireann and I think I was absolutely right in doing so.'

The NFA cited the RTE affair not only as an attempt 'to hinder the democratic right of freedom of speech' but also as 'one further example of the arrogance of Mr Haughey'. The latter suddenly found himself embroiled in a controversy over the freedom of broadcasting.

RTE journalists had been uneasy for some months over the station's role in the recent presidential election campaign. In his mid-eighties and almost totally blind, de Valera was unable to wage a campaign to match his younger opponent, so it was decided that he would not campaign at all. As his director of elections, Haughey sought to minimise the Fine Gael candidate's physical advantages by persuading RTE not to cover the campaign. Haughey contended that the President would not campaign as he was above politics, so RTE should then ignore his opponent's campaign in the interests of fairness. RTE's news department accepted the argument, which was unfair to O'Higgins. Unlike the President, he campaigned actively but got practically no news coverage, whereas the various government ministers that Haughey despatched to rallies around the country were able to secure publicity for de Valera's campaign by using their own official positions to make news-worthy pronouncements. Haughey had pulled another political stroke, but now the pent-up frustration of RTE journalists were suddenly released in the midst of the latest controversy.

Matters were further compounded when Haughey withdrew from a scheduled television appearance on the current affairs programme *Division*, on which he was supposed to debate the cattle situation with Deasy. RTE decided to go ahead with the programme anyway, using one of its own reporters, Ted Nealon, to put forward the minister's case.

Haughey protested against this decision. He made it clear that he had no reservations about Nealon's integrity or professional competence, but he did take exception to him being allowed to put forward government policy. 'I emphatically reject the right of any person not authorised by me to do so to purport to outline the policy of this department', Haughey declared. But the programme went ahead in spite of his objections. No doubt those objections would have been even stronger if he could have foreseen that Nealon would one day be elected to the Dáil as a Fine Gael deputy and would be Minister of State to the future Taoiseach, Garret FitzGerald.

With the Minister for Agriculture refusing to meet the NFA leadership, the latter decided to exert pressure by enlisting public support for a protest march. On 7 October Deasy set out on foot with other members of the NFA to walk the 210 miles from Bantry to Dublin, where it was planned to hold a protest rally outside Leinster House in Merrion Square twelve days later. In the following days other marchers set out from different centres to join with those coming from Bantry, and the various marches gathered support as they made their way to the capital. By the time they reached Merrion Square on 19 October, there were several thousand protesters. After their rally Deasy and eight other leaders went over to the Department of Agriculture and asked to meet Haughey, but he refused.

Deasy and his colleagues had walked a long way, so the Minister's refusual to meet them seemed churlish, at least to NFA members if not to the general public. It would quickly become apparent that Haughey had made a tactical blunder because they set about dramatising his refusal in a novel way. Deasy promptly vowed that he and his colleagues would wait outside the Department of Agriculture for 'a bloody month' if necessary until the minister met them. The nine of them thereupon camped outside the front door of the department for the next three weeks while the quest to find a successor to Lemass reached its climax within Leinster House.

Haughey travelled to the continent and tried frantically to find a market for Irish cattle. He was actually depicted as a cowboy driving cattle to the ends of the earth on the cover of the next issue of *Dublin Opinion* magazine. But the only firm concession he came up with was a German promise to purchase 2,000 head. He promptly announced this to the Dáil much to the embarrassment of the Germans, who had not had time to clear the matter with their European partners.

Haughey and Colley were initially seen as the main contenders to succeed Lemass, while others like Jack Lynch, Donagh O'Malley, Neil Blaney, and Paddy Hillery were only mentioned as outsiders. 'Almost all agreed that Mr Colley starts with an advantage as the first choice of the Taoiseach at the present time,' wrote Michael McInerney, the political correspondent of the *Irish Times,* 'but there is great appreciation of the sheer ability of Mr Haughey in the Dáil, in the party, and in the government. The only snag, it is generally agreed, is that his public image is not favourable.'

And that image was not being enhanced by either the RTE controversy or his refusal to meet the farmers camped on his office doorstep. When he went to Athlone for a party meeting on 21 October, his car was attacked by a mob of protesting farmers. Four days later the same thing happened outside the Intercontinental Hotel in Dublin.

'Rat, rat, come out of your sewer, sewer rat,' many of the 200 farmers chanted as they tried to prevent his car entering the hotel grounds. Later they tried to prevent him from leaving by standing in front of the car and pounding on it.

'Go on, go on,' an elegantly dressed woman shouted from the sidelines. 'I hate him.'

Such scenes were not helping Haughey's leadership chances, though the Taoiseach did come to his aid by endorsing what he had done. In the course of a blistering denunciation of the intimidatory tactics, Lemass contended that the farmers were actually challenging the elementary principles of democracy. 'In these circumstances,' he added, 'it would be a matter for the government and not the minister to decide when and in what manner discussions with the National Farmers' Association representatives would be resumed.'

Colley was in the United States when he suddenly cut short his mission. He had been called home by the Taoiseach, who disclosed his intention of resigning within a week.

There is a certain amount of confusion about the role Lemass played in the succession drama. He led some correspondents to believe he was supporting Colley, but it has been argued that this was a deliberate ploy to help Haughey by discouraging others from entering the fray. Colley, with the backing of senior party figures like Aiken and MacEntee, was seen as the candidate of party traditionalists in the mould of de Valera, who were more concerned with the revival of the Irish language than with economic matters. Haughey's support, on the other hand, came largely from those interested in a more pragmatic, business-minded approach.

According to Tim Pat Coogan, Haughey was 'the epitome of the men in the mohair suits' who were changing the face of Fianna Fáil. The Minister for Agriculture and fellow ministers like Donagh O'Malley and Brian Lenihan were urban realists with little time for the pastoral idealism which inspired de Valera's dream of comely maidens dancing at the cross roads. Instead, they hung out at the Russell Hotel in the company of self-made men, speculators, builders and architects, hard-nosed go-getters whose past was often in the countryside and small towns but whose future was tied to the concrete and brick with which Dublin was being transformed.

Haughey worked hard but he also played hard, and he became the subject of an elaborate mythology of rumours, many ribald and vicious. His bonvivant lifestyle with its aristocratic trappings commanded attention, though not always the approval of those he seemed to be imitating. Among many of the staid, county set, he was despised as *nouveau riche*. Such rejection hurt him but he was able to overcome the pain by immersing himself in his work and his play. Others, some probably jealous of his successful rise, questioned how in a relatively short time he made the money to live in such opulence, especially when much of his career was in public life, where practitioners were not particularly well paid — at least not until later when their salaries increased significantly. Haughey was secretive about his business dealings, so the unanswered questions led to speculation and a situation easily exploited by enemies who spread some of the most scurrilous, defamatory rumours.

Of course, given the country's strong libel laws, which Haughey had rewritten himself, the rumours were not published. He had already shown he was not afraid to take legal action in the case of the *Sunday Independent* cartoon in August 1964. But there was little or nothing he could do about the rumours circulating in Leinster House, where the succession contest would be decided.

All agreed the contest would be close but there was a general feeling that Colley was ahead, which was hardly surprising in view of the amount of controversy surrounding Haughey at the time. Several deputies from Munster pressed Jack Lynch, the Minister for Finance, to be a candidate but he refused. Then suddenly on 3 November Kevin Boland announced he would be nominating Neil Blaney, the Minister for Local Government. Blaney indicated his willingness to stand if Lynch could not be persuaded to run. Donogh O'Malley, who had been acting as Haughey's campaign manager, promptly switched to Blaney. He apparently did so because he concluded that Colley would win in a straight contest against Haughey. With that the latter's chances quickly evaporated. James Dillon later recalled seeing him that night.

'I took one look at his face, white as parchment, and I said: "Haughey is down the sink".'

With the entry of Blaney into the race, Lemass finally moved and personally asked Lynch to stand. The Corkman agreed. Blaney and Haughey then promptly told Lemass they would support Lynch. Haughey even offered to nominate him. Only Colley held out, but the result was a foregone conclusion. Lynch won a comfortable majority when the party finally voted.

His selection was widely welcomed, even in opposition circles, where there was obvious relief that Haughey had not succeeded. James Dillon, who had confidently predicted back in July that Lynch would succeed Lemass, now rejoiced openly, as he predicted that Haughey would never be Taoiseach. 'Remember,' Dillon told the Dáil, 'when he failed to land his fish last Wednesday night, he will never land it. He is finished. He stinks, politically, of course.'

Having backed Lynch in the end, Haughey was rewarded with a prestigious promotion to what was generally seen as the second most powerful post in the government. He was appointed Minister for Finance.

5
A Popular Taxman

Minister for Finance
1966-70

'It's a little joke, sir, which you might be able to work into your Budget speech.'

Dublin Opinion, March 1967

OVER the years, ever since he delivered his maiden speech in the Dáil during the budget debate of 1957, Haughey had clearly felt his greatest expertise was in the area of finance. As a cabinet member he normally confined himself to speaking on items relating to his own portfolio, but when he did intervene in other matters, these were usually connected with finance. Hence his appointment as Minister for Finance should not have surprised anyone, but it was roundly criticised in opposition circles. Indeed the appointment became the focal point for opposition criticism of the new government.

Fine Gael leader, Liam Cosgrave, accused Haughey of being an embarrassing failure who had to be moved as Minister for

Justice because the 'Succession Bill as originally drafted would have wound up every farm and every small business in this country'. He was then moved to Agriculture where, according to Cosgrave, he made another mess and 'got involved with the farmers and not merely nearly upended the government but certainly cost himself the position of future Taoiseach'.

Patrick J. Lindsay of Fine Gael accused Haughey of being a political mercenary who caused chaos in the Department of Justice and then got into trouble with the farmers because of 'his arrogance and insolence'. Although Seán Dunne of the Labour Party refused to join in what he described as 'the beagle hunting for Charlie', his condescending remarks must have been cold comfort for Haughey. 'I think he has had enough punishment,' Dunne said. 'Everybody makes mistakes and when you become a hate symbol in society, you want a bit of sympathy, do you not?'

Haughey left himself open to further criticism when he made a *faux pas* in his first official act in the Dáil as Minister for Finance. On introducing a supplementary estimate to defray the expenses for President de Valera's state visit to United States and Canada, he mistakenly explained that the expenses had been in connection with President John F. Kennedy's visit to Ireland in 1963. James Dillon immediately exploited the mistake to berate the new minister for not having read his own department's documentation before asking for the money. 'If the minister is prudent,' Dillon continued, 'he will express his regret to the house and his resolve not to offer gross discourtesy'.

'As you would say yourself,' replied Haughey, 'go and fish.'

As Minister for Finance he had landed what was probably the second most powerful job within the government, and he could hardly have secured it at a better time. For one thing the new Taoiseach was slow to assert his authority over his ministers, with the result that they were all given 'their head to an unusual degree,' according to one commentator, who described the cabinet as 'a coalition between the various strong headed ministers each bent on the achievement of particular ambitions.' Haughey has always been keenly ambitious, so his new post accorded him real scope, especially in the prevailing economic climate. The country was actually in the midst of a boom, though it was not fully recognised at the time because the economy had just suffered a slight reversal. Nevertheless this turned out to be a mere hiccup when the figures were published for the financial year ending on 31 March 1967.

The government actually ended up with an annual surplus of £800,000 as opposed to a defecit of ten times that amount the previous year. According to Haughey, the first priority of the previous budget had been to achieve a substantial reduction in the balance of payments deficit, which was in fact reduced by almost 62 per cent. Hence he announced his first budget would reverse his predecessor's deflationary course. He was not going to raise taxation on any capital items. Instead he hoped to raise the money needed either domestically or by 'foreign borrowing if necessary'.

Haughey was making no excuses for increasing government spending on a wide range of programmes like local authority housing, where almost a quarter of the allocated £12.5 millions was being spent on the Ballymun project in Dublin. There had been an increase in unemployment, but he attributed this to a substantial drop in emigration (down by over 60 per cent since the previous year), as a result of problems in the British economy. 'The slowing down of economic activity in Great Britain,' he suggested, 'has had the result of people not emigrating from here and thereby increasing the unemployment figure by the amount of the decrease in emigration figures.'

In each of the budgets introduced by Haughey there were increases in the duty on drink, tobacco, and petrol for which he made no apologies, because consumption continued to rise as did the state's revenue from each. 'As long as they continue to come up smiling,' he said, 'they cannot expect to escape the attention of any Minister of Finance.'

These price rises were cleverly cloaked with strokes of political genius that involved imaginative yet comparatively cheap give-aways. In the budget of 1967, for instance, Haughey announced that old age pensioners would be given 100 free units of electricity every two months and that they would be allowed to travel free on public buses and trains during off-peak hours. The ESB and CIE would then be compensated for these concessions by the exchequer.

Other measures designed to help the needy included welfare and pension increases which more than offset the previous year's inflation. Moreover, as Minister for Agriculture Haughey had been appalled by the poverty he had seen in the west of Ireland. 'Up till that time,' he later explained, 'I had more of a tourist knowledge of the west than anything else. Then I saw the uncertainties of the situation and the conditions under which families were trying to live on small farms.' He therefore took steps to help the less well off among the farming community by announcing a complete derogation from rates on holdings of agricultural land valued at or less than £20 under the poor law valuation system. There would also be scaled down relief for those with land holdings valued at between £20 and £33 under the same system. Moreover, he announced that 10,000 farm owners who had been debarred from drawing unemployment assistance from March until October would henceforth be able to draw this assistance throughout the year. 'As a result,' he explained, 'small holders are not only protected against hardship throughout the year, but, because the payments are not adjusted for variations in farm output, they have every incentive to increase their incomes by more intensive use of their land.'

Some opposition deputies saw those measures as Haughey's way of repairing his damaged relations with the farming community in general. In effect, they were contending that he had been browbeaten by the ICMSA and NFA, but he denied this.

'Nobody will ever browbeat me into anything,' he declared.

Faced with the obvious popularity of so many of the budget measures, the opposition was reduced to creating what Haughey called 'a political smoke-screen' by making murky insinuations about Fianna Fáil's business dealings with property developers. Richie Ryan of Fine Gael called the concessions made to the public as a 'payment of conscience money,' and he referred to the overall financial proposals as 'this conscience money budget.'

'You are a reflection on the dignity of this house,' Haughey snapped. 'You are only a gutty.' Later Haughey exclaimed rather flippantly, 'we will string the deputy up.'

It seemed as if Ryan had struck a nerve so other colleagues, who were apparently unwilling to challenge the popular measures just announced, resorted to similar tactics.

'Our people will get the government they voted for,' James Dillon declared. 'If it is *Animal Farm* they want, they should vote for Fianna Fáil, but if it is democracy and decency they want, I suggest they will have to look elsewhere. I think the acceptance of corruption as the norm in public life is shocking.'

'Is it not another form of corruption to take people's character away, to spread false rumours about them?' Haughey asked and then went on to charge that Fine Gael had been villifying and slandering him with their malicious rumours. 'That is all you are good for, the lot of you,' he said.

Haughey explained that he would have liked to reform the whole tax system, but he could see no way of doing it. 'I have a suspicion that, by and large, there is roughly the same amount of complexity in all income tax codes because the process goes on interminably of revenue commissioners trying to close loopholes and clever accountants and lawyers finding other loopholes and revenue commissioners seeking to close these again,' he explained. 'Basically, I suspect what really annoys people about income tax is not the complexity of the code but that it has to be paid.'

No doubt there was a great deal of validity to what he said, but he was conveniently ignoring the discontent of urban workers who felt the system discriminated in favour of farmers who were exempt from paying income tax regardless of the extent of their profits. It seemed anomalous that farm labourers should be liable to income tax, while their employers were exempt. The inequity of the system was further evident in the case of the working wives of farmers.

For example, a woman teacher who married a farmer would automatically be exempt from paying income tax, no matter how much profit her husband was making on the farm. On the other hand, a single teacher, or even one married to an unemployed industrial worker would have to pay income tax. This was clearly a grave inequity, but Haughey had already been badly burned in his dealings with farmers and he showed no inclination to take them on again.

Instead he bragged about helping to raise farm incomes, which increased by an average 8.78 per cent during the year, whereas the cost of living rose by only 2 per cent. 'The increase in farm income,' he said, 'is in large degree due to government measures of various kinds including price supports for all the main farm products, fertiliser subsidies, rates relief and schemes for improving the structure and productive capacity of farms.'

Haughey's first full year as Minister for Finance was a fairly hectic one. For some time the government had been trying to prepare the country for eventual entry into the EEC and this issue came very much to the fore following Prime Minister Harold Wilson's announcement that Britain intended to apply for membership in the near future. That news came on the same day that Lemass announced his decision to resign as Taoiseach, with the result that Irish preparations for EEC membership assumed a new urgency once Lynch took over. Part of the previous preparations involved taking a greater interest in international economic matters like the General Agreement on Tariffs and Trade (GATT). Haughey's department became deeply involved in incredibly detailed negotiations which culminated in June 1967 with the drawing up of a draft agreement for Ireland's accession to GATT. Haughey later noted that one American legislator was 'on record as saying that anybody who attempts to wend his way through the intricacies of the GATT in all its developments will undoubtedly go mad.'

By this time moves were already underway for Ireland to join the EEC. On 11 May 1967 the Taoiseach formally applied for membership on behalf of the country. Britain, Denmark and Norway also applied the same day. As Minister for Agriculture in 1964 Haughey had engaged in some exploratory talks with Jean Rey, a Vice-President who had since taken over as President of the European Commission, so he became an obvious choice for the Irish delegation which was selected for preliminary talks on a bilateral basis with leaders of each of the EEC's six member states.

The Irish delegation consisted of Lynch and Haughey, together with two senior civil servants, T. K. Whitaker, Secretary of the Department of Finance, and Hugh J. McCann, Secretary of the Department of External Affairs. These bilateral talks began with meetings with Dutch Premier Petrus de Jong in The Hague on 21 and 22 June 1967. Five days later the Irish delegation met with West German leaders Chancellor Kurt Kiesinger and Finance Minister Franz Josef Strauss, in Bonn. The Dutch and German leaders expressed support for Irish membership but warned that Britain's application posed real problems because of the likely opposition of President Charles de Gaulle of France. Italian leaders like Prime Minister Aldo Moro and Foreign Minister Amintore Fanfani expressed basically the same views on 21 July when the Irish delegation met them in Rome.

The fate of the Irish application was inevitably bound up in the British request. If Britain joined the EEC, Ireland could not afford to stay out, or *vice versa*, because the Irish economy was heavily dependent on trade with Britain. When the Dáil debated the government's decision to apply for EEC membership the following week, Haughey acknowledged it was 'basically true' that Ireland had no choice economically, but he contended it was psychologically wrong to argue this way. He wanted to be positive, so he spoke forcefully in favour of membership.

'We are now at a turning point in our history,' he declared. 'Either we go on and give our people, and especially our young people, access to new horizons and give them the chance to live and work in the stimulating climate of the new Europe or we decide to remain isolated, with very little prospect of progress or opportunity for development. I submit that there is no question as to where our choice should be.' He explained that one of the most attractive aspects was the budgetary freedom which would result from relieving the national exchequer 'of the burden of supplementing the export of agricultural surpluses'. At the time over 26 per cent of the agricultural budget actually went on export subsidies. Consequently, the removal of this burden from the exchequer would, he said, provide 'very great scope for the development of social services, health services and education services to European levels'.

'We believe that possibility of membership of the Community offers us an opportunity unparalleled in our history,' Haughey continued. 'It offers us an opportunity to take part in the building of a new Europe. Inside that new Europe I think we could feel a great deal more secure in this troubled world because this new United Europe would be a potent influence in world affairs in the promotion of international peace in our time.' He left no doubt that the country's avowed policy of neutrality should not be allowed to prevent involvement in the military allignment which seemed an inevitable aspect of EEC membership. The Treaty of Rome, for instance, envisaged that the EEC would eventually become a political union, and Haughey noted that such a union 'would be utterly meaningless' without a common defence policy. He therefore favoured 'the working out of common defence arrangements'.

While Haughey remained in Dublin for the conclusion of this Dáil debate Lynch went to Brussels for talks with Belgian Prime Minister Paul van den Boeynants, who voiced misgivings about Ireland's neutrality. He noted that all six members of the EEC were part of the North Atlantic Treaty Organisation (NATO) and he said that they were anxious that all new members of the EEC should also be in NATO.

The question of Irish neutrality was raised again the following day when the Irish delegation met members of the European Commission in Brussels. Lynch explained that his government had no reservations about the political union envisaged in the Treaty of Rome. And Haughey, who by this time had rejoined the delegation, supplemented the Taoiseach's remarks by summarising his own comments in the Dáil the previous day. President Rey was obviously impressed by the assurances, which he described as 'very important'. The commissioners left the Irish in no doubt that they were favourably disposed towards admitting Ireland to the EEC, as did Prime Minister Pierre Werner of Luxembourg next day. But none of them was optimistic about the chance for early membership because of the attitude of the French government towards Britain's application.

Three full months passed before the Irish delegation was able to get together for talks in Paris with French leaders — President de Gaulle, Prime Minister Georges Pompidou, and Foreign Minister Maurice Couve de Murville. De Gaulle explained to Lynch on 2 November that France had no objections in principle to Ireland joining the EEC but he had strong reservations about admitting Britain at the time. Those reservations could only have been strengthened within a fortnight when the British decided to devalue sterling. Hence the French President effectively vetoed Britain's application to the EEC and with it the Irish application had to be postponed until after de Gaulle departed the political scene in 1969. (By the time the formal negotiations were restarted in May 1970 Haughey was out in the cold politically.)

The extent of Ireland's economic dependence on Britain was highlighted on 14 November 1967 by the Dublin government's decision to devalue the Irish currency by 14.3 per cent in line with a similar devaluation announced simultaneously in Britain. If the Irish had not followed suit it would have meant placing an effective tariff of 16.7 per cent on all Irish exports to Britain. Although the *Sunday Independent* reported that Haughey believed there was 'no reason why the cost of living' should be affected by devaluation, he admitted in the Dáil that there would be a modest increase of about 2 per cent. He expected it would remain that low because most of Ireland's main trading partners had also devalued. In fact, only 14 per cent of Irish imports came from non-devaluing countries. While such items as petrol, tea, fruit, coal, fertilisers, tobacco and animal feeding stuffs would increase in price, he argued that the rise should be gradual because stocks would already have been purchased at a pre-devaluation price.

As usual opposition speakers were critical of Haughey's actions, but their criticism lacked conviction. T. F. O'Higgins deprecated the fact that the Minister for Finance was 'in effect like a puppet on a string' held by the British Chancellor of the Exchequer. Fine Gael speakers relied heavily on the *Sunday Independent* report to accuse Haughey of complacency in the whole affair. He denied saying that the cost of living would not be affected, but he had no apologies for giving an air of complacency.

Mindful that people elsewhere had previously committed suicide as a result of fears that a devaluation had wiped out their life savings, he had deliberately cultivated an air of complacency. 'My concern was', he said, 'to point out as calmly and as objectively as I could precisely what was involved and to show that there was no need for either panic or hysteria.'

In his next budget statement on 23 April 1968, for instance, Haughey would be able to contend that the cost of living had only risen by 2 per cent, but the real effect of devaluation had not yet made its way through the system and he failed to appreciate its true impact.

Some of Haughey's new financial proposals went down very well with all sides of the house. For instance, he introduced a bill to allow him to provide pensions for the widows of deputies and senators. It promptly passed all stages of the house, taking up less than four columns in the official report. A member of the Dáil's Committee on Procedures and Privilege also asked him to accord a £500 salary increase to deputies, who were being paid £1,500 per annum at the time. His reaction was to offer them double the amount because, he said, he would get just as much stick from the public for proposing a 66 per cent increase as he would get for 33 per cent. He also introduced legislation to accord himself and other members of the government comparatively similar increases.

As the effects of devaluation began to make themselves felt in the economy, there were widespread demands for wage increases, and workers showed little receptiveness to government calls for pay moderation, especially after the politicians had voted themselves such handsome increases. Consequently it became necessary to introduce a mini-budget in the autumn, but the rectifying measures were deliberately delayed for political reasons while the government pushed through a bill for a constitutional amendment to abolish the system of proportional representation on the grounds that it was not conducive to stable government. As his party's campaign director, Haughey realised early that the amendment was in deep trouble and he privately expressed fears that he would be blamed for the setback. But, following a car accident in Co. Wicklow on 20 September 1968, he was hospitalised for the final weeks of the campaign, so he missed out on the referendum's ignominious conclusion as the government's proposal was soundly defeated at the polls. He also missed out when the Taoiseach introduced the mini-budget that had the immediate effect of causing unpopular price rises. As a result, *Hibernia* noted that he was 'relatively untainted by the odium of recent setbacks.'

The corrective measures proved successful, at least as far as Haughey was concerned. He proudly declared that '1968 was the best year in our economic history.' Industrial production increased by 11 per cent to reach a record level, and 'the value and volume' of agricultural output also 'broke all previous records'. As a result farm income increased by 16 per cent.

In 1969 the budget was clearly constructed with one eye on the forthcoming general election, which was then less than six weeks away. As usual Haughey included some giveaways. His most celebrated stroke in the budget of 1969 was his proposal to grant income tax exemptions to writers and artists.

'As a further encouragement to the creative artists in our midst and to help create a sympathetic environment here in which the arts can flourish,' he announced, 'I will provide in the Finance Bill that painters, sculptors, writers and composers living and working in Ireland will be free of tax on all earnings derived from work of creative merit.' This measure secured international publicity for Haughey as a patron of the arts.

In the same budget address he also announced that disabled drivers would henceforth be permitted to buy up to 350 gallons of duty-free petrol annually. The travel concessions already given to old age pensioners were extended to those on British and Northern Ireland pensions, the cheap fuel scheme was extended to cover the months of October and April, and children's allowances were increased. Haughey also announced that the exchequer would pay £100 on the birth of triplets and £150 for quads.

'The Minister is the best gimmick raiser in the business,' Paddy Donegan of Fine Gael exclaimed in reaction to the grants for triplets and quads. The whole thing would not cost even £1,000 because very few triplets were born in a year and Haughey admitted no quads were born in Ireland. Describing the whole thing as 'typical of the minister's approach to life and politics,' Donegan noted that Haughey was so anxious to please voters that he 'would chase a vote from where he lives right across the city to Dun Laoghaire'.

This, of course, was the art of politics, as far as Haughey was concerned. With such measures — whether gimmicks or not — he distracted attention from the more unpalatable aspects of the economic situation. From the previous year's surplus, there had been a swing of £35 millions into the red, which he conveniently glossed over by saying that the deficit was not as high as projected.

He was making no apologies for his policy of borrowing. 'The public capital programme of investment by the government in desirable social and economic projects has been increasing year by year,' he explained. 'We have been borrowing money to finance that programme and we are very proud to be able to do that. The public capital programme this year is the highest on record.'

Haughey was again national director of elections for Fianna Fáil in the June general election. This was Jack Lynch's first general election as Taoiseach and Haughey sought to exploit the leader's popularity by having him tour the country in the style of an American presidential candidate.

The Fianna Fáil's fund raisers had already been adopting American methods in the form of Taca, a support group made up mostly of businessmen who were invited to join at £100 per year. The money was then deposited in a bank until election time, while the interest was used to fund lavish dinners at which members of Taca could mix with cabinet ministers.

Taca was 'a fairly innocent concept', according to Haughey. 'In so far as it had any particular motivation it was to make the party independent of big business and try to spread the level of financial support right across a much wider spectrum of the community.' For instance, some members had previously been subscribing 'substantially more' to the party at election time than even the £500 which would accumulate in Taca subscriptions if there were five full years between elections.

Although Haughey was the politician most associated with Taca in the public mind, the idea had come from somebody else and the funds were controlled by the Taoiseach, Boland and Blaney. Nevertheless the Minister for Finance embraced the scheme with enthusiasm and took on the organisation of the first dinner, which was a particularly lavish affair with the whole cabinet in attendance.

'We were all organised by Haughey and sent to different tables around the room', Kevin Boland recalled. 'The extraordinary thing about my table was that everybody at it was in some way or other connected with the construction industry.'

Opposition deputies promptly began asking questions about the propriety of this cosiness between the property developers and members of the government. In particular, there were questions about the selection of property being rented by government departments and agencies as they mushroomed in the midst of the unprecedented economic growth. Boland was adamant that he 'never did a thing' within his department for members of Taca, but he admitted that other ministers might have been 'susceptible.' A cloud of suspicion was cast over the operations of Taca and it 'unfortunately provided a basis for political attack which', Haughey said, 'did us a lot of damage at the time'.

Insinuations of corruption were widespread and these were fuelled in May 1967 when George Colley urged those attending a Fianna Fáil youth conference in Galway not to be 'dispirited if some people in high places appeared to have low standards'. In view of the intensity of their rivalry over the party leadership some months earlier, it was widely assumed that Colley was alluding to Haughey in particular.

Liam Cosgrave neatly linked the remarks to the activities of Taca in his presidential address to the Fine Gael ard fheis a few days later, when he challenged Colley to name names. But if the Fianna Fáil minister *had* been referring to a cabinet colleague, he promptly backtracked. Colley denied that he had been alluding to any member of the government. Instead, he cited Cosgrave's own ard fheis speech as an example of the kind of thing he had in mind.

In the middle of the general election campaign of 1969, Haughey found himself more openly implicated in the Taca controversy following a sensational report in the *Evening Herald* about the sale of his Raheny home. The newspaper stated that it was sold to his developer friend, Matt Gallagher, for over £200,000.

The Minister for Finance promply issued a statement complaining about the report. 'I object to my private affairs being used in this way,' he declared. First of all, he noted that none of the figures could be given with certainty, because he did not give details to any reporter. 'It is a private matter between myself and the purchaser.'

But the whole thing became a national issue when Gerard Sweetman, the former Fine Gael Minister for Finance, announced that a senior counsel had advised him that Haughey might have been liable for income tax on the sale of the land had he not recently introduced legislation to repeal the relevant part of the 1965 Finance Act. Thus, Sweetman charged, the Minister for Finance had personally benefited from legislation he introduced himself without explaining his own position to the Dáil.

Suddenly Haughey was forced into the position of having to discuss his private business dealings as a result of the charge by Sweetman. 'Because he has impugned my reputation,' the

Minister for Finance explained, 'I have felt obliged to refer the matter to the Revenue Commissioners, under whose care and management are placed all taxes and duties imposed by the Finance Act 1965.' The Revenue Commissioners promptly reported 'that no liability to income tax or surtax would have arisen' under any provision of the 1965 act. Although this should have killed the issue, one of his opponents in his Dublin North Central constituency — the Labour Party candidate, Conor Cruise O'Brien — raked it up repeatedly during the campaign in an effort to expose what he described as 'the Fianna Fáil speculator-orientated oligarchy.'

The media was enthralled by the contest. The *Irish Times* gave an in-depth biographical profile of both Haughey and O'Brien extending over three days each. As a result it was hardly surprising that both men did well in the election.

Haughey again increased his vote to top the poll with 11,677 votes, while Cruise O'Brien was a distant second over 4,000 votes behind. Although Fianna Fáil's overall vote throughout the country dropped by 2 per cent, the party actually gained two seats through the vagaries of the PR system which it had so recently tried to scrap.

Lynch was therefore re-elected as Taoiseach and he again appointed Haughey as Minister for Finance. This was a particularly critical time as the situation in Northern Ireland, which had been smouldering for the past year as the civil rights campaign gathered momentum, erupted into large-scale violence during August. The nationalist minority in Northern Ireland was exposed to the threat of a concerted attack from the RUC, the B Specials and loyalist mobs. Pressure mounted on the Dublin government to take some kind of effective action on behalf of the threatened nationalists. The immediate response came in the form of an offer of financial help to relieve their distress. This was how Haughey initially became involved in the events that eventually led to the Arms Crisis the following year. His involvement and the circumstances surrounding it will be discussed at length in the following chapters.

Partly as a result of the Northern troubles the economy began to slow down, but speaking in December, Haughey was still able to describe it as 'a reasonably good year'. Industrial exports rose by 20 per cent, but the economic boom of the past few years was having some undesirable consequences. 'The problems we have stem from growth and from expansion', he explained. 'We could solve all our problems simply by stopping growth, by turning off the tap.' In particular, the demand for wage increases was outstripping the economic advances and the new found wealth had led to an increased demand for consumer imports and thus to a severe trade deficit. He played this down at the time saying that 'what really matters is the trend, and that can only be identified over reasonably long periods.'

But it continued to rise in the following months to the extent that the annual deficit reached £60 millions, or nearly three times worse than the previous year. In the three full years that Haughey had served as Minister for Finance, the deficit had quadrupled and he intended to tell the Dáil in his next budget address that the deficit could be 'substantially higher' in 1970.

Haughey complained about unrealistic wage demands. 'Scarcely a year passes without claims for increases well above what the rise in national production would justify,' he believed. 'Under threats of disruption of their business, the tendency of employers has been to buy industrial peace at too high a price in labour cost.' In fact, the annual rise in wages was more than twice the increase of national production.

Among the giveaways or strokes that Haughey planned in the new budget was the introduction of a deserted wives allowance equivalent to the non-contributory old age pension. He also intended to announce the extension of the free electricity and free travel schemes to widows of veterans of the War of Independence. All told he would need £20 millions to finance various increases and he intended to recoup the bulk of this by doubling the turnover tax to 5 per cent. 'I have come to the conclusion,' he wrote, 'that the added-value tax is the most efficient system of collecting a turnover tax extending to the retail stage.'

'There was a hushed silence as Mr Haughey rose from his usual seat and walked across to the Taoiseach's place on the front bench to open his briefcase,' the *Evening Herald* reported. 'The minister, who began his budget speech earlier than usual because of the small number of queries during Question Time, started off with a review of the economy in general.'

Over the years Haughey had complained more than once about the unreliability of the evening newspapers and now the

Evening Herald was making his case for him in spectacular style, because far from starting his budget address early, the Minister for Finance was not even in the Dáil. Instead Lynch announced that Haughey had had an accident that morning and was in hospital, where he had been 'ordered to remain under medical observation for some days'. As a result the Taoiseach read the budget address himself.

According to Haughey, the injuries resulted from a fall from a horse, but contrary rumours began circulating almost immediately. The gárda commissioner informed Peter Berry that 'a strange rumour was circulating in North Co. Dublin that Mr Haughey's accident occurred on a licensed premises on the previous night.' Berry related this to the Taoiseach, who 'was emphatic' that there should be no gárda enquiries into the 'accident'.

'Within a couple of days,' Berry noted, 'there were all sorts of rumours in golf clubs, in political circles etc., as to how the accident occurred, with various husbands, fathers, brothers or lovers having struck the blow in any one of dozens of pubs around Dublin.' The rumours were so persistent that Haughey took the unusual step of having one of the stable hands who had witnessed the riding accident talk to the press.

But by then the rumours of Haughey's other activities were already rampant as the country found itself in the midst of the Arms Crisis which led to his dismissal as Minister for Finance on 6 May 1970.

6
'Not even the Slightest Suspicion'

The Arms Crisis
1969-70

Lynch's wives must be above suspicion.

Hibernia, May 1970

IT was around three o'clock in the morning of 6 May 1970 when Jack Lynch issued a statement to the press that was to shock the Irish public and lead to a major political crisis. 'I have', he began, 'requested the resignation of members of the government, Mr Neil T. Blaney, Minister for Agriculture, and Mr C. J. Haughey, Minister for Finance, because I am satisfied that they do not subscribe fully to government policy in relation to the present situation in the Six Counties as stated by me at the Fianna Fáil ard-fheis in January last.'

This was not all. On learning of the Taoiseach's decision, Kevin Boland had resigned as Minister for Local Government and Social Welfare in protest, and Paudge Brennan, his Parliamentary Secretary, did likewise. The country was suddenly awash with rumours that the Taoiseach had discovered plans for a coup d'état. It was not until hours later that Lynch explained to the Dáil that he had acted because security forces had informed him 'about an alleged attempt to unlawfully import arms from the continent'. As these reports referred to the two cabinet ministers, he decided to ask them to resign on the basis 'that not even the slightest suspicion should attach to any member of the government in a matter of this nature'.

To understand what happened one must go back to events surrounding serious violence which erupted in Derry following the Apprentice Boys' parade on 12 August 1969. The parade was attacked by nationalist protesters. The police, supported by unionist thugs, then beseiged the nationalist area. What became known as the Battle of the Bogside had begun and quickly spread to other nationalist areas of Northern Ireland, which seemed on the brink of a full-scale civil war.

Amid the escalating violence the cabinet met in Dublin. Lynch arrived with a draft speech which he intended to deliver during a television address that evening. Several members of the cabinet objected that the speech was too weak. Haughey, Blaney, and Boland, together with Jim Gibbons, Brian Lenihan and Seán Flanagan, all called for something stronger, so a new address was prepared at the cabinet meeting.

'The Stormont government evidently is no longer in control of the situation, which is the inevitable outcome of policies pursued for decades by them,' Lynch told the nation that evening. 'The government of Ireland can no longer stand by . . .'

The statement had an electrifying impact on the situation in the North. The beseiged nationalists in the Bogside thought that the Republic was going to come to their aid militarily, while the unionist population — blinded by an irrational fear of the South — reacted hysterically in the belief that Northern Ireland was about to be invaded. Lynch's speech really had most unhappy consequences, because the Dublin government never had any intention of invading.

The Irish army was woefully unprepared. Even Kevin Boland, one of the cabinet's most outspoken proponents of assisting the northern nationalists, believed it would be 'disastrous' for the Irish army to become involved. 'Places contiguous to the border could obviously be assisted effectively,' Boland contended, 'but to do so would mean the wholesale slaughter of nationalists [or Catholics] in other areas where there was no defence available. I feel reasonably certain that the others also saw this and that none of them visualised an actual incursion.'

Faced with the irrational frenzy of the heavily armed unionist community, northern nationalists were extremely vulnerable. They had few arms, while the unionists had at their apparent disposal the armed Royal Ulster Constabulary (RUC) and the dreaded paramilitary police reserve, the B Specials.

Defence Committees were established in nationalist areas and their representatives came south to Dublin for help. All had the same message; they needed arms to protect themselves. Even a renowned moderate like Gerry Fitt, the future leader of the Social Democratic and Labour Party (SDLP), was among those asking for guns.

'We asked for guns,' explained John Kelly, a Belfast republican who came on some of the deputations. 'No one from Taoiseach Lynch down refused that request or told us this was contrary to government policy.' But neither did Lynch ever promise guns.

At the time the government was reacting to the crisis in a number of ways. It launched a massive propaganda campaign to enlist international sympathy for the nationalist position. Experts were seconded from various state companies and sent abroad to conduct the campaign. But, other than this moral support, the only tangible assistance offered to the people on the other side of the border was in the form of financial help to relieve the distress.

'There was a feeling among the government, and among the community as a whole, that we could not do a great deal to help the people of the North', Haughey explained. 'We knew that a lot of people were suffering very severe hardship and distress and the government decided to be generous in coming to their aid. I was appointed as the person to see that this aid was given as freely and generously as possible.' The actual terms of the cabinet decision were that 'a sum of money — the amount and the channel of disbursement of which would be determined by the Minister for Finance — should be made available from the

Exchequer to provide aid for the victims of unrest in the Six Counties'.

'There was no sum of money specified,' according to Haughey. 'I was instructed by the government to make money available on a generous scale to whatever extent we required.' In short, he was given virtual *carte blanche* to help the nationalists financially.

'In my experience,' explained Charles H. Murray, the secretary of the Department of Finance, 'I have never seen a government decision that was drafted in such wide terms.'

The cabinet also decided to set up a committee consisting of Haughey, Blaney, Padraig Faulkner and Joe Brennan to cope with the government's lack of reliable information about what was happening in Northern Ireland. 'We were given the instruction that we should develop the maximum possible contacts with persons inside the Six Counties and try to inform ourselves as fully as possible on events and on political and other type of developments in the Six County area,' Haughey later testified.

It was also decided that plans should be drawn up in case the government later decided to intervene militarily in Northern Ireland. The Minister for Defence, Jim Gibbons, was told to get the army to prepare contingency plans. And, as the army had been starved of money for years, Haughey and Gibbons were charged with ensuring that the forces were properly prepared with the best equipment the state could afford.

'It was an amazingly irresponsible thing to do,' according to Boland. Both Haughey and Gibbons had been advocating a hardline policy with which Lynch did not agree.

The Taoiseach should have seen the danger signs within a week. On 20 August 1969 Peter Berry, the secretary of the Department of Justice, gave Michael Moran, the Minister for Justice, a seven-page document outlining, among other things, details of a meeting between a cabinet minister and a prominent member of the IRA. According to the report, the minister, who had not been identified by the police sources, promised that the authorities would not interfere with IRA operations planned for Northern Ireland, if the IRA called off all the activities within the twenty-six counties. Moran read out this document at the next cabinet meeting.

'That could have been me,' Haughey volunteered. 'I was

asked to see someone casually and it transpired to be this person. There was nothing to it; it was entirely casual.'

Initially on hearing this Berry 'was completely reassured', because he remembered Haughey had taken such a strong stand against the IRA on becoming Minister for Justice back in 1961. Now it seemed inconceivable that he would act in such a manner, but the security people were not reassured at all. 'They repeated that their sources had proved reliable in the past,' Berry noted. Moreover, in subsequent reports Haughey was accused of having supposedly promised the IRA leader £50,000 at the meeting.

There were also some disturbing reports about the activities of Haughey's brother, Pádraig (Jock), who had been selected by the Minister for Finance to go to Britain as part of an official team to galvanise 'those disposed to be friendly' to help relieve the distress in Northern Ireland. While in London, the Special Branch believed, Jock Haughey engaged in negotiations to purchase arms.

The unarmed nationalist people in the Six Counties were undoubtedly living in dread of armed, hostile loyalist thugs, so that the provision of arms for defensive purposes could be seen as a legitimate means of relieving distress. Jock Haughey and John Kelly opened negotiations with one Captain M. Randall, who just happened to be an undercover British agent. Sensing that something was wrong, the two of them returned to Ireland. Randall was invited for further talks in Dublin, where the Englishman stupidly betrayed himself by trying to recruit a republican as a British agent. At that point Randall might well have been murdered by the IRA except for the intervention of an Irish military intelligence officer, Captain James J. Kelly, who was soon to play a central role in the developing drama.

When the Battle of the Bogside began, Captain Kelly happened to be in Derry on vacation. On returning to Dublin he wrote a report of his impressions of events for Colonel Michael Hefferon, the director of military intelligence. The latter was delighted to get the report, especially from someone like Captain Kelly, who had twenty years experience in the army, with the last ten years in military intelligence. At the time, even military intelligence had been caught unawares by the ferocity of events north of the border.

The situation had developed 'like a thunderclap on top of everybody,' according to Hefferon. 'I was very glad of any information. I had to run around and try to find out the people that would give me the most because you had a whole lot of rumours going which had no foundation to them.' He therefore instructed Captain Kelly to maintain his northern contacts, and the captain made another visit to the North in the first half of September, along with Seamus Brady, a journalist working on the government's propaganda campaign.

Gerry Fitt was among those whom Captain Kelly met in Belfast. 'Fitt made clear the urgency of the situation and that it was of paramount importance to get in arms immediately,' the captain reported.

On returning to Dublin he and Brady discussed their visit with the latter's friend, Neil Blaney, who — as a member of the cabinet committee charged with finding out what was happening in the North — was particularly interested in what they had to say. He then arranged for them to meet Haughey. Brady broached the Minister for Finance with the idea of establishing a newspaper and a pirate radio station to direct propaganda at the Six Counties in order 'to maintain the new-found morale of the minority and to keep pressure up against the Unionist authorities.'

'I brought the idea to Charles Haughey for a preliminary discussion because I valued his judgment,' Brady wrote. 'As director of elections for the Fianna Fáil Party in two successive general elections, he had acquired, in my opinion, considerable expertise in regard to publicity and propaganda work.' Haughey endorsed the newspaper idea and even suggested it be called *The Voice of Ireland,* an idea which was partially adopted when Brady launched the *Voice of the North* a few weeks later.

Haughey was having difficulty selecting reliable people to ensure that relief money would get to the right quarters in the North. Initially it had been envisaged that most of the money would be distributed by the Irish Red Cross, but the latter was refused permission to function in Northern Ireland by its British counterpart. Haughey therefore turned to military intelligence for help.

'About the end of September,' Colonel Hefferon recalled, 'I was asked by Mr Haughey to see him at his residence and to bring Captain Kelly along.' The Minister for Finance was looking for advice in order to establish a committee of reputable individuals who would oversee the distribution of financial relief, so Captain Kelly briefed him on the position in the North.

'At this stage', the captain later explained, 'there were delegations coming down to see government members and primarily the conversation was about the members of these delegations, any of them I had met, what information I had concerning them and so on.' He told the Minister for Finance that he had arranged to meet between fifteen and twenty representatives from the various defence committees in nine days time at a hotel in Bailieboro, Co. Cavan, but he needed money to cover his expenses. On Haughey's instructions, the Department of Finance provided £500.

Captain Kelly's activities had already aroused the suspicion of the Special Branch, which was disturbed that he had been meeting with known members of the IRA. Berry was actually in hospital for tests when he learned that the captain was in Bailieboro for a meeting with a group of IRA people, including the Chief of Staff Cathal Goulding. Berry immediately tried to notify Moran and then the Taoiseach, but neither was at home. He therefore telephoned Haughey, who promptly called to the hospital.

Although Berry had been having some distinguished visitors, like President de Valera and Archbishop McQuaid, he noted that Haughey's visit caused more excitement among the nursing staff than any of the other visitors. Believing the information was of critical national importance, the secretary felt he had to warn a member of the cabinet as soon as possible and, in the absence of the others, Haughey was an obvious choice. After all the Minister for Finance had experience of the Justice portfolio.

'I told him of Captain Kelly's goings on and of the visit planned for Bailieboro,' Berry noted. 'He did not seem unduly perturbed about Captain Kelly but was quite inquisitive about what I knew of Goulding. I felt reassured.'

Of course, Berry did not know at the time that the Minister for Finance had actually provided money to cover the expenses of the Bailieboro meeting, and Haughey did not enlighten him. If the meeting in Co. Cavan was the genesis of the plot to import arms, as Captain Kelly later contended, then this meeting between Berry and Haughey can be seen as the genesis of the Arms Crisis itself. Berry had taken Haughey into his confidence, but the Minister had not reciprocated. If Haughey's actions and intentions were above-board, Berry could well ask why the minister had not put him fully into the picture? It was only a matter of time before the Special Branch learned of Haughey's involvement, and Berry undoubtedly felt a sense of betrayal. It was he who then did most to frustrate the gun-running plans first hatched at Bailieboro. Indeed, it was because of Berry's opposition that the whole thing was called off at the eleventh hour, and then his personal attitude towards Haughey was clearly a factor in his determination to ensure the whole affair was not hushed up.

Although Haughey had been warned by Berry, he had no reservations about turning to Captain Kelly for advice and help in the coming weeks. 'I had no hesitation in receiving assistance from Captain Kelly in briefing me on the situation in the North of Ireland and letting me know who the different groups were and all that sort of thing,' Haughey declared. It was with Captain Kelly's advice and help that a relief committee of three northern nationalists was selected to administer the government's relief funds following the Bailieboro meeting. A bank account under their joint control was opened in Clones, and Haughey personally telephoned the secretary-general of the Irish Red Cross to deposit £5,000 in the account. Thereafter Haughey's personal secretary, Anthony Fagan, would transfer money to the Red Cross with instructions that it be forwarded to the relief account.

The Irish Red Cross was basically being used to launder the money, so that the committee could pretend its funds had nothing to do with the Dublin government. 'If there were any questions in the North then they would say "We got it from the Irish Red Cross",' Fagan explained. 'In other words, it was a ruse, if you like, but a deliberate one to protect these people.'

Haughey was anxious to insulate his department from any apparent involvement in Northern Ireland. He instructed his staff to ensure 'that no communication should go north of the border which indicates that we are interested in helping out these people'. Captain Kelly acted as an unofficial liaison between the Minister for Finance and the northern nationalists. Whenever Haughey wanted information or to pass on a message about the North, he would call on the captain.

'Get Kelly to do it,' he would tell Fagan.

When money was needed Captain Kelly would go to Fagan, who would forward a note like:

> Minister,
> Kelly wants another £3,500 from the Bank a/c in the usual way.
> Is this OK please?

Haughey would then simply write 'OK' on the note. A few times he did baulk temporarily. 'This cannot go on for ever,' he said to Fagan. But each time he authorised the requested payments after discussing them with Captain Kelly.

Meanwhile Berry learned the details of what had happened at the Bailieboro meeting from his sources. Again he could not get in touch with Moran, so he telephoned Lynch, who called at the hospital on the morning of 18 October as Berry was undergoing tests. Although 'a bit muzzy' at the time, Berry was certain he told the Taoiseach of Captain Kelly's activities.

'I told him of Captain Kelly's prominent part in the Bailieboro meeting with known members of the IRA, of his possession of a wad of money, of his standing drinks and of the sum of money — £50,000 — that would be available for the purchase of arms.'

Lynch later denied the conversation ever took place, but this was apparently one of those occasions on which he was suffering from political amnesia. He actually told Gibbons about Berry's report, and the Minister for Defence, in turn, questioned Colonel Hefferon, but that was apparently the end of the matter.

In the last week of December 1969 there was a curious incident following the arrest of some Derrymen with weapons just on the southern side of the border. Moran told Berry the Taoiseach wanted 'to throw the book' at those arrested, so charges were preferred against them, much to the annoyance of the Minister for Finance.

'Twenty-four hours later Mr Haughey was on to me furiously enquiring who had given the gardaí the *stupid* direction to arrest the men,' Berry wrote. 'I told him that the decision came from the very top'.

'Do you mean the Taoiseach?' Haughey asked.

'Yes.'

Berry explained what had happened but said the charges would be thrown out if the men recognised the court. Otherwise he said they would be committed for contempt. Haughey remained furious. 'His language,' according to Berry, 'was not the kind usually heard in church. He said that he would ensure that there would be no contempt.'

As a result of the arrest Berry concluded that the Taoiseach wanted it to be seen publicly that he would not condone such conduct, but at the same time his failure to make 'any more than a cursory enquiry' about the Bailieboro meeting prompted the secretary of the Department of Justice to conclude that Lynch 'was not thankful' for being told of the plot to import arms. In short, Berry suspected the Taoiseach wished to be able to turn a blind eye to the planned gun running, and this assessment was shared by more than one member of the cabinet. There had already been such persistent rumours of an earlier importation of small arms destined for Northern Ireland that members of the government were certain the gun running had occurred. Consequently, when nothing effective was done about Berry's warning, Kevin Boland concluded that the Taoiseach privately approved of smuggling arms. 'As far as I could see,' Boland explained, 'everyone assumed everyone else knew and the matter was spoken of as if it was a case of the government assisting in the only way a government could assist without a diplomatic breach.' Nevertheless he did believe that Lynch would veto such gun running if someone brought it up in cabinet. 'I felt sure', Boland admitted, 'this importation would not be agreed to by the Taoiseach, if it had come up for specific government decision.'

Whether the Taoiseach had been deliberately turning a blind eye to all of this may be open to question, but there could be little doubt that his wishes were deliberately circumvented on the question of financing *Voice of the North*.

'Brady understood that the Government Information Bureau wished him to publish this newspaper', Haughey explained. But the bureau refused when he asked for support. He therefore turned to the Minister for Finance for help. 'He came to me,' Haughey said, 'and indicated that he had put £650 of his own money into the publication and he was now in difficulty with the Government Information Bureau because they were not prepared to pay up.'

Haughey talked to the Taoiseach about the matter, but Lynch was adamant 'that public monies were not to be used for this publication.' Nevertheless more than £5,000 of public funds, allocated for relief of distress in Northern Ireland, was secretly given to Brady to support the publication in the following weeks.

Initially the funds from the Department of Finance were laundered simply to protect the committee supervising the account, but some twists were soon added to the laundering procedure. On 7 November Captain Kelly made arrangements to transfer most of the money from the Clones bank account to a new account at the Munster & Leinster Bank in Baggot Street, Dublin. This time the three people supposedly controlling the account were each listed under assumed names. And a further twist was added to the laundering method a couple of days later when two other accounts were opened at the same bank in the respective names of George Dixon and Ann O'Brien.

Relief money allocated by the Department of Finance would be sent to the Red Cross with instructions that it be transferred to the relief account in Baggot Street. Some of this money was then transferred to the Ann O'Brien account, from where the payments were made to Brady. Other transfers were made to the George Dixon account, from which the money was withdrawn to purchase arms.

During February and March 1970 Captain Kelly visited Germany where he purchased a variety of machine guns, grenades and pistols, as well as flak jackets and ammunition. It was planned to ship the arms from Antwerp on the *City of Dublin,* which set sail on 19 March and docked in Dublin six days later.

As Minister for Finance, Haughey gave instructions for the cargo to be cleared through customs without being inspected. Captain Kelly and John Kelly were at the Dublin docks with a lorry to take the arms to a hiding place, but the weapons had not been loaded aboard in Antwerp because the papers for them were not in order.

Captain Kelly therefore made further trips to the continent, and he brought Albert Luykx, a Dublin-based businessman of Belgian origin, to act as his interpreter. At first the captain planned to have the cargo transferred to Trieste for shipment to Ireland, but while it was en route he had it offloaded in Vienna so that it could be flown directly to Ireland on a chartered plane.

Plans were made for the weapons to be flown to Dublin on Tuesday, 21 April 1970. But the Special Branch staked out the airport with the aim of seizing the cargo.

Haughey learned that the Special Branch were at the airport with instructions to seize the incoming cargo unless someone in authority told them to do otherwise. He therefore telephoned Berry, who confirmed that the cargo would be seized as soon as the plane landed. The Minister for Finance then said that he would have the whole thing called off.

Berry really found himself in a tricky position. He was supposed to report to the Minister for Justice, but Moran had been ill in recent months and his illness was compounded by heavy drinking, with the result that the secretary did not feel that he could depend on him to pass on his warning to the government. The Special Branch had been pretty much on top of matters for the past few months but the government had done nothing about its warnings. Moran did complain to at least one colleague that he had been trying to get Lynch to act on the matter, but the Taoiseach would do nothing.

Berry had his own doubts about Lynch after nothing had happened following the warning he had given about Captain Kelly back in October. 'I had some lingering doubt that all this could not have gone on for several months without the knowledge of the Taoiseach unless he was wilfully turning the blind eye,' Berry wrote. He therefore decided the time had come to get in touch with President de Valera in order to force Lynch's hand.

Berry did not actually give de Valera any details. He just asked him what he should do about some information 'of national concern' when he was not sure the information would get to the Taoiseach by the normal channel. He knew the President would tell him to go directly to Lynch, so he was not actually looking for advice. His real aim was simply to bring de Valera into the picture in the hope of getting some action from Lynch.

'By consulting the President, and telling the Taoiseach that I had consulted the President,' Berry wrote, 'I would be pushing the Taoiseach towards an enforcement of the rule of law.'

Berry told the Taoiseach on the morning of 20 April 1970. Lynch immediately instructed him to have the whole matter investigated thoroughly and to report again the following morning, when Berry confirmed that Haughey and Blaney had been involved in the plot.

Lynch decided he would interview the two ministers the following day, but that was the day on which Haughey had his accident, so the Taoiseach did nothing about it until he could speak to Haughey.

'I ultimately got the doctor's permission and I decided to interview Deputy Haughey in hospital on Wednesday 29 April,' Lynch explained to the Dáil. Before the meeting the Taoiseach was very agitated.

'What will I do, what will I do?' he kept muttering as he paced about his office.

'Well, if I were you,' Berry said, 'I'd sack the pair of them and I would tell the British immediately, making a virtue of necessity, as the British are bound to know, anyway, all that is going on.'

But Lynch had not been looking for advice. He was just talking to himself and he abused Berry for having the impertinence to advise him.

The Taoiseach spoke to Blaney first and then went to the hospital to speak to Haughey. 'Each of them denied he instigated in any way the attempted importation of arms,'' Lynch told the Dáil. 'They asked me for time to consider their position. I agreed to do so.'

At this point Lynch apparently hoped that the whole thing could be swept under the carpet. He sent for Berry next day and told him that he had talked to the two ministers and that the matter was therefore ended as there would be no repetition. Berry was stunned.

'Does that mean Mr Haughey remains Minister for Finance?' he asked incredulously. 'What will my position be? He knows that I have told you of his conversation with me on 18 April and of the earlier police information.'

'I will protect you,' replied Lynch.

Next day the Taoiseach told his cabinet that he had decided to accept the denials of the two ministers. But he warned, according to Boland, 'that henceforth no minister should take any action in regard to requests for assistance from the Six Counties without approval.'

Boland went straight over to Haughey afterwards and told him the news. Although Boland thought the crisis was over, it was really only beginning. The story had been leaked to Liam Cosgrave, the Fine Gael leader, who tried to interest the *Sunday Independent* and the *Irish Independent* in the story, but their editors thought it too hot to handle.

On 5 May Lynch announced in the Dáil that Moran had resigned as Minister for Justice on the grounds of ill-health. Although rumours were already circulating about the arms plot, the Taoiseach successfully managed to skirt questions about further possible resignations. At eight o'clock that evening, however, Cosgrave confronted Lynch with the story.

'I considered it my duty in the national interest to inform the Taoiseach of information I had received which indicates a situation of such gravity for the nation that it is without parallel in this country since the foundation of the state,' Cosgrave told the Dáil. He did not bother to mention that he had first tried to interest the press.

That night Lynch demanded the resignation of Haughey and Blaney, but both refused. He therefore requested President de Valera to remove them from office in accordance with the constitution. After this was done, the Taoiseach made his early morning announcement to the press. There was a ceremony commemorating the Easter Rebellion next morning, so the Dáil did not convene until the early evening. First there was a meeting of the Fianna Fáil parliamentary party, at which Haughey joined Blaney and the other members of the party in unanimously upholding the Taoiseach's right to remove them.

The Dáil then began a continuous sitting that was to last for over thirty-seven hours as it debated the crisis. Tension was running high afterwards and scuffles actually broke out in the lobbies. 'It was not clear who was directly involved, but some deputies had to restrain others,' the *Irish Independent* reported.

Haughey did not take part in the debate but he voted with the government, as did Blaney and Boland. Members of Fianna Fáil seemed preoccupied with retaining power. 'The necessity to keep the Fianna Fáil government in power at all costs was the overriding consideration', Berry concluded. 'What was happening in the Lynch regime would have been unthinkable under Mr Lemass or Mr de Valera. The naked face of self-interest in ministerial circles was on exhibition without any attempts at concealment from the serving civil servants.'

After the Dáil vote Haughey simply issued a statement in which he categorically denied having 'taken part in any illegal importation or attempted importation of arms into this country.' On 25 May he repeated this in a further statement in which he concurred with the Taoiseach's view that 'not even the slightest suspicion should attach to any member of the government.'

'I have fully accepted the Taoiseach's decision, as I believe that the unity of the Fianna Fáil Party is of greater importance to the welfare of the nation than my political career,' Haughey emphasised. He was facing possible criminal charges and this was a desperate appeal to Fianna Fáil's traditional solidarity. But the appeal was in vain.

On 27 May Captain Kelly, John Kelly and Luykx were arrested, and it was clearly only a matter of time before Haughey would be charged. Next day, when the gardaí arrived at Kinsealy to arrest him, Haughey's solicitor and friend, Pat O'Connor, was at the house. He offered to drive the former minister to the Bridewell, but the police refused. As a result Haughey, with his hand still in a sling, had to suffer the indignity of being arrested and taken from his home in a police car like a common criminal.

7
'Whatever it is'

The Arms Trials
1970

The A.G.: 'W-would you G-gentlemen be k-kind enough to s-s-step inside for q-q-questioning ... if you please.

Hibernia, 29 May 1970

ON 28 May 1970 Haughey and Blaney were formally charged with conspiring to import arms into the country illegally. They were then promptly released on bail.

Although the media as a whole had been slow to question Lynch's motives in dismissing his two ministers, there could be little doubt that political considerations had played a major part in determining the subsequent timing of their arrest. Both still enjoyed support within the parliamentary party, so there was a danger their supporters might react emotionally to the arrests and bring down the government in a fit of pique. It was therefore decided that the two men should be arrested on Thursday, 27 May, because the Dáil would be breaking up early that day for the bank holiday weekend and would not reconvene until the following Wednesday. This would afford deputies an opportunity to get over their initial shock and give them time to ponder the consequences of bringing down the government. Whether they would ever have done so can only be a matter for speculation because they made no attempt once the Dáil reconvened the following week. Lynch had survived another crisis and his popularity was soaring, while Haughey's political career seemed in tatters.

A public opinion poll showed that 72 per cent of the electorate agreed with Haughey's dismissal. He was actually more popular — or rather, less unpopular — outside Fianna Fáil than he was within the party. He was the preferred choice for Taoiseach of just 3 per cent of the electorate and a mere 1 per cent of those who had voted for Fianna Fáil last time, while Lynch was the choice as Taoiseach of 82 per cent of the electorate as a whole and a staggering 89 per cent of those who had voted for Fianna Fáil last time. Without Lynch in the race for party leader, Haughey was only fourth as the choice of 11 per cent just behind Blaney and well behind Colley and Hillery. Comparatively few people could have thought that he would eventually replace Lynch as leader of the party, much less as Taoiseach.

Notwithstanding the enormous popularity enjoyed by the Lynch government in the polls, there was considerable political unease during the summer of 1970. In fact, on 5 July there was an emergency meeting of senior cabinet ministers and the security chiefs as a result of some unfounded rumours of a possible *coup d'état*.

The gárdaí placed an armed guard on Berry's home and began escorting him to and from work in a police car with an armed guard. He was also furnished with a pistol and was instructed on its use. Ever since the Book of Evidence was circulated on 17 June, he and his family had become the target for particular abuse.

Andreas O'Keefe, the President of the High Court, eventually assigned himself to the case but not before stating publicly that none of his colleagues wanted to preside at the arms trial. 'It is a question of finding a judge who is not reluctant,' he explained. His own reluctance was understandable because, as

Attorney-General, he had served in government and worked closely with Haughey, while the latter was Minister for Justice.

Throughout the summer Haughey kept a fairly low profile, avoiding public contact with either Blaney or any of his co-defendants. The Special Branch, which kept Haughey and his home under surveillance, reported in early September that he was seen with some cabinet ministers at the Festival of Kerry in Tralee.

Berry told Desmond O'Malley, the new Minister for Justice, that Haughey was seen with Brian Lenihan, the Minister for Transport and Power. With the arms trial due to begin later in the month, Berry commented on the inadvisability of ministers consorting with Haughey before the trial, because the Special Branch officers watching the former minister might get the wrong impression. This was obviously a subtle admonishment of O'Malley himself, because the secretary knew that O'Malley had also met with Haughey in Tralee.

O'Malley promptly volunteered this information and added that he planned another such meeting at Haughey's Kinsealy home later in the week. Berry objected to the meeting, especially at Haughey's home. If O'Malley was determined to go ahead then he suggested the meeting should be in the Minister' own office in Leinster House, where it could take place without the knowledge of Special Branch people.

Following a half-hour meeting with Haughey in Leinster House on 9 September, O'Malley told Berry the conversation had concentrated on Berry's own statement in the Book of Evidence and on the testimony which he was likely to give at the trial.

'He said that Mr Haughey's principal worry was over my evidence and that he had asked if I could be "induced", "directed" or "intimidated" into not giving evidence or changing my evidence,' Berry recalled. The secretary asked if 'induced' meant bribed, but O'Malley did not answer that question.

O'Malley has been particularly secretive about this meeting, but he flatly rejected any suggestion of impropriety surrounding the affair. 'I thought it quite appropriate at the time,' he explained. 'I had told Mr Berry beforehand that I was meeting Mr

Haughey and I told him afterwards what had transpired. But unfortunately the connotation is put on it that I made some kind of request to him which I certainly didn't. I factually reported what had happened because I thought it was appropriate that he should know.'

Berry had been given an assurance that his evidence against Haughey would not be highlighted at the start of the trial, but the assurance was ignored when the trial began on 22 September 1970. In his opening statement the chief prosecutor appeared to sensationalise Berry's forthcoming testimony for the benefit of the media by quoting what Berry would have to say about his telephone call from Haughey on 18 April. Tom MacIntyre, who had been commissioned to write a book about the trial, concluded from the opening statement that the tactics of the prosecution were 'Gut Haughey and gut him fast.'

All the defendants stood indicted of having 'conspired together and with other persons unknown to import arms and ammunition illegally into the State' between 1 March and 24 April 1970. To prove the case against Haughey the state was depending on the testimony of three prosecution witnesses, Gibbons, Berry, and Anthony Fagan, Haughey's personal secretary while he had been Minister for Finance.

Fagan was the first to testify. He told the court that Captain Kelly came to see Haughey on 19 March but the minister was engaged, so Kelly informed Fagan that the cargo, which he had told Haughey about the previous month, would be arriving on the *City of Dublin* on 25 March and he was wondering if the customs people could be instructed to admit the consignment without inspecting it. In passing on the message Fagan assured the minister it was within his power to authorise this, so Haughey told him to go ahead.

On taking the stand on the third day of the trial Gibbons testified that he had been uneasy about what Captain Kelly was doing so he had asked Haughey in March to find another job for him. 'I have an officer I want to get rid of immediately, and I want your assistance,' Gibbons said. 'I want a job found for him.'

'We'll make a pig smuggling prevention officer of him,' Haughey suggested some days later.

In early April, Gibbons testified that he again talked with

Haughey, who told him he was not aware of any conspiracy to import guns. They both agreed at this meeting that collective government action was the only way 'in matters of this kind'.

Berry testified about his conversation with Haughey on 18 April. With the permission of the court he read from notes he made in his diary at the time. He said that he answered the telephone himself and immediately recognised Haughey's voice.

'You know about the cargo that is coming into Dublin Airport on Sunday?' Haughey asked.

'Yes, minister.'

'Can it be let through on a guarantee that it will go direct to the North?'

'No.'

'I think that is a bad decision,' Haughey said. 'Does the man from Mayo know?'

'Yes.'

'What will happen to it when it arrives?'

'It will be grabbed,' replied Berry.

'I had better have it called off.'

Haughey then hung up, according to Berry, who was confident about the exact wording because, he said: 'I made notes there and then in my personal diary as to what Mr Haughey said.'

Gibbons testified that he also had a conversation with Haughey about this arms shipment around the same time, but he was not as clear about the details. He was not sure, for instance, whether the conversation took place on 17 or 20 April. Moreover his statement in the Book of Evidence described their discussion as a telephone conversation, but corrected this on the witness stand.

He had telephoned Haughey to say he wanted to talk to him about a matter of great urgency, and the Minister for Finance invited him to come over to his office. 'I told him of certain telephone calls that had come to the Department of Defence concerning the shipment of weapons and ammunition into the country,' Gibbons testified, 'and I asked him if he knew this, and he said, "The dogs in the street are barking it." I asked him if he were in a position to stop it, and he said, "I'll stop it for a month" or words to that effect. I said, "for God's sake, stop it altogether".'

Although the prosecutor had amassed impressive evidence

about Haughey's involvement in the whole affair, the state's overall case against the defendants was already in deep trouble. In order to make the charges stick against any of the accused the prosecution had to prove beyond a reasonable doubt that Gibbons had not authorised the importation of the arms, because if he had, then the attempt to bring them in was legal and there was no basis for the conspiracy charge.

While on the witness stand, Gibbons admitted that Captain Kelly had told him at their first private meeting that he intended to help the northern people looking for guns. He also admitted that the captain had given him details of the *City of Dublin* fiasco and the fact that he had another plan to bring in the guns.

'I seem to have a recollection of Captain Kelly mentioning the possibility of having them shipped through a port in the Adriatic because I suggested to him — would that port possibly be Trieste', Gibbons told the court. In addition, he admitted that he did not even suggest that Captain Kelly should have nothing to do with the gun-running.

By the time Gibbons left the stand on the fifth day of the trial, the prosecution's case was clearly in trouble. And it was to receive a further damaging setback later the same day when the state called Colonel Michael Hefferon to the stand. He had retired from the army just before the arms crisis began, after almost eight years as Director of Military Intelligence.

Hefferon's testimony was devastating. He established that Captain Kelly had not acted independently but with the knowledge and approval of Hefferon himself. Moreover, he added that, as Director of Military Intelligence, he had reported directly to the Minister for Defence on a regular basis and kept Gibbons fully briefed on Captain Kelly's activities. Indeed he testified that he told Gibbons the captain was going to Frankfurt in February 1970 to make enquiries about purchasing weapons.

'From what Captain Kelly said to you, who were these arms to be for?' Hefferon was asked.

'They were to be for the Northern Defence Committees, in the event that a situation would arise where the government would agree to them going to them' he explained. Captain Kelly first suggested storing the weapons in Cathal Brugha Barracks, but Hefferon thought it would be impossible to keep their presence there a secret. If the arms were to be handed over secretly, in line with the army's contingency plans, then it was thought best to store them in a Cavan monastery. As part of this effort to keep the whole thing as secret as possible he said that he told Captain Kelly to see Haughey about having the arms cleared through customs without being inspected.

On retiring from the army Hefferon admitted that he did not inform his successor about what had been happening. 'I felt' he said, 'that the whole project of importing arms was one of very great secrecy in which some government minister, to my mind acting for the government, was involved, and I felt that it should more properly be communicated to him by the Minister for Defence.'

'Were you satisfied at that time that the Minister for Defence had full knowledge of the activities of Captain Kelly?' Hefferon was asked.

'Yes,' he replied emphatically.

The prosecution's case was limping badly next day by the time Hefferon left the stand, but very shortly afterwards the whole proceedings were in disarray when the judge declared a mistrial after he had been accused of conducting the trial in an unfair manner by Luykx's counsel. The latter, no doubt sensing that the case was already as good as won, offered to withdraw from the proceedings, but O'Keefe rejected the offer and discharged the jury.

Haughey was understandably livid. 'Resign from the front bench,' he shouted at the judge.

Afterwards a member of the jury came up to Captain Kelly outside the court and told him he 'had the case won'. The various defence teams had not even begun to present a defence, but the juror had already made up his own mind. 'It was a not guilty verdict, even at this stage,' he explained.

'As the trial went on,' *Private Eye,* the satirical British magazine noted, 'it became clear that if Mr Haughey and his co-defendants were guilty of importing arms into Ireland, so was the entire Irish cabinet.'

There was a lot of speculation about O'Keefe's motives in declaring a mistrial. 'Was it that having heard the critical evidence he did not want to have to direct the jury?' Boland later asked. Many people thought the judge was simply giving the state an opportunity to drop the case without having to suffer the indignity of losing it in open court. But by declaring a mistrial the judge afforded the prosecution an opportunity of reorganising its case by dropping Hefferon as a state witness. In that event the prosecution would have a chance to discredit his testimony under cross-examination, if the defence called him as a witness.

A new trial began on 6 October 1970 with Mr Justice Seamus Henchy presiding. At the outset there was controversy over the status of Hefferon, who was subpoena'd to attend the trial, but the prosecution indicated it would not be calling him as a witness. Counsels for the defendants naturally objected. They were anxious to be able to cross-examine him, so they did not want to call him as their witness. He was like the potato that was too hot to handle.

The controversy was eventually resolved by the judge calling Hefferon as a witness, with the result that both the state and the defence could cross-examine him. The former Director of Military Intelligence again turned out to be a very effective witness for the defence, as did Captain Kelly when he elected to take the witness stand in his own defence.

Gibbons had admitted that Captain Kelly told him about the plan to bring in the arms and he made no effort even to suggest his disapproval, with the result that this might have been sufficient to create a reasonable doubt in the minds of jurors as to whether or not the inaction of the Minister for Defence amounted to approving the scheme under the circumstances. If this was not sufficient to raise the necessary doubt, there was the testimony of Captain Kelly and the invaluable corroboration of Hefferon, an independent witness, that Gibbons actually approved of the whole arrangement.

The two army officers had been very effective witnesses. 'No one in Dublin with whom I discussed the case — and I discussed it with many people of widely different views,' Conor Cruise O'Brien wrote, 'had any hesitation in believing Captain Kelly and Colonel Hefferon.'

At this point Haughey really did not need to testify at all. But he was anxious to play down his whole role in the affair. Captain Kelly's testimony had hardened the evidence of Haughey's involvement because he testified that he told the Minister for

Finance about the plans to bring in guns, which were financed out of the money provided by the Department of Finance for relief of distress in Northern Ireland.

On the stand Haughey gave an added twist to his own defence. Like the others he contended that what was being done was legal because it had the sanction of the Minister for Defence, but he also stated that he did not know that a consignment of arms was actually involved. He assumed the cargo was something 'needed by the army to fulfil the contingency plans', so he authorised its clearance through customs without knowing or, for that matter, caring about the actual nature of the consignment. He said it would have made no difference if he had been told that guns were involved.

'If you had known that they were intended for possible ultimate distribution to civilians in the North would that have made any difference?' his counsel Niall McCarthy asked.

'No, not really,' he replied, 'provided, of course, that a government decision intervened. I would have regarded it as a very normal part of army preparations in pursuance of the contingency plans that they would provide themselves with, and store here on this side of the border, arms which might ultimately, if the government said so, be distributed to other persons.'

Haughey said he had no reason whatever to suspect Captain Kelly. He admitted that he had suggested making him a special customs officer to deal with pig smuggling but, he said, he believed Gibbons had asked him to arrange a job not because of any qualms about the captain's behaviour but because British intelligence might be on to the captain's activities.

'My view of the situation was that Captain Kelly was a very valuable intelligence officer.' Haughey explained. 'I never heard any suggestion that he did not have Mr Gibbons's complete confidence, but that he was a useful person and that if at all possible we should retain him in some guise where he could pursue his activities and not be picked up as an Irish army intelligence officer by the British army.'

While that seems plausible enough, Haughey was not as convincing when it came to the matter of not knowing that the consignment being imported consisted of arms. Fagan and Berry had testified that they each talked to Haughey on the telephone about the consignment due to arrive at Dublin Airport. They knew it was a consignment of arms and each assumed Haughey also knew, but neither actually said that arms were involved.

'Did you ask Mr Fagan any questions as to what this consignment consisted of?' Haughey was asked.

'No,' he replied. 'We were speaking on the phone, and, as far as I can recollect, Mr Fagan told me he had already been in touch with Colonel Hefferon. I had no doubt in my mind that this was a consignment which was coming in as a result of the direction which we had given in pursuance of the contingency plans.'

'Did you appreciate that it was arms and ammunition?'

'No. I did not appreciate or know at that point of time, and, even when I spoke to Mr Berry, the words 'arms and ammunition' were never used.'

In dealing with his telephone conversation of 18 April with Berry, Haughey tried to give the impression of having a very vivid memory of the discussion. For instance, Berry said that he had answered the telephone himself, whereas Haughey contended that a child answered it first.

To remember a small point like that, which had absolutely no bearing on the subsequent conversation, would indicate a clear recollection of the call. He went on to say that Berry had omitted a number of things in his account of the call. For instance, Haughey testified that the secretary had asked at the outset if he had a scrambler and mentioned that the consignment weighed 'seven or eight tons' and had also said that 'it was the most stupidly handled affair he had ever known in his civil service days.' None of these points were important except that, if true, they would indicate that, even without contemporary notes, Haughey had a better recollection of the conversation than Berry. All this was important because Haughey was categorially contradicting Berry's testimony on two vital points. Firstly, he was contending he had never said anything about guaranteeing the arms would be sent to the North, and secondly, he stated that Berry had missed his concluding words. After saying 'it had better be called off,' he had added, 'whatever it is.'

He said he called off the shipment in order to avoid bad publicity. 'It was made clear to me,' he explained, 'that the Special

Branch wished this cargo to come, and wished to seize it. I was quite certain in my mind that evening that something had gone wrong, and that Army Intelligence was clearly at cross-purposes with the Special Branch, and there was a grave danger of an unfortunate incident occuring at Dublin Airport with, as I said, all the attendant publicity.' But throughout all this he said that he still did not know that a consignment of arms was actually involved.

He did not ask about the cargo because, Haughey testifed, they were speaking on an unsecured telephone line without a scrambler and Berry 'was very conscious of the need not to be talking in any careless terms.' It was understandable that there could be such confusion under the circumstances, but this would not explain why Haughey did not ask Gibbons what the whole thing was about when they met privately.

'Do you tell us that a conversation took place with your colleague the Minister for Defence, in the privacy of your office — with nobody else present — and you decided between you to call off the importation of a certain consignment, and that that conversation began and ended without you knowing what the consignment was?' Haughey was asked.

'Yes,' he replied. 'Nor did he mention what the consignment was.'

'Did you not ask him what it was?'

'No. It did not arise. In my mind was present the fact that this was a consignment being brought in by Army Intelligence in pursuance of their own operations.'

'As a matter of simple curiosity, were you not interested at that stage in finding out what the cargo was that all the hullabaloo was about?'

'No,' replied Haughey, 'the important thing was that the Army and Special Branch were at cross-purposes, and that it had better be stopped. I don't rule out the possibility that it could well have been in my mind that it could have been arms and ammunition — but it could have been a lot of other things.'

'If your evidence is correct,' the prosecutor said, 'I suggest that when Mr Gibbons came to see you on Monday your reaction would have been, "I have already called this off for you but now, please, tell me what it's all about?"'

'That's not what happened,' Haughey maintained. 'It may

be what you think should have happened — but it did not happen.'

In his opening statement the prosecutor stated 'that Mr Haughey's involvement — while of a lesser degree, because he was only there briefly — was of a vital nature because it was he who had given directions to Mr Fagan that this consignment was to be cle___d without customs examination.' But now in his closing statement Haughey's counsel contended that the defendant had merely facilitated a legitimate request from Army Intelligence, seeing that it was actually Colonel Hefferon who suggested that Captain Kelly should approach Haughey in the matter in the first place. Haughey's counsel tried to dismiss the damaging evidence given by Gibbons by contending that Gibbons was now posturing as having been opposed to importing the arms when he never so much as suggested to Captain Kelly that the whole thing should be called off. 'I think', counsel continued, 'it is hard to find anywhere — and I mean anywhere — in the evidence of Mr Gibbons anything convincing in his action and in his deeds consistent with what he now says was his view of what was happening at the time.' For instance, he continued, Gibbons admitted that Captain Kelly told him about the *City of Dublin* fiasco and told him that it was planned to use an Adriatic port next, and the Minister for Defence mentioned Trieste.

'But, gentlemen,' Haughey's counsel said to the jury, 'if Mr Gibbons's attitude to what was happening was as he now declares it to be, surely he would there and then have said, "Captain Kelly, you cannot go on with this — this must stop."' But Gibbons did nothing. He left the captain go out of his office without a reprimand, a rebuke or a warning.

Delivering his summation to the jury, the prosecutor challenged Haughey's testimony. 'For the purpose of establishing the case made by Mr Haughey in his defence, it is necessary.' he said, 'to disbelieve the evidence of four other witnesses: Captain Kelly, Mr Fagan, Mr Berry, and Mr Gibbons.' He then outlined some of the discrepancies.

For one thing, Captain Kelly testified that he told Haughey of the nature of the consignment, which flatly contradicted an integral part of Haughey's defence. Moreover, there was 'one piece of evidence which is crucial to the case, crucial in the sense that a verdict in favour of Mr Haughey cannot be reconciled with this piece of evidence,' the prosecutor continued. 'Mr Berry said that Mr Haughey said on the telephone, could the consignment be let through if a guarantee was given that it would go direct to the North.' 'Gentlemen,' he added, 'if it was just Mr Haughey and just Mr Berry, or just Mr Haughey and just Mr Fagan, or just Mr Haughey and just Mr Gibbons, or just Mr Haughey and just Captain Kelly, nobody could quarrel with the decision that you are not prepared to reject Mr Haughey's account. But I think you have to consider the cumulative effect of the evidence: is he right, and all they wrong? Because you, gentlemen, have got to hold that they are all wrong.'

In his charge to the jury on the final day of the trial, 23 October 1970, the judge directed that 'in fairness to Mr Haughey' in particular, the whole question of the financing of the guns should be ignored. He then spent some time on the conflict of testimony between Gibbons and Haughey, and Berry and Haughey. In each instance, he contended, one of them committed perjury. 'Either Mr Gibbons concocted this and has come to court and perjured himself, or it happened,' the judge said. 'There does not seem to me to be any way of avoiding a total conflict on this issue between Mr Haughey and Mr Gibbons.' The discrepancies were so great that he did not think they could be attributed to a simple memory failing of one of the participants.

'I would like to be able to suggest some way you can avoid holding there is perjury in this case,' Henchy continued. 'You have a solemn and serious responsibility to decide in this case, firstly, whether Mr Gibbons's conversation took place or not, and, secondly, whether Mr Berry's conversation took place or not. I shall not give any opinion on these crucial matters because, were I to do so, I might be thought to be constituting myself the jury.'

As far as the conspiracy charge went, however, all this would be important only if Captain Kelly were found guilty. If Haughey's testimony was believed he could be found not guilty while all the others could be convicted. Thus the crucial issue was whether Gibbons had authorised the importation. If he had, then the operation was legal. Henchy told the jury that they could conclude that when Gibbons 'got information about the attempted importation into the Port of Dublin, and the projected importation from Vienna, and when he did not say No, in categorical terms, Captain Kelly was entitled to presume that Mr Gibbons was saying Yes. That is a view that is open to you.'

The verdict was a foregone conclusion, according to Kevin Boland. What he called the 'establishment representatives who had attended each other day of the case' were conspicuous by their absence from the court on the last day. 'Everyone had come to cheer the inevitable result', he wrote.

It took the jury less than a hour to reach a verdict. The foreman handed a slip of paper to the clerk of the court who announced that each of the four defendants had been found 'not guilty'.

'Immediately the court erupted into a wild scene of cheering and shaking hands,' Captain Kelly recalled. 'People jumped for joy and I pushed through the exuberant crowd to arrive on the street, battered and in disarray.'

Haughey was surrounded by a force of gardaí who escorted him out of the courtroom. Outside in the foyer his supporters were ecstatic. 'We want Charlie,' they shouted. 'Lynch must go.'

'I am grateful to you all, every one of you, particularly my constituents, for the loyalty you have shown me during this difficult time,' he told them. 'I will take another occasion to thank you all.' Then, with the help of the gardaí, he slipped out a side door of the Four Courts: a free man.

8
Down but not out

The Road Back
1970-77

Sunday Independent, 25 October 1970

IN the Four Courts Hotel after the trial, Haughey was in a
defiant mood. 'I was never in any doubt that it was a political
trial,' he told the press. 'I think those who were responsible for
this debacle have no alternative but to take the honourable
course that is open to them.'

'What is that?'

'I think that is pretty evident,' he replied. 'There is some dissatisfaction with the Taoiseach at the moment.' And Haughey
said he was 'not ruling out anything' when he was asked if he
would be a candidate for Taoiseach himself.

These remarks were 'unanimously interpreted by the media
as a dramatic throwing down of the gauntlet to the Taoiseach',

according to Kevin Boland. 'After a long silence, Mr Haughey was exploding into action and coming out with all guns blazing.'

But Lynch seemed confident of coping with any challenge to his leadership. 'If the issue is raised,' he told newsmen in New York, 'I look forward to the outcome with confidence.'

Lynch's supporters were ready for a showdown. As a test of strength they called on all members to show their loyalty to the Taoiseach by going to Dublin airport to welcome him home from the United States. 'Everyone had to be there unless he or she had a doctor's cert,' according to Boland. As a result a comfortable majority of the parliamentary party turned out, which dealt a devastating blow to Haughey's challenge.

In his short biography (or what might more appropriately be called a hagiography) Tadgh Kennedy wrote that Haughey's 'good name, integrity and reputation were completely vindicated' with the verdict of the trial, but this was a gross oversimplification. There were still some questions to be answered. Captain's Kelly's testimony had raised a new issue concerning the expenditure of the public money to purchase arms, and Haughey had been ultimately responsible for ensuring that this money was spent properly.

The Dáil decided the Committee of Public Accounts should investigate the whole affair in order to determine whether money allocated for relief of distress in the North had been misappropriated. Legislation was passed by the Oireachtas allowing a select twelve-man committee to subpoena witnesses to testify under oath. Members of the committee included Ray MacSharry, Jim Tunney, Ben Briscoe, and Sylvester Barrett of Fianna Fáil, Garret FitzGerald, Dick Burke and Eddie Collins of Fine Gael, together with Justin Keating and Seán Treacy of the Labour Party.

Most of the witnesses at the Arms Trial were called and the hearings inevitably covered much of the same ground. Some of the witnesses were actually cross-examined on testimony they had given at the trial. But court rules did not apply during the committee hearings, so witnesses were able to give hearsay testimony that would have been inadmissible in court. For instance, Chief Superintendent Fleming of the Special Branch admitted at the outset that all his pertinent information was second-hand 'from confidential sources' whom he was not at liberty to name. He then proceeded to make some sensational disclosures.

'I know', Fleming declared at one point, 'that Mr Haughey had a meeting with one of the leading members of the IRA' and promised him £50,000.

'For what purpose?' the committee chairman asked.

'For the IRA, for the North.'

But when asked for further details of the alleged meeting, the Chief Superintendent explained he was 'not sure of the date or the place' of the meeting. All he could say was that it took place somewhere in Dublin in either August or September 1969. Later he was asked if he thought Haughey had any more meetings.

'I am not sure about further meetings,' he replied. 'I know his brother Pádraig was deeply involved.' In fact, the chief superintendent said that he believed Pádraig (Jock) Haughey was George Dixon.

Charlie Haughey was suddenly back in the eye of the storm. He vehemently denied either meeting the IRA leader or having promised to pay him money. 'No such meeting ever took place, and no such promise was ever made by me,' Haughey declared in an open letter to the committee chairman.

'Chief Superintendent Fleming's evidence, if one may properly so call it,' he continued, 'included such phrases as — "I had other confidential information" — "I take it that" — "I am not sure but" — "I would imagine" — "as far as my impression goes" — "as far as I am aware": all, plainly, indications that his "evidence" was based on rumour, reports, and other hearsay. No court would ever permit such an abuse of privilege quite apart from the fact that such "evidence" would be inadmissible.'

When Charlie Haughey appeared before the committee to testify on 2 March 1971, he explained it was impossible to give a full and proper accounting for the expenditure. 'None of us ever envisaged that any such accountability would ever be required,' he explained. 'We administered this particular money more of less along the same lines as we would administer the Secret Service Vote.' In short, he felt this was like money voted for famine relief in Biafra about which few questions would be asked once the money was handed over for others to administer. Indeed when the Dáil formally authorised the expenditure in

March 1970, it did so without comment. 'Nobody asked me questions,' Haughey said, 'and it went through without any discussion whatsoever.'

It is important to remember that the events in question took place before the first British soldier had been shot in Northern Ireland. At the time the British army was being generally welcomed as a protector of the nationalist people. It was also before the establishment of the Provisional IRA. Indeed, as of October 1969 the *United Irishman*, the mouthpiece for the IRA, accused Haughey and Blaney of promising help to nationalists in order to undermine the standing of the IRA north of the border. Some people later contended that those two politicians were responsible for the split that led to the establishment of the Provisional IRA. Whatever validity there is to this contention, southern politicians lost whatever influence they had over the situation following the Arms Crisis.

The money voted by the Dáil was intended for relief of distress in Northern Ireland. A valid case could have been made for arguing that certain propaganda activities or providing arms were each a means of relieving mental distress, but Haughey did not argue on these lines. Instead, he accepted that using money for such purposes was 'absolutely' out of order and irregular. 'Public funds were misappropriated,' he declared. 'That is a criminal offence.'

There were doubts about the validity of expenditure in four different areas: (1) financing the visit of Jock Haughey and others to London in August 1969; (2) the money which Captain Kelly used for the Balieboro meeting; (3) the funds from the Ann O'Brien account used to finance *Voice of the North;* and (4) the money from the Dixon account used to purchase the arms.

Haughey admitted that his brother and three others were selected to go to Britain by himself. 'The purpose of the visits', he explained, 'was to mobilise assistance over there for relief of distress in the North'. He added that he knew nothing of Fleming's allegations that his brother had engaged in arms talks. 'If the evidence which Chief Superintendent Fleming gave to this committee about my brother is as false and misleading as it is about me,' the former Minister for Finance said, 'then I think the committee should throw it into the waste paper basket.'

104

The money used by Captain Kelly for the Bailieboro meeting had actually been paid to Colonel Hefferon by the Department of Finance. The captain had asked for the money, so the two army officers believed the £500 was for the Balieboro meeting, but Haughey — who instructed the department to give the money to Hefferon — said that he believed the funds was just part of payments made to Colonel Hefferon to fund an office to help Northern refugees.

The circumstances surrounding the financing of *Voice of the North,* however, were more complicated. Brady had submitted a bill to the Information Bureau which was forwarded to the Department of Finance. Haughey thought the Taoiseach's department should look after the bill, so he instructed Fagan to enquire into the matter. But the Taoiseach's department, under which the Information Bureau functioned, refused to have anything to do with the bill.

'I felt Mr Brady was unfairly treated,' Haughey told the committee. 'Mr Brady understood that the Government Information Bureau wished him to publish this newspaper. Whether he was right or wrong, or did not understand it, I cannot say.' But Brady 'certainly' thought he was being wronged. 'He came to me and indicated that he had put £650 of his own money into the publication and he was now in difficulty with the Government Information Bureau because they were not prepared to pay up,' Haughey continued. 'I went to the Taoiseach on the matter. The Taoiseach gave me a direction and a ruling that public moneys were not to be used for the publication.'

Although there was no hope of Lynch agreeing to spend public money on the project, Haughey indicated that he would personally make sure Brady would not be out of pocket on what had already been spent but he said it might be necessary to suspend publication for the time being. 'You had better hold it,' the Minister for Finance said. 'I myself will see you all right with what you have spent if it comes to that.'

Brady then went over and told Captain Kelly that *Voice of the North* would have 'to fold as no money was coming in for it'. But within a couple of days Captain Kelly came back to him with financial support in the form of a cheque drawn on the Ann O'Brien account. Brady said that he had no idea this was government money.

Fagan told the committee that shortly afterwards he saw Brady's original bill on Haughey's desk. 'What is being done about this?' he asked.

'Oh, that is being looked after', the Minister replied. 'Ask Kelly how Brady's affairs stand?'

Fagan duly contacted the captain who told him to 'tell the Minister he is OK'. Thus, contrary to the specific direction of the Taoiseach, government funds were used to support *Voice of the North*, but Haughey swore that he did not know who helped Brady out. He also testified that he knew nothing about the O'Brien account, or indeed any of the three accounts opened at the Munster & Leinster Bank in Baggot Street. The first he heard of them, he said, was during the Arms Trial.

Two of the witnesses felt Haughey must have known about the main account in Baggot Street, but neither witness was definite. For instance, Captain Kelly testified that he 'certainly' told Fagan about this account. 'And,' he added, 'I should imagine Mr Haughey would know too. I cannot see any reason why not.' Fagan thought it 'inconceivable' that he would not have told the minister but added that he could 'not honestly recall' mentioning it at any specific time. 'It is possible,' Fagan said, 'that on one or more occasions that Baggot Street might have come into our discussions but I do not specifically recall that.'

Haughey explained that he had selected the three northern nationalists to distribute the relief money in Northern Ireland when it became apparent that the Irish Red Cross could not operate there. He was aware of the bank account opened in Clones, but did not know — or for that matter, care — that the money was transferred to Baggot Street. 'If they nominated someone else to administer the fund, that was not really any particular concern of mine,' he argued. 'We were not concerned with the mechanics of the payments.'

He forcefully denied knowing that any of the relief money had been spent on buying weapons. 'I have no knowledge whatever,' he emphasised, 'that any of these moneys, any halfpenny of these moneys, went for the procurement of arms.'

'I have no personal knowledge of this,' he continued, 'but I am informed that it can be proved beyond any doubt that my brother Pádraig was not George Dixon.'

'You are satisfied that he was not?' Ray MacSharry asked.
'He has so informed me and I accept his word.'

Jock Haughey had by then told the committee under oath that he had never used 'the name of George Dixon in any connection with any financial or banking dealings,' but he then refused to answer any questions. 'I am advised,' he explained, 'that by giving evidence before this committee I might be liable in civil law and under the laws of the land for any answer I might make.' In American parlance, he was taking the Fifth Amendment, but the United States Constitution did not operate in Ireland, so Pádraig Haughey was cited for contempt and sentenced to six months in jail by the High Court. He appealed successfully to the Supreme Court, which overturned the conviction on constitutional grounds.

'This judgment deprived the committee,' in the estimation of its own members, 'of any effective powers in the event of a witness refusing to attend, to produce documents or to answer questions.' Opposition members of the committee wanted to ask the Oireachtas for the necessary powers, but this was blocked by Fianna Fáil members, with the result that the hearings sputtered to a rather ineffective conclusion with the presentation of the committee's final report on 13 July 1972.

The report was incomplete; the committee was only able to conclude 'definitely' that a little over £29,000 was 'expended on or in connection with the relief of distress' in Northern Ireland. It found that a further £31,150 may have been spent in the same way, but over £39,000 had, in effect, been misappropriated. There was no definitive conclusion on who was directly responsible for the misappropriations, but the committee was specifically critical of Haughey on two counts. Firstly, it concluded that 'the misappropriation of part of the money which is now known to have been spent on arms might have been avoided' if either Haughey, Blaney or Gibbons had 'passed on to the Taoiseach their suspicion or knowledge of the proposed arms importation'. Secondly, the committee was 'not satisfied' that Haughey's actions in connection with the £500 given to Captain Kelly for the Bailieboro meeting 'was justified under the terms of the Fund'.

Meanwhile Haughey was already struggling to regain his standing with Fianna Fáil. He kept a low profile as he meticulously toed the party line, always dutifully voting with the government in divisions even when it came to opposing a motion of no confidence in Jim Gibbons as a member of the government. This Fine Gael motion, which was clearly designed to embarrass Fianna Fáil in general and Haughey in particular, was a blatant effort to widen the rift within the governing party.

On dismissing Haughey, the Taoiseach had said back in May that there could not be 'even the slightest suspicion' about the activities of a minister, but he then seemed to apply a different standard to Gibbons. If the latter's testimony about not having approved the importation of arms had been accepted by the jury, it is difficult to see how all the defendants could have been acquitted, so their acquittal at least raised the spectre of a reasonable doubt, or put another way, cast at least 'the slightest suspicion' on his role in the controversial events. Moreover, during the trial Gibbons had seemed to admit that he had deceived the Dáil back in May when he denied any knowledge of an attempt by Captain Kelly to import arms. 'I wish emphatically to deny any such knowledge', he told the Dáil in May 1970. Yet in court he not only admitted that Captain Kelly had already informed him, and he implied that a different degree of veracity was required in Leinster House.

Rather than vote confidence in the Minister for Agriculture, Kevin Boland took the extraordinary step of resigning from the Dáil. In the circumstances all eyes were on Haughey, but he dutifully voted with the government, thereby affording his critics another opportunity of slating him.

'Whatever charisma attached to the name of C. J. Haughey', *Hibernia* noted, 'was very seriously, perhaps irrevocably tarnished by his decision to vote with the government on the Gibbons censure. For a man who so terribly badly wanted to be leader, his epitaph may well read that he tried too hard.'

Boland went on to found a new party, *Aontacht Éireann*. He hoped to persuade Haughey to join the party. 'I went to Haughey and tried to persuade him that even if he did succeed in taking over Fianna Fáil, he would be dealing with people who were incompetent, inadequate and unreliable,' Boland recalled. 'But he didn't see it that way.'

Instead Haughey decided to work to re-establish himself

within Fianna Fáil. At the party's ard fheis in February 1972 he was elected as one of the party's five vice-presidents. This was the first real step in his comeback. His supporters were ecstatic as he arrived on the platform to be greeted by many of the party hierarchy, but there were some determined exceptions. Erskine Childers sat silently reading his newspaper. Dismayed at the prospect of Haughey's return to prominence, he constantly urged Lynch not to restore the man from Kinsealy to the front bench of the parliamentary party.

Another of the party elders, Frank Aiken, one of the principal founders of Fianna Fáil back in 1926, wanted to block Haughey's nomination as a party candidate in the general election of 1973, but Lynch refused to go that far. Aiken was so annoyed that he refused to stand himself. Initially he threatened to tell the press of his real reason for quitting politics, but, under pressure from President de Valera and others within the party, he soon relented and allowed Lynch to announce that he was retiring 'on doctor's orders'. It was a sad end to the long political career of a particularly courageous man, and it was all the sadder that he should leave politics quietly while some of those of whom he was critical distorted the truth about his going.

Although Conor Cruise O'Brien hammered away at the unanswered questions about the gunrunning and the misappropriated funds, Haughey again headed the poll with an increased vote. In fact, his personal tally was the second highest in the country, but Fianna Fáil lost its majority in the Dáil and was replaced by a coalition government.

At the 1974 ard fheis Haughey was confident enough to run for and gain election to the prestigeous post of joint national secretary of the party. As secretary he then travelled about the country helping to boost flagging morale and assiduously ingratiating himself with grassroots members of the party. He went on what has been called 'the rubber chicken circuit' accepting invitations to party functions throughout the length and breadth of the country. He said later he attended so many dinners that he could readily identify the factory from which the chicken had come. He was now clearly a force to be reckoned with and his supporters began clamouring for his return to the front bench of the parliamentary party.

In February 1975 Lynch's line on the Northern Ireland

question seemed to come in for questioning when Michael O'Kennedy, his spokesman for foreign affairs, called on the British to make a declaration of their intent to withdraw from Northern Ireland in order to 'concentrate the minds' of unionists and cause them to look more favourably on an offer from Dublin to negotiate a solution to the partition question. The Taoiseach, who had been merely calling on the British to express their interest in a united Ireland, was annoyed at the pronouncement but, rather than confront O'Kennedy, he simply dismissed the difference as a mere change of emphasis. Lynch had clearly backed down rather than confront the hard-liners on the northern issues, and this became all the more apparent a few days later when he restored Haughey to the front bench as spokesman for health. The appointment was generally believed to have been the result of a 'kind of republican rebellion inside Fianna Fáil'.

This led to an extraordinary outburst from the widow of President Erskine Childers, who had died some weeks earlier. She had been invited to a mass that the party had arranged for her late husband and other recently deceased party deputies, but in a fit of pique over Haughey's restoration, she declined the invitation in an open letter. 'The late President would not benefit from the prayers of such a party,' she wrote. 'Happily for him he is now closer to God and will be able to ask His inter-cession that his much loved country will never again be governed by these people.'

Although the spokesmanship for health had generally been considered a minor post, it had an added significance at the time because the Minister for Health and Social Welfare, Brendan Corish, was both Tánaiste and leader of the Labour Party. In his new role, therefore, Haughey was given a chance to shine by contrasting his own performance with those of his less capable colleagues, as well as the lack-lustre performance of Corish.

Normally, for instance, the vote on the estimates of each department allowed the minister to outline his own plans, but Corish made poor use of the opportunity afforded to him in 1975. His department had been considering a hospital develop-ment plan for the past eighteen months, but he was only able to say that he hoped to announce the new programme soon. 'In the whole speech,' Haughey complained, 'the minister could not announce one single significant new development.' The delay was probably well advised, because when the proposals were published later in the year they were rejected piecemeal by a succession of different interest groups.

Corish had pledged to bring in a system of free hospitalisation, but he was unable to get the scheme off the ground. He also had difficulties with the Misuse of Drugs Bill, which was first introduced in 1973 but only had its second reading after Haughey's return to the front bench. The drugs issue was highly emotive with enormous potential for an unscrupulous politician who might wish to whip up public emotions and thereby secure considerable publicity, but Haughey adopted a highly constructive approach. 'This is a situation', he said, 'which calls for enlightenment, understanding, maturity, judgment and wisdom.' He approved of the 'humane' approach which recognised a difference between unfortunate addicts who were coerced into selling drugs in order to feed their own habits and those 'cold, calculating pedlars' who pushed drugs just for money without being personally addicted.

Haughey's criticism of the bill was that it did not lay enough emphasis on the different categories of drugs. Many uninformed people often become quite vehement in their blanket condemnation of the use of drugs for non-medical purposes, yet they would be totally oblivious of the fact that such drugs include tea, coffee, tobacco and alcohol. Haughey was particularly mindful of the manner in which tobacco and alcoholic drinks were being advertised in a way that actually encouraged their misuse.

'Can we regard it as satisfactory that we promulgate these penalty provisions in regard to drugs, while at the same time we permit the expenditure of vast amounts of money every year on the promotion of other drugs, which are, in their own way, perhaps, just as harmful?' he asked. 'We will have to have a fundamental sorting out of our priorities in regard to this whole situation.'

As opposition spokesman Haughey concentrated his criticism on what he believed was the government's failure to do enough in the health area because of its unwillingness to allocate sufficient money for the purpose. When Corish introduced a supplementary estimate to cover cost overruns by his department, Haughey was able to say that he had warned him. 'It was obvious to everyone', he said, 'that the provisions being made were inadequate.'

The Fianna Fáil spokesman was quite positive in his overall approach. He moved a Private Member's Bill to extend the eligibility for medical cards to a wide range of people, including all those over sixty-five years of age, widows, people with long-term illnesses and people whose earnings were under a certain level, but the government defeated this legislation on financial grounds. Politically the whole exercise had been a brilliant tactical move. Haughey got the credit for trying to introduce the measures, while the government were blamed for killing them. But this was not just a cynical political exercise. He obviously believed in what he was doing, and he later proved his sincerity by introducing legislation to give effect to his various suggestions when Fianna Fáil returned to power.

Although Haughey had foreshadowed some of the legislation he would later introduce, there was little indication of any of this in the famous Fianna Fáil election manifesto of 1977. Privately Haughey was known to have reservations about some of the extravagant promises made in the manifesto, but those had nothing to do with the health area. Instead the health clauses were largely platitudinal with little more than lip service being paid to aspirations. There were no specific promises.

Public opinion polls conducted during the campaign showed that the electorate thought Fianna Fáil would handle various aspects of the economy better, but the coalition was preferred in the whole security area. Thus Conor Cruise O'Brien tried to exploit the security issue by raising questions about Haughey's previous behaviour. In an interview with the London *Times* he predicted that a Fianna Fáil government that included the man from Kinsealy would 'turn a blind eye' to the activities of the IRA in Northern Ireland. The remarks promptly generated media interest, and O'Brien was interviewed for news programmes on both the RTE and BBC. He also spoke out publicly at a rally in Raheny the same day.

'Can an alternative government which included Mr Haughey be trusted on security?' he asked. 'Can it be trusted in relation to the Provisional IRA? Can it be trusted in relation to Northern Ireland? Can it be trusted — indeed, will it be trusted — in the field of Anglo-Irish relations?' He contended it was right to bring up such issues because many young people 'simply do not know that when Mr Haughey was Minister for Finance large sums of public money voted for the relief of distress in Northern Ireland were diverted in the purchase of arms and ammunition.' Even though only a minor member of Lynch's team, Haughey obviously enjoyed an enormous influence within his party. In fact, Cruise O'Brien continued, 'many people believe that before very long Mr Lynch will retire from the leadership of Fianna Fáil and that Mr Haughey will succeed him. Are the people of this country prepared to entrust their security into the hands of a government which might turn out to be led by a person with the record of Mr Charles J. Haughey?'

Dismissing what he described as 'unfounded allegations', Haughey contended the electorate showed their contempt for such charges by giving him the second highest vote in the country in 1973. 'I believe they will treat them in the same way on this occasion,' Haughey continued. 'That Dr O'Brien should go to the London *Times* to launch a piece of character assassination against a fellow Irishman is not surprising in view of that newspaper's role in Irish history.'

If Haughey had been allowed to choose a member of the government to make the charges against him, he probably could not have chosen anybody better from his own standpoint than Cruise O'Brien, because the latter had a highly negative rating with many sections of the electorate. Indeed the *Irish Times* published a poll a couple of days later which showed that Cruise O'Brien was the member of the cabinet that most people would least like to see as Taoiseach. On the other side, Haughey was the person that most people would least like to see lead the country if Fianna Fáil were returned to power. But Haughey's critics must have found cold comfort in the statistics, because the same poll indicated that while he was not nearly as popular as Lynch, he was now clearly the second most popular figure in Fianna Fáil. And, in the event that Lynch decided to step down, Haughey was a full 12 points ahead of Colley as the choice to succeed.

In the last two general elections Haughey and Cruise O'Brien had run against each other in the same constituency, but this time they were separated as a result of the drastic restructuring of the constituencies by the coalition government. Haughey choose to run in Artane, where he stormed home with more than

113

11,000 votes from a greatly reduced electorate. With 37 per cent of the first-preference votes, his tally was up by almost 7 per cent. Cruise O'Brien's dropped, on the other hand, and he lost his seat by a narrow margin as Fianna Fáil swept to power with the largest majority in the history of the state.

Lynch was duly elected Taoiseach when the Dáil reconvened. He then appointed Haughey Minister for Health and Social Welfare. There were apparently some objections, but the Taoiseach felt the man from Kinsealy had purged his past indiscretions and behaved himself since being brought back on the frontbench. 'I felt that I was doing the right thing, the Christian thing and the fair thing in giving him a chance again,' Lynch explained some years later.

Although Haughey had argued while in opposition that the two departments of Health and Social Welfare were too much for one man, he apparently made no objection when Lynch offered him the dual posts. He did not even ask to be assigned a parliamentary secretary. He was obviously intent on demonstrating to the full his own political skills.

9
Balls in the Air

Minister for Health and Social Welfare
1977-79

The Irish Times, 13 December 1979.

MOST of Lynch's people would probably have preferred to have excluded Haughey from the cabinet, but he was simply too influential to be ignored. As President Lyndon Johnson said after re-appointing an individual he would have preferred to have retired, it was better to have him inside the tent pissing out, than outside pissing in.

The Taoiseach appointed a cabinet committee to deal with major economic matters. It consisted of himself; Martin O'Donoghue, the Minister for Economic Planning; George Colley, the Minister for Finance; and Desmond O'Malley, the Minister for Industry and Commerce. They would take many of the most important economic decisions and present the rest of the cabinet with a *fait accompli*. Thus Haughey was distant from the real centre of power, and he had no involvement in security matters.

At first sight it might have appeared that the Departments of Health and Social Welfare would offer little scope for the new minister to construct a power base, because the various promises made in the Fianna Fáil manifesto had little to do either with health or social welfare, but the new appointment did afford Haughey enormous opportunities of building up a power base within the back benches of the party.

As a result of the Fianna Fáil landslide, there were many deputies arriving at Leinster House for the first time. It took them a while to settle in. Those who sought Haughey's help found him highly approachable and helpful, often in marked contrast with other ministers who were aloof and showed little concern. He had always had the reputation of being prepared to go to extraordinary lengths to win votes and now he realised it was important to win the support of those on the backbenches, because they were going to have a vital say in the election of the next Taoiseach if, as there were already indications, Lynch decided to step down at mid term. This would then probably be Haughey's last chance to fulfil his ambition of becoming Taoiseach.

Deputies anxious to cut bureaucratic red tape for constituents looking for medical cards or having problems with welfare payments found Haughey very helpful. And this helpfulness was not just part of a calculated plan to build up support for his bid for the office of Taoiseach. He behaved the same way towards opposition backbenchers who sought his assistance. Such behaviour came quite naturally to him because helping out deputies obviously gave him a sense of power that he enjoyed. He could be concerned, courteous and charming — a far cry from the waspishness that some might have expected as a result of his reputation.

During the next two and a half years Haughey kept a very high profile and generated a considerable amount of publicity to enhance his own political image. He used his administrative and legislative experience to telling effect not only in securing funding for a wide range of programmes that he had the skill and initiative to get off the ground, but also in implementing some legislative measures for which he received enormous, if not always favourable, publicity. Of course, critics charged that he was just campaigning for Taoiseach.

'Charlie has no plans for health,' one old hand at medical politics was quoted as saying. 'What he's done is to keep ten balls in the air at the same time and protect his own.'

Within a couple of years he had the most favourable rating of any minister in the government. He did this by working hard and ensuring that he was given credit both for the achievements and for the popular measures introduced by his departments. For instance, he inherited the draft of a major bill to consolidate the whole range of social welfare legislation, which consisted of more than sixty acts beginning with the Old Age Pension Act of 1908 and stretching right through the 1976 Social Welfare Act. Frank Cluskey, the Minister for State at the Department for Social Welfare under Corish, had worked on drafting this legislation, but now Haughey took the credit for the new Social Welfare (Consolidation) Bill, which ran to more than 200 pages in length. Because there had been so many acts with so many changes over the years, social welfare legislation had become very complex, and Haughey contended it would be best to amalgamate all the legislation in one act that would 'provide all interested individuals with a readable and legislative framework.'

As Minister for Finance before the Arms Crisis, he had got the credit for various concessions to pensioners and now, as Minister for Social Welfare, he again demonstrated his ability to generate publicity for himself by claiming credit for the same kinds of concessions in the budgets introduced by Colley. In fact, he assumed responsibility for such extensive changes that the Fine Gael spokesman, John Boland, accused him of 'endeavouring to introduce a budget of his own'.

The changes included an easing of the five-year residency requirements for people applying for the old-age pension, deserted wives allowances, or widow's pensions. A provision was also introduced which allowed a relative taking care of the child of a deserted wife who dies to collect an orphan's pension even though the father might still be alive, and there was a provision to allow the father in a broken marriage to claim his family as dependants while supporting them. Hitherto, the father could not claim them as dependants if they were living under a different roof. There were also some of the imaginative giveaways for which Haughey was renowned during his tenure as Minister for Finance. There was a provision for the elderly to get free bottled gas in lieu of their free electricity allowance, if they wished. In addition, pensioners living alone were being given free rental on their telephones. 'I think,' Haughey explained, 'we must give increasing attention to the problems of loneliness in so far as the old are concerned and see if we can devise by community action or otherwise, ways of mitigating this feeling of loneliness and isolation.'

The annual cost of the total increase in social welfare improvements was estimated at £55 millions, while the health budget was up by £45 millions to bring the total estimated expenditure of Haughey's two departments to around £967 million, or about one third of the government's total budget. He proudly declared that more money than ever was being spent on health and social welfare, and he stated that 2,400 new jobs were being created as a result.

'His greatest coup,' according to the *Irish Medical Times*, 'was bought for the modest expenditure of £1 million — the cost of dramatically expanding the role of the new Health Education Bureau', which had been set up by Corish in 1975. Through the bureau Haughey launched imaginative publicity campaigns aimed at promoting better standards of fitness and hygiene. His approach, which included the distribution of a free toothbrush to all school children in the country, was to promote positive health measures based on the assumption that prevention was better than cure. He was credited with bombarding the public with exhortations to walk rather than drive, to jog, dance, play games, to quit smoking and to cut down on alcohol.

Through skilful propaganda Haughey managed to introduce the country to a new era of happy health consciousness. 'I am not interested in promoting a concept of health that is joyless and based on a narrow moralistic approach', he told a Fianna Fáil Youth Convention in Dundalk. 'I take it as a basic fact of life that neither young nor old are prepared to be told dogmatically what they should do about their health, nor do they wish to be lectured constantly or badgered about it.'

To many people it was as if he invented health education with the publicity campaigns. And he led by example in announcing that he himself had given up smoking cigarettes and drinking alcohol. This was not the old authoritarian administrator but a New Haughey. Although his overall approach was to provide positive encouragement, rather than rely on negative legislation, he was prepared to introduce such legislation to cope with the problem of cigarette advertising when it interfered with the positive approach.

'In attempting to implement such a positive health policy,' he explained, 'we immediately came up against the problems of cigarette smoking and the widespread intensive, glamorous advertising of tobacco products'. In such circumstances efforts to warn the population of the hazards of smoking could 'only be of doubtful value in an environment saturated with the advertising of tobacco and alcohol — advertising which continues to grow in volume and sophistication'. He therefore introduced the Tobacco Products Bill which sought to control 'the advertising and sales promotion of tobacco products and of sponsorship by the tobacco industry'.

The opposition criticised the bill on the grounds that the powers it gave to the Minister for Health were too sweeping, but Haughey was making no apologies. 'It gives him complete, absolute power at his discretion to deal with this problem of the promotion and advertising of tobacco products', Haughey admitted. 'There is no doubt that under this legislation any Minister for Health can do almost anything he wants to control, regulate or prohibit the advertising and promotion of the sale of tobacco products. Whether any Minister for Health would wish to avail of these powers to the full or not at all is entirely a matter for the judgment and discretion of the Minister for Health.' Following the passage of the bill he introduced regulations prohibiting cigarette companies from sponsoring events for people under eighteen years of age, and also made it illegal for competitors in show jumping events or cars participating in motor races to carry the name of a tobacco company or its products.

The groundwork had already been done for a new hospital programme by the previous government, but Haughey demonstrated a greater ability than his predecessor to implement the programme as he cut through reams of red tape. For example, he took the design of Cork Regional Hospital and had it used for

119

the new Beaumont Hospital, thereby speeding up the construction of the new building by some years. He commissioned a new regional hospital in Wilton, Cork, secured funds for a £5 million development at Mullingar General Hospital, authorised an extension to double the size of Sligo General Hospital, and had funds provided to start construction of a new regional hospital in Tralee.

In July 1978 Haughey announced a new scheme providing for free hospitalisation for all those earning under £5,500 per year. His predecessor had been anxious to introduce free hospitalisation and the department had drawn up a scheme which was ready for implementation, but consultant doctors refused to implement it. Haughey realised the scheme was ready for implementation with the consultants. He compromised by allowing them to charge patients earning at least £5,500 annually. Thus the scheme was given practical effect. It was another major achievement getting the cabinet to approve of his scheme, because free hospitalisation had not been part of the 1977 election manifesto and was not therefore high on the party's list of priorities.

Before the scheme could be implemented, however, O'Donoghue conceded to union demands in the National Understanding that the earnings ceiling should be raised to £7,000 annually. This, of course, amounted to a reneging on Haughey's commitment to the consultants and led to some heated cabinet exchanges between himself and O'Donoghue. The whole affair was really indicative of the shabby way in which Haughey and a number of others were being excluded from the government's decision making process when it came to major economic matters. As a result of the National Understanding with the unions, Haughey's credibility — or to be more precise, his ability to deliver — was called into question by the Irish Medical Association. But he did not allow his political standing to be undermined so easily. Instead he delivered to the consultants by getting the Department of Finance to produce a special payment scheme to cover patients earning between £5,500 and £7,000 per annum.

In November 1978 hundreds of uniformed nurses descended on Leinster House in a demonstration for salary increases. Like the gárdaí during the Macushla Affair, the nurses did not have a right to strike, but their protest could be damaging if not handled properly. Haughey certainly did not want a repetition of his disastrous refusal to meet the farmers when they marched on his department back in 1966. Some 300 nurses in uniform were invited into Leinster House and they packed the Dáil chamber, which was turned into a veritable circus by deputies playing to their audience.

John Boland proposed a motion 'to set up a commission of enquiry on nurses' pay and conditions.' Then, much to the delight of the nurses, Haughey figuratively stole the clothes of the Fine Gael spokesman by introducing an amendment asking the Dáil to 'approve the measures taken by the government to improve the pay, conditions and status of the nursing profession and to welcome the recent decision to establish a commission of enquiry.'

Before the end of the year Haughey also introduced his controversial family planning bill, which was drawn up after exhaustive consultations with the Catholic hierarchy and other interested parties. The bill immediately came in for some strong criticism in liberal and left-wing circles.

'This is a sectarian bill with sectarian intent', thundered the editor of *Hibernia*. 'It is the product of weak politicians bending in front of the most reactionary element in Irish society today.' Critics took particular exception to provisions restricting the sale of contraceptives to married people and requiring that they have a doctor's prescription, even for non-medical contraceptives like condoms.

On introducing the bill for its second reading in the Dáil, Haughey admitted that, far from providing easier access to contraceptives, his bill was actually designed to restrict availability. 'It is clear to me from my consultations that majority opinion in this country does not favour widespread uncontrolled availability of contraceptives,' he explained. 'It emerged clearly that the majority view of those consulted was that any legislation to be introduced should provide for a more restrictive situation in relation to the availability of contraceptives than that which exists by law at present.' The Family Planning Bill therefore required that the person seeking to purchase any kind of contraceptives should first secure a medical prescription from a doctor, who had to be satisfied 'when giving the prescription or authorisation, that the person required the contraceptives for the purpose, *bone fide,* of family planning or for adequate medical reasons and in appropriate circumstances.' Haughey realised everybody was not happy with the legislation but then he did not believe it was possible to find a solution that would satisfy everyone. 'This bill seeks to provide an Irish solution to an Irish problem,' he said. 'I have not regarded it as necessary that we should conform to the position obtaining in any other country.'

When it came to voting on the bill four Fianna Fáil deputies defied their party's three line whip and failed to vote on the measure. Three of them later apologised but the fourth, Haughey's arms trial adversary, Jim Gibbons, was recalcitrant. As Minister for Agriculture he could easily have arranged to be away on business, and his absence would not have been noticed because his vote was not needed. Instead, he stayed around the Dáil until just before the vote was due to take place and then he left. Afterwards he announced defiantly that he would not be supporting any stage of the bill. This was seen as a clear challenge to Lynch's authority, but the Taoiseach took no action. It was the first time since the foundation of the state that any minister had publicly defied the government of which he was a member in such a blatant manner. The first nail had been driven into Lynch's political coffin, and the man responsible was not Haughey, but the latter's implacable critic, Jim Gibbons.

The Minister for Health and Social Welfare was riding the crest of a political wave at the time. John Kelly of Fine Gael, a long time critic, admitted he did not like Haughey. 'But,' Kelly continued, 'I hand it to him that he has made an impact on his department. In a sense it is a telling reflection on the government of which he is a member that he has made more impact in his office than any of his colleagues have in theirs, and only a small-minded person would deny that.'

A public opinion poll conducted by MRBI during the controversy over Gibbons's absence from the Dáil found that Haughey had the most favourable rating of all the members of the government, including the Taoiseach. Some 75 per cent expressed the opinion that Haughey had done well or very well in his ministry, while only 20 per cent were not favourably impressed with the job he was doing. On the other hand, Colley had a dismal approval rating of just 38 per cent with 53 per cent

High point and low point. Haughey's career has been an extraordinary mixture of ups and downs. The photograph left shows him at his first press conference after his election as leader of Fianna Fáil. The one below shows him walking out of the Four Courts after the Arms Trial, a free man but with his political career apparently in ruins.

On the island. Innishvicillaun offers Haughey a private retreat from the pressures of public life. He is shown here en route to the island by helicopter (*above left*), on the balcony of his island home (*above right*) and sailing in the Blasket Sound (*below*).

Family man. At breakfast in Kinsealy (*above*). At home with his mother (*below*).

A man with a past or a man with a future? Haughey enters his third term as Taoiseach facing greater difficulties and greater opportunities than any other Taoiseach in peacetime.

feeling that he had been doing a poor job as Minister for Finance. He had the poorest rating of all, with the exception of Padraig Faulkner, the Minister for Posts and Telegraphs, who was plagued at the time by a protracted postal strike.

Colley's standing had undoubtedly suffered from a debacle surrounding his effort to get farmers to shoulder a more equitable share of the tax burden. In the February budget he had announced a 2 per cent levy on all agricultural produce. The farming community immediately raised an outcry and, under pressure from rural deputies, the plan was scrapped, much to the irritation of PAYE workers who took to the streets in a massive nationwide protest against being saddled with a disproportionate share of taxation. At one stroke the government had alienated both farming and urban voters.

Public disillusionment with the government became apparent in June when Fianna Fáil's vote dropped to 34.6 per cent in the European elections. Down from the 50.8 per cent of two years earlier, it was the worst showing in the party's fifty-three-year existence. And nervous backbenchers began to look for a change of leadership.

Fianna Fáil's majority in the Dáil really sowed its own seeds of instability, because the party was left holding many marginal seats. Backbench deputies from those marginal constituencies became noticeably uneasy as things began to go wrong for the government. Fearing for their seats, they became restless for change.

Five deputies stood out in this movement. Dubbed 'the gang of five,' they were Tom McEllistrim, Jackie Fahey, Mark Killilea, Seán Doherty and Albert Reynolds. Beginning with a slow, relentless campaign to secure Haughey's election as Lynch's successor, they soon found enthusiastic supporters in deputies like Paddy Power, Síle de Valera, Charlie McCreevy, Seán Calleary and Bill Loughnane. Haughey knew the campaign was being conducted on his behalf, but he stayed very much in the background as the dissidents started sniping openly at the leadership. He knew that it could be counter-productive if he was seen to be trying to undermine Lynch, so he left all the running to those on the back benches.

During a speech in Fermoy on 9 September 1979 Síle de Valera delivered a thinly veiled attack on Lynch's Northern

Ireland policy. A month later, Tom McEllistrim raised the issue of allowing the British military to overfly Irish territory. In November Lynch suffered the humiliation of having Fianna Fáil lose two by-elections in his native Cork — including one in his own constituency after he had campaigned there personally. His magic seemed to have deserted him. Soon Bill Loughnane was accusing him of lying to the Dáil about the government's security co-operation with the British. Lynch was in the United States at the time, so Colley, as acting leader, tried to have Loughnane expelled from the party but had to settle for a compromise in which the deputy from Clare merely withdrew the accusation. The dissidents next began circulating a petition calling for Lynch to step down. Deputies were asked to sign without being allowed to see the other names on the petition unless they first signed. Although more than twenty signed, they were still well short of a majority.

Had Lynch wished to stay on as Taoiseach, there was little doubt he could have continued, but he intended to go in a few months anyway and he no longer had much stomach for the party in-fighting. Moreover, he was persuaded by Colley and O'Donoghue that the time was opportune to retire because Haughey would be caught on the hop. On Wednesday, 5 December 1979, therefore, Lynch announced his intention of resigning as Taoiseach.

In an obvious effort to prevent the Minister for Health and Social Welfare organising a proper campaign, the meeting to select Lynch's successor was called at just two days' notice. Thus the campaign was very short and was over so quickly that the media had little chance to exert much influence.

Far from being caught by surprise, however, Haughey had been preparing for the day ever since he withdrew from the leadership contest back in 1966. He was supremely confident when he met with Doherty, McEllistrim, Killilea and McCreevy shortly after Lynch's announcement. There were few people on the back benches for whom he had not done favours and now he expected them to return the compliments by backing him. He also anticipated support from some members of the cabinet like Lenihan and O'Kennedy. Sitting in his office he totted up his likely support and concluded that he would get 58 votes to Colley's 24.

'Do you know,' Doherty exclaimed after a thoughtful pause, 'you're the worst fucking judge of people I ever met.'

The contest was going to be much closer than Haughey first expected. The bookies initially installed him and Colley as joint favourites, but Haughey was the punter's choice. He was promptly backed down to a money-on favourite in most of the Dublin betting shops, with the exception of Seán Graham, who had Colley as favourite after taking two sizeable bets on him.

None of the daily newspapers took a committed editorial stand in support of any candidate, but the *Irish Press* seemed to be leaning towards Haughey with an editorial stressing some negative implications of the recent by-election defeats in Cork. The *Irish Independent*, on the other hand, obviously favoured Colley in ways that were probably intended to be subtle but were blatant in their intent. For instance, on the moring of the crucial parliamentary party meeting, the newspaper carried an editorial which while not naming anyone, stressed that 'the need to convince the Northern majority to come down from their battlements and mingle with the rest of us is an absolutely essential task facing any Taoiseach of this country, and he, therefore, must be someone they are not suspicious of.' If that hint were not enough, there was a photograph on the front page of Colley on the elevator in Leinster House under the caption 'Going Up'.

The *Cork Examiner* betrayed a similar bias. On the eve of the parliamentary party meeting in a lead story headlined, 'Taoiseach George?', the newspaper carried a ridiculous estimate of Colley holding a lead of 45 to 24, even though its own political correspondent only gave him a lead of four or five votes with many left undecided. It was later charged that the story had been telephoned to the newspaper by Bart Cronin, the press officer in Colley's department.

Press speculation about the support for each candidate was mixed. Both Chris Glennon and Bruce Arnold of the *Irish Independent* had Colley in the lead, as did Liam O'Neill, political correspondent of the *Cork Examiner*, while Dick Walsh of the *Irish Times* had Haughey with 'a paper-thin lead' but only one vote short of the needed majority. His tally was 41 for Haughey and 35 for Colley, with 6 undecided.

Most of the cabinet seemed solidly behind Colley, but they

were obviously out of touch with their backbenchers, who were terrified lest Colley's low standing in the polls and his close identification with some unpopular moves would lead to a repetition of the party's poor showing during both the European and the recent Cork by-elections. Under such circumstances the party back benches would probably be decimated. Haughey, on the other hand, not only had a high standing in the polls, but had been excluded from the major economic decisions that had recently turned sour, so he had the advantage of being seen as an outsider within the cabinet.

Haughey's people set his bandwagon rolling with some announcements that were timed to give him a boost at the right psychological moments. First of all there was the news that Colley's Parliamentary Secretary, Ray MacSharry, would be proposing Haughey. This was followed at the eleventh hour by a declaration that the Minister for Foreign Affairs, Michael O'Kennedy (who was regarded as a possible compromise candidate) would be voting for Haughey. Suddenly Colley's people realised they were in trouble.

Cabinet members made frantic efforts to persuade deputies to support Colley by threatening to cut off funds already allocated for local projects. The campaign threatened to become dirty, but there was not enough time. Colley had really outmanoeuvred himself by rushing the election because the dissidents backing Haughey were not only organised, but superbly organised.

It turned out to be a contest between the government and its backbenchers. 'They were voting to save their jobs and we were voting to save our seats,' was how one backbench member summed up the division. When the votes were counted Haughey had won by 44 to 38.

The ballot papers were immediately burned, and the resulting smoke set off the fire alarm in Leinster House. This was, no doubt, seen by his critics as a portent of things to come, but his supporters were absolutely jubilant. 'Nixon's comeback,' one of them said, 'may have been the greatest since Lazarus, but there is only one resurrection that beats Charlie's.'

At a press conference afterwards there was little sign of any members of the cabinet as Haughey surrounded himself with backbenchers, but he said that Colley had pledged him loyalty and support. Reporters questioned the new leader on issues on which his silence over the years had been interpreted as a sign of ambivalence. In particular they were interested in his attitude towards the Provisional IRA.

He had not spoken out before, he said, because he had no authority from the party to speak on the Northern Ireland question. Now he was unequivocal. 'I condemn the Provisional IRA and all their activities,' he declared.

Another reporter asked about the Arms Crisis, but this was a wound he had no intention of re-opening. 'This is very much now a matter for history,' he replied. 'I am leaving it to the historians.'

Would he help the historians?

'I will write my own.'

While Fianna Fáil had a comfortable majority in the Dáil, the divisions within the party were so great and the bitterness between Haughey and Colley so intense that the new leader's election as Taoiseach could not be taken as a foregone conclusion. There were still some slight doubts about whether he could actually win the necessary confidence of the Dáil.

The speech made by the Fine Gael leader, Garret FitzGerald, following Haughey's subsequent nomination for the post of Taoiseach on 11 December, should be seen in the context of a botched play for the support of disillusioned Fianna Fáil deputies. 'I must speak not only for the opposition but for many in Fianna Fáil who may not be free to say what they believe or to express their deep fears for the future of this country under the proposed leadership, people who are not free to reveal what they know and what led them to oppose this man with a commitment far beyond the normal,' the Fine Gael leader declared. 'He comes with a flawed pedigree. His motives can be judged ultimately only by God but we cannot ignore the fact that he differs from all his predecessors in that those motives have been and are widely impugned, most notably but by no means exclusively, by people within his own party, people close to him who have observed his actions for many years and who have made their human, interim judgment on him. They and others, both in and out of public life, have attributed to him an overweening ambition which they do not see as a simple emanation of a desire to serve but rather as a wish to dominate, even to own the state.'

Nowhere in the speech did FitzGerald make any specific charges as to why Haughey was unsuitable for office. All he made were vague, unsupported accusations and then cloaked those with the pretence that he could not be more specific 'for reasons that all in this House understand'. But of course all remarks made in the Dáil are privileged, so there was no justification whatever for underhanded insinuations. If, as he implied, he had reasons for saying what he did, then he should have had the gumption to substantiate his charges.

Others like John Kelly and Richie Ryan of Fine Gael also made caustic comments, as did the longtime maverick Noel Browne, who described Haughey as a dreadful cross between former President Richard Nixon and the late Portuguese dictator, Antonio Salazar. 'He has used his position unscrupulously in order to get where he is as a politician', Browne told the Dáil. 'He has done anything to get power; does anybody believe that he will not do anything to keep power?'

Even back in 1932 when the political climate was still poisoned by civil war bitterness, Eamon de Valera had not been subjected to such abuse. Throughout most of the invective, Haughey sat alone on the government benches, treating his tormentors with contempt by refusing to reply, and restraining others from replying on his behalf. His actions were a silent assertion that the charges were so ludicrous as not to merit a reply.

Since Haughey's family, including his seventy-nine-year-old mother, were in the public gallery, the attacks were seen as most ungracious and were resented by the general public. Fitz-Gerald's own genial image was tarnished and there was a lot of sympathy for Haughey — even among people who had serious reservations about him. Some of them might have agreed with the sentiments expressed, but they thought the occasion most inappropriate.

10
'Rise and follow Charlie'

Taoiseach At Last
1979-81

The Irish Times, 15 February 1980

FOLLOWING his election as Taoiseach Haughey went to great lengths to bind up the wounds within Fianna Fáil by re-appointing most of the outgoing cabinet, even though only one, or at most two, of them supported his candidacy. Only Albert Reynolds of 'the gang of five' who had orchestrated Haughey's campaign was given a cabinet post, but Haughey did reward the loyalty of the others by appointing them as Ministers of State. Ray MacSharry also joined the cabinet.

The two ministers dropped were Gibbons and O'Donoghue. The latter's Department for Economic Planning was also scrapped. Most of its sixty administrative grade officials were transferred back to the Department of Finance from whence they had been recruited, but the permanent secretary and strategic planners moved to the Department of the Taoiseach, which 'changed almost beyond recognition in the few months following Haughey's election as Taoiseach'. When he took over, the department had only three units — the government secretariat, government information service, and a private office staff — but this was rapidly expanded with divisions to handle foreign affairs, economic and social policy, cultural and legal affairs, together with a personnel division. Within a year the Taoiseach's staff had more than doubled and it had virtually tripled by 1981 as Haughey gathered more of the decision-making functions to himself.

Although Colley was appointed Tánaiste and was given a virtual veto over the appointments of the Ministers for Defence and Justice, he was still far from placated, as was evident within a fortnight when he made a most extraordinary speech stressing that he had pledged neither loyalty nor support to Haughey after the latter's election as party leader.

'In my speech at the party meeting,' Colley explained, 'I referred to Mr Haughey's ability, capacity and flair and I wished him well in the enormous task he was taking on. I did not, however, use the words 'loyalty' or 'support' which he attributed to me.' Colley fully understood how, 'in the excitement and euphoria' of victory, Haughey had misunderstood him, but now the Tánaiste was setting the record straight. As far as he was concerned the traditional loyalty normally given to the leader of the party had been withheld from Lynch, so it was now legitimate to withold 'loyalty to, and support for the elected leader.' He did qualify this slightly by adding that 'The Taoiseach is entitled to our conscientious and diligent support in all his efforts in the national interest.'

While some of Haughey's old enemies were more implacable than ever, he was the 'media's darling'. His victory was clearly welcomed by influential editors like Douglas Gageby of the *Irish Times*. Tim Pat Coogan of the *Irish Press*, and Michael Hand of the *Sunday Independent,* as well as Vincent Browne of *Magill* magazine.

One of the young, energetic reporters who initially welcomed the election of the new Taoiseach was Geraldine Kennedy of the *Irish Times*. She was rewarded with the rare privilege of an exclusive interview, but Haughey became quite agitated when she began asking questions about the Arms Crisis. At one point he threatened to terminate the interview if she persisted with her line of questioning. She wrote about this in her article but her editor excised the material. The seeds of future discord had now been sown. She had seen Haughey close up and was apparently not impressed, while his distrust of journalists was probably strengthened by what, in his eyes, must have amounted to the defection of a previous admirer. In the following weeks he repeatedly put off requests for interviews without actually refusing them. As a result the requests built up to the point where there were over 250 applications from journalists to interview him.

Marking the tenth anniversary of the Arms Crisis in May 1980 Vincent Browne of *Magill* began a series of articles that re-opened the whole controversy. The articles, which were based largely on the reminiscences of Peter Berry (who had died in 1975), provided an extraordinary insight into the controversial events. A number of people tried to block publication by threatening to sue the publisher, distributors, and sellers of the magazine. Although publication was temporarily delayed, the controversy helped to generate public curiosity and the issues carrying the Berry story were in great demand. As a result Haughey's role in the whole crisis became the focus of public attention and the Dáil held another debate on the Arms Crisis, ten years after the traumatic events.

Although the *Magill* articles raised serious questions about Haughey's conduct, the disclosures were probably even more damaging to some of his critics within Fianna Fáil because Berry had already told the court virtually all he knew about Haughey's involvement in the affair during the two arms trials. Thus his most startling posthumous disclosures related to others.

Browne was actually quite restrained in his own criticism of Haughey's alleged activities. In fact, he concluded that Haughey 'could easily and justifiably defend what he did at the time' but was so anxious to put the whole affair behind him that he glided over the facts.

Thus Browne tended to be more critical of the activities of others. 'While Mr Haughey certainly behaved improperly,' the editor concluded, 'he was and has been innocent of the more

131

colourful charges that have been laid against him concerning the crisis. It can be argued with some force that he was more a victim of the Arms Crisis than anything else.'

Even a vociferous opponent like John Kelly of Fine Gael had concluded that Haughey's alleged involvement in gun running back in 1970 could have been justified when seen in the perspective of the time, rather than in the light of the subsequent murderous campaign conducted by the Provisional IRA. It should be remembered that Gerry Fitt was one of those clamouring for guns for defensive purposes at the time, and Fitt later demonstrated the value of carrying a gun. On more than one occasion he used a licensed pistol to face down a rabble that broke into his home with the intention of attacking him.

In the course of the *Magill* articles, which were dragged out in four different issues of the magazine, Browne wrote that Kevin Boland had tried to persuade Haughey to secure cabinet approval for the planned importations of the arms in March 1970. This assertion cannot be reconciled with Haughey's arms trial testimony both about believing that the importation was totally proper and not knowing that guns were involved. Of course, this would not alter the fact that his actions prior to his arrest were justifiable. It was his actions following his arrest that were most open to question.

Some of the disclosures in *Magill* raised questions about the conduct of others, particularly Jack Lynch and his Minister for Justice, Desmond O'Malley. The articles demonstrated conclusively that despite assertions to the contrary, Lynch had been informed of Captain Kelly's activities before 20 April 1970. And Gibbons now publicly admitted that in 'October-November 1969' he had informed the Taoiseach 'that there were questionable activities on the part of certain members of the government making contact with people they should not make contact with'. Berry's account also gave rise to serious questions about O'Malley's judgment in connection with his private meeting with Haughey less than a fortnight before the arms trial was due to begin.

Having initially welcomed Haughey's election as Taoiseach, Browne gradually became quite critical of him, because he suddenly seemed to become uncharacteristically indecisive. It was not that the new Taoiseach was confused about the best course to follow, but that he lacked the political courage to stand by his convictions once faced with opposition. This vacillation was apparent on the political, economic and diplomatic fronts.

Politically, for instance, he ignored Colley's extraordinary renunciation of loyalty and support, while on the economic front he identified serious problems confronting the country but then did little about them. 'We have been living at a rate which is simply not justified by the amount of goods and services we are producing,' he told the nation during a special television address in January 1980. 'To make up the difference we have been borrowing enormous amounts of money, borrowing at a rate which just cannot continue.'

Haughey did not give any details of how he hoped to cope with the economic problems that night, but in the following months his government indicated it would be restricting the free bus service to rural school children and would be limiting wage increases in the public sector. It was also announced that a resource tax would be introduced in order to get farmers to bear a fairer share of the tax burden, but these proposals were quickly abandoned under political pressure. The most dramatic capitulation was on the public service pay issue on which the government conceded a staggering 34 per cent increase. As a result of this and other extravagant policies the budget deficit ended up more than 50 per cent over target.

Some Fianna Fáil deputies were allowed to announce extravagant schemes. Tom McEllistrim, Haughey's self-styled campaign manager, made so many announcements in his own constituency that he was dubbed 'MacMillions' by a local newspaper. Another staunch supporter, Pádraig Flynn, the Minister of State for Transport, pushed the building of a major airport in his own constituency on a mountain-top near Knock, Co. Mayo. The plan went ahead with the local airport company being asked to put up only £100 for the multi-million pound project. While all this was happening Haughey turned his attention to the Northern Ireland problem.

He declared at the Fianna Fáil ard fheis on 16 February 1980 that his government's 'first political priority' was to end partition. To further his aim he intended to enlist international help to put diplomatic pressure on the British. As far as the Taoiseach was concerned, Northern Ireland had failed as a political entity, so a new beginning was needed. But it was note-worthy that he did not call on the British to announce their intention to withdraw from the area. Rather, he asked them to declare 'their interest in encouraging the unity of Ireland by agreement and in peace'. He explained his policy would be to seek the development of 'some new free and open arrangement in which Irishmen and women, on their own, without a British presence but with active British goodwill, will manage the affairs of the whole of Ireland in a constructive partnership with the European community.'

Haughey went over to London to meet Prime Minister Margaret Thatcher in May. His chances of securing any kind of advance seemed remote from the outset because, on the eve of their meeting, she told the House of Commons that the con-stitutional affairs of Northern Ireland were 'a matter for the people of Northern Ireland, this government and this par-liament and no one else'. In short, she was saying that the Northern question was none of Haughey's business. Neverthe-less, the two of them got on quite well together next day. He brought a silver Georgian teapot to her as a present, and she was apparently surprised by his charm. One member of her cabinet later told friends 'he was sure he detected a "sexual" attraction for the smallish, rather worse-for-wear Irishman.'

After their meeting the two leaders issued a joint com-muniqué emphasising that they had decided to have regular meetings in order to develop 'new and closer political co-operation between our two countries.' The most significant aspect of the communiqué was their agreement that 'any change in the constitutional status of Northern Ireland would only come about with the consent of a majority of the people of Northern Ireland'.

Part of Haughey's overall plan was to wage an international campaign to have diplomatic pressure exerted on the British government to work for a settlement. Traditionally the Irish-American community had been the Dublin government's most influential supporter, but the Irish-Americans were bitterly divided on the Ulster question, with a large, vocal and well-organised minority supporting the campaign of the Provisional IRA. Ever since his appointment as Irish Ambassador to the United States in 1978 Seán Donlon had sought to isolate these

134

militants and in the process he ran foul of them and the organisations they controlled, like Noraid, the Irish National Caucus, and the Ancient Order of Hibernians. Hence Haughey decided to replace Donlon with someone who could work with all the Irish-American elements so that the Irish-American voice could be consolidated behind his plans for an Irish settlement. He therefore arranged for Donlon to be transferred to the United Nations, but word of the move was leaked and some powerful voices were raised in Washington, where Donlon was held in high esteem by influential Irish-American political figures like Thomas 'Tip O'Neill, the Speaker of the House of Representatives, Senators Edward Kennedy of Massachusetts and Daniel Patrick Moynihan of New York. Other admirers included Governor Hugh Carey of New York and the former Governor of California, Ronald Reagan, then engaged in his successful bid for the Presidency. Faced with opposition from such influential people, Haughey backed down and Donlon was allowed to remain at his post in Washington.

So with Haughey's first year in office as Taoiseach coming to a close, he desperately needed some kind of real achievement. He was obviously indebted for his reinstatement within Fianna Fáil to the so-called green wing of the party which wanted the government to take a more active part in seeking a solution to the Northern problem. The whole question took on added significance on 26 October 1980 when seven republican prisoners went on hunger strike as part of their H-Block protest for what amounted to political status. Little over a week later, Haughey watched aghast from a by-election platform in Letterkenny, Co. Donegal as Síle de Valera revived memories of her Fermoy speech by denouncing 'Mrs Thatcher's lack of compassion' and her 'callous, unfeeling and self-righteous statements'.

Although Haughey made no reference to Síle de Valera's speech during his own address moments later, he was obviously taken aback. Immediately after the rally he and some senior colleagues retired to a local hotel to discuss it. About an hour later Ray MacSharry, as director of elections, issued a statement to the press emphasising that neither the Taoiseach nor any member of the government had seen her script in advance and that her remarks had not reflected the views of the government.

Síle de Valera later expressed surprise at the statement dissociating the party from her remarks. She said that following her Fermoy speech in 1977 Lynch had banned her from making any public comments on the Northern situation, but Haughey lifted this ban when he became Taoiseach. 'Mr Haughey told me when he assumed office that the ban no longer applied,' she explained. 'I was working under the assumption that there was no ban when I spoke in Letterkenny.'

Privately Haughey may well have agreed with her sentiments, but he clearly did not like her timing. Since he was beside her on the platform when she made the remarks, it would appear that he was openly endorsing what she said unless some kind of repudiation was issued. He was anxious to dissociate himself from her remarks because he did not want them to impair his relations with the Prime Minister before their next meeting.

This meeting took place in Dublin Castle on 8 December. Thatcher was accompanied to Dublin by Chancellor of the Exchequer Geoffrey Howe, Foreign Secretary Lord Carrington, and Humphrey Atkins, the Secretary of State for Northern Ireland. The inclusion of Carrington gave rise to speculation because he had recently played a major role in changing the direction of Britain's Rhodesian policy. Prompted by the Foreign Secretary, Thatcher had agreed to a settlement which brought one of the guerrilla leaders to power. Haughey, with his almost messianic belief in his own capability, seemed to think he had a real chance of persuading the British to settle the Irish question for once and for all.

The Taoiseach was accompanied by Lenihan and O'Kennedy, his respective Ministers for Foreign Affairs and Finance. They were included in most of the day-long discussions, though not in the private meeting lasting an hour and a quarter between Haughey and Thatcher.

Afterwards the two leaders issued a joint communiqué describing their talks as 'extremely constructive and significant'. In relation to Northern Ireland, they 'accepted the need to bring forward policies and proposals to achieve peace, reconciliation and stability'. And to further these aims they agreed to promote 'the further development of the unique relationship between the two countries' by commissioning 'joint studies covering a range of issues including possible new institutional structures, citizenship rights, security matters, economic co-operation and measures to encourage mutual understanding'.

Some one hundred reporters from around the world were present at a press conference afterwards when Haughey explained that there had been 'an historic breakthrough,' but he was not prepared to elaborate publicly. Instead he repeatedly referred the reporters to the text of the communiqué. But he was more forthcoming immediately afterwards in an 'off-the-record' briefing for Dublin political correspondents. According to Bruce Arnold, the Taoiseach indicated 'by implication and innuendo' that the British leader had agreed that the joint studies could reconsider Northern Ireland's whole constitutional position; he also anticipated an early end to partition. Moreover, Lenihan said in an RTE interview that the partition question was on the verge of being resolved.

The British Prime Minister promptly denied there was any intention of altering the constitutional position of the Six Counties, but Ian Paisley, the Democratic Unionist (DUP) leader, exploited unionist unease by taking to what he called the 'Carson Trail' in order to demonstrate the intensity of unionist opposition to constitutional change. A whole series of demonstrations were organised throughout Northern Ireland to rail against the joint studies. Paisley vented his spleen particularly at Haughey, a long-standing unionist hate figure. The DUP leader talked about the ancestors of the unionist people cutting 'civilisation out of the bogs and meadows of this country while Mr Haughey's ancestors were wearing pig skins and living in caves'. At a Newtownards rally he conjured up a picture of the Taoiseach with 'a green baton dripping with blood' in one hand and 'a noose specially prepared for the Protestants of Ulster in the other'.

No doubt the bitterness with which Paisley and his followers reacted to the outcome of the Dublin Castle summit encouraged some optimism in nationalist circles. It was noteworthy that the H-Block hunger strike was called off within ten days. Whether the exaggerated significance attached to the Dublin Castle summit had encouraged those advising the hunger strikers to engage in some wishful thinking is a matter for speculation, but in time it would become apparent that Haughey and his people

137

had, either wittingly or unwittingly, grossly oversold the significance of the summit.

Opposition leaders criticised the Taoiseach for not being more specific about his talks. According to Frank Cluskey, leader of the Labour Party, 'evasiveness' was the single most distinguishing characteristic of the government. 'Everything has come under the heading of confidentiality and secrecy', he contended. FitzGerald complained that the government seemed to be trying to bring about Irish unity without the prior consent of the Northern majority, which he believed was a recipe for civil war.

Yet Haughey made no apologies for the secrecy surrounding the joint studies. 'To suggest that permanent officials engaged in such studies should try to carry out their task in the full glare of publicity is nonsense,' he later declared. 'We were accused of trying to settle matters over the heads of people of Northern Ireland when in fact we were seeking to set up a political framework in which they could participate without prejudice to their principles.' At the time, however, he allowed his own people to encourage the belief that he was close to a settlement that would end partition, notwithstanding all the rantings of Paisley.

There was considerable speculation that the joint studies on security matters were aimed at drawing up details of an Anglo-Irish defensive pact which Haughey would sign in return for the ending of partition. This, of course, would undermine the country's avowed neutrality, Joseph Carroll, author of *Ireland in the War Years, 1939-1945*, observed that there was actually 'more heated debate about Ireland's neutrality outside the Dáil during 1981 than during the years of the Second World War'. Although Haughey denied 'unequivocally' that his government was 'discussing or negotiating any kind of secret agreement on defence with Britain or with any other country or group of countries', the speculation continued, fuelled by the misgivings voiced by FitzGerald together with the Taoiseach's own admission that if partition were ended, his government 'would of course have to review what would be the most appropriate defence arrangements for the island as a whole'. He also reiterated his own longstanding conviction that the country should align completely with its European partners once the EEC developed 'into a full political union'. 'We could not, and would not wish to opt out of the obligations and aims inherent in the achievement of the ideal of European unity', he emphasised.

FitzGerald must have known that Irish neutrality was never much more than notional. Despite appearances Ireland was not really neutral during the Second World War, because the de Valera government secretly gave the Allies virtually all the help it could. In the circumstances the country's policy should more appropriately have been described as non-belligerency, rather than neutrality. So why did the Fine Gael leader make a fuss about the joint studies on security being a threat to the country's supposed neutrality?

Haughey later contended that FitzGerald 'was merely pandering to those who do not want the studies to succeed anyway'. The charge was reminiscent of one made in the 1930s by de Valera who accused the Fine Gael leadership of deliberately trying to frustrate his efforts to negotiate an Anglo-Irish agreement. This charge of near treasonable behaviour was not without substance. Official documents released in line with Britain's thirty year secrecy rule contain clear evidence that Fine Gael leaders (no doubt convinced they were acting in their country's best interest) secretly pleaded with the British not to conclude an agreement with de Valera because it would enhance his reputation and thereby destroy Fine Gael politically. In 1981 Haughey seemed to think that history was repeating itself.

In the aftermath of the Dublin Castle summit the Taoiseach was clearly looking towards an early election, even though the existing Dáil still had eighteen months to run. In January 1981 the government introduced a budget which did not reflect the country's economic plight. Fianna Fáil was due to have its ard fheis in mid-February, and there was speculation that Haughey would use the occasion to foreshadow the calling of a general election. But on the eve of his planned ard fheis speech disaster struck in the form of the Stardust tragedy in which forty-eight young people were killed in a discotheque fire in the Taoiseach's own Artane constituency. Given the magnitude of the disaster, the remainder of the ard fheis was postponed. When it was reconvened in April, Haughey referred to 'ending the age-old problem of partition' in his presidential address. 'A year from this ard fheis if we persevere faithfully,' he said, 'we may begin to see in a clearer light the end of the road on which we have set out.'

By this time, however, the political climate had already been poisoned by the start of the second H-Block hunger strike on 1 March 1981. This hunger strike, which was in support of the same demands as the one called off in December, received massive international publicity following the election to Westminster of one of the men, Bobby Sands. The hunger strikers vowed to fast to death and other colleagues pledged to replace them on the fast until their demands were met. Sands expected that Haughey would be compelled to support their demands publicly, but the Taoiseach refused to be pressurised, even after Sands and his colleagues began to die. Privately Haughey indicated to the sister of one of those who was about to die that he would like to be helpful but did not see how he could be of assistance.

'What can I do?' he asked her.

She replied that he should ask Thatcher to implement the five demands, but he said it would do no good to become embroiled in a propaganda battle. When she asked point blank if he believed in the five demands, he refused to answer the question.

When Haughey called a general election for 11 June 1981 some of those connected with the hunger strikers believed the date was chosen because, if the hunger strike was still on, the first group would be dead and none of their replacements would yet be nearing death. Although this factor may well have been a consideration in choosing the actual day for the election, other factors undoubtedly weighted more heavily with Haughey.

First, a considerable amount of the money allocated for 1981 had already been spent and it was going to be necessary for the government to introduce legislation to secure supplementary funding in the near future. This would almost inevitably lead to increased taxes, which were not likely to be popular with the electorate. Secondly, Fianna Fáil's private polls were indicating that the party was in good standing with the electorate, which was tending to be rather volatile at the time. In early March 1981, for instance, Fianna Fáil had enjoyed a comfortable lead over the combined opposition. The situation was reversed during April, but on the day after Haughey called the election an IMS poll detected a massive swing back to Fianna Fáil, which enjoyed a 17 per cent lead over Fine Gael, with the Labour Party a further 19 per cent behind. When the 15 per cent 'don't knows' were excluded, the poll estimated that Fianna Fáil would get 52 per cent of the vote, an even higher percentage than 1977. In addition, Haughey's own position had improved dramatically. In the April poll he had trailed FitzGerald by 10 per cent as the preferred choice for Taoiseach, but now he actually led him by 43 to 40 per cent. So things were looking well for him and for Fianna Fáil generally.

Haughey ran a high profile, presidential-style campaign. The party adopted 'Charlie's Song,' a catchy song written and recorded just for the election, as its campaign anthem. It was played at all party rallies, calling on voters to 'rise and follow Charlie'. He toured the country in a whirlwind fashion and travelled by helicopter to maximise his exposure. Still, the party lost ground during the campaign.

This was due to a number of factors. For one thing, Fine Gael ran a very effective campaign on their own, with some promised giveaways and tax cuts reminiscent of Fianna Fáil in 1977. Secondly, Haughey was confronted with a hostile media, and thirdly, the party was seriously hurt by the H-Block issue.

Bruce Arnold contended that the media's hostility towards Haughey stemmed from the latter's exaggeration of the significance of the Dublin Castle summit. But the Taoiseach also suffered by being contrasted with the Fine Gael leader.

Reporters found Haughey the more exciting to cover because he was so unpredictable. 'You don't know when he might lash out and clock someone or suddenly take a flying leap and start biting the furniture,' wrote Gene Kerrigan in *Magill*. They also had the unwanted excitement of trying to keep up with him as he was whisked off to the next destination by helicopter, while they scrambled frantically for transport to the next stop with no hope of getting there on time.

Haughey really had a mixed relationship with those covering his campaign. He was very co-operative with photographers and had an inexhaustible appetite for photo calls. He did not feel threatened by the photographers; they did not ask awkward questions. He could also be charming and friendly with reporters, but he was clearly ill-at-ease when they asked awkward questions, as they were wont to do.

Olivia O'Leary of the *Irish Times* noted that while Haughey usually found time to talk to reporters, he gave them very little information and his speeches were 'a series of genial banal declarations' without much substance. He just trotted out well-worn phrases to evoke applause when desired. According to her, he confidently used this refined hustings technique 'with the ease of a veteran performing monkey'. This assessment was essentially endorsed by Vincent Browne, who complained that Haughey uttered 'the same clichés again and again to a point where reporters on tour with him could anticipate his every utterance'. Almost all those reporters 'developed a deep personal dislike of him, in a manner reminiscent of "The Boys on the Bus" with Richard Nixon in 1968'.

Although Garret FitzGerald was not as exciting, most reporters preferred to cover him because, as a former journalist, he understood and sympathised with their need both to get a story and file it by their deadline. Moreover, as the country's only helicopter-hire service was run by Haughey's son Ciarán, FitzGerald confined himself to the more conventional modes of travel. Reporters therefore had no problems keeping up with him. Indeed they often travelled with him on the campaign bus, where he was readily available to answer questions, and he even flattered them by asking their advice on certain issues. As a result he got on well with them. 'FitzGerald was the darling of the media', Bruce Arnold wrote.

Towards the end of the campaign there was a 'television debate' in which the main party leaders were questioned separately by a team of four journalists. One of the questioners, Vincent Browne, admitted afterwards that Haughey handled himself very well and clearly outwitted his interrogators, who were immediately despondent at having let him off 'very lightly'. During a commercial break before interviewing FitzGerald, the journalists decided not to overcompensate by being too rough on the Fine Gael leader. They therefore 'tacitly agreed to go easy'. Later when they viewed a tape of the programme they realised they had not been as easy on the Fianna Fáil leader as they had first imagined.

'We were surprised to see that we had been much tougher than we had thought,' Browne explained. By going deliberately easy on FitzGerald, therefore, the journalists had been unfair to

Haughey and their unbalanced questioning was clearly evident. This certainly lent substance to Haughey's charge that the media were biased against him and quite probably contributed towards whittling away the lead he had enjoyed in the IMS poll at the start of the campaign. But the last straw was the presence of H-Block candidates on the ballot papers.

In nine different constituencies H-Block prisoners, including some of the hunger strikers, were registered as candidates in an attempt to secure publicity for their cause. Wherever Haughey went during the campaign he was taunted by supporters of the H-Block candidates. In Navan, for instance, he was heckled by Bridget Rose Dugdale, recently released from jail.

'Murder, murder,' she shouted repeatedly. 'Who killed Ray McCreesh?' The latter was one of the four hunger strikers who had already died.

The Taoiseach received a particularly stormy reception when he went to Ballyshannon, Co. Donegal, on 28 May. His rally was disrupted and he was jostled by protesters. He also suffered the indignity of being hit on the head with an egg, and when he tried to leave the town his car was blocked by protesters who kicked and pounded on it while the gárdaí strove to clear the way for him. Later in Dun Laoghaire he narrowly escaped when another protestor tried to dump a can of paint on him.

Supporters of the H-Block campaign had targeted Haughey in the blind belief that FitzGerald could not be more unsympathetic than him from their standpoint. They had allowed their emotions to run away with them because the Fine Gael leader was even less likely to endorse their demands seeing that he had already publicly urged the British government not to accede to them. It was therefore ironic that the Fine Gael leader was one of the principal political beneficiaries of the H-Block campaign, which probably made the difference that led to Haughey's defeat in his bid for re-election as Taoiseach.

As expected Haughey easily won re-election to the Dáil with more than a quota to spare, but Fianna Fáil's first-preference vote nationwide was down significantly (by 5.1 per cent overall and 8.6 per cent in Munster) from 1977. However, it was grossly unfair to blame the drop on Haughey. The party had already lost considerable ground before he took over as Taoiseach in 1979 and it would have been more appropriate to compare the latest showing with its dismal performance in the European elections of 1979. Moreover, the Cork by-elections of the same year should also be remembered. In comparison with those 1979 performances, the latest Fianna Fáil showing under Haughey was little short of phenomenal.

The party had actually secured a higher percentage of first-preference votes than it had under Seán Lemass in his first general election as Taoiseach in 1961. Moreover, it came within half a percentage point of its share of the 1969 vote when it secured an overall majority. In the end, Fianna Fáil (with 78 seats) finished just two seats short of the combined total of Fine Gael and Labour. That situation could actually have been reversed with just 250 extra votes spread over two constituencies in which Fianna Fáil candidates lost the last seats to Fine Gael. It was that close.

The balance of power was held by the one Workers' Party deputy and five Independents. One of the latter, John O'Connell, who had recently resigned from the Labour Party, was elected Speaker of the Dáil, so FitzGerald needed the support of two of the others, whereas Haughey needed the support of four. Two of the Independents, Noel Browne and Jim Kemmy, were highly critical of Haughey, so the outcome was a virtual foregone conclusion. They duly voted against him, as did the Workers' Party deputy, with the result that Haughey's nomination to remain as Taoiseach was defeated by 83 votes to 79. FitzGerald was then elected, and Haughey graciously accepted the verdict. He was again out in the cold, but this time he was leader of the opposition.

11
Sojourn in the cold

Leader of the Opposition
1981-82

Sunday Independent, 28 February 1982

HAVING confidently anticipated his re-election as Taoiseach, Haughey was not prepared for the role of leader of the opposition. In the following months he appeared to drift without a positive approach of his own as he just reacted negatively to the coalition government's policies.

Although he had remained fairly quiet about the H-Block campaign as Taoiseach, he did speak out following the collapse of the hunger strike after it had claimed the lives of six more hunger strikers, including one of those elected to the Dáil. Despite his supposedly warm relations with the British Prime Minister, Haughey now blamed much of the tragedy on her intransigence. He said that she should have conceded the demands of the hunger strikers. The campaign had focused considerable attention on the northern question, with the result that it was to remain in the forefront of Irish politics for some time.

FitzGerald wanted to adopt a positive approach towards ending partition by trying to win over the Northern majority with concrete assurances that Northern Protestants would have nothing to fear in a united Ireland. Like Haughey, he accepted that Irish unity should only be brought about with the consent of the Northern majority, but unlike the Fianna Fáil leader, he was prepared to make the Republic more attractive without first waiting for the Northern majority to come to the conference table.

FitzGerald proposed changing what he believed were sectarian aspects of the Irish constitution and legal system which, he said, were 'inbred with the ethos' of the Catholic majority. For years Irish nationalists had been blind to their own discriminatory behaviour towards Protestant values while complaining about the manner in which the Protestant majority discriminated against the minority in Northern Ireland. The Republic was therefore a sectarian state, 'though not in the acutely sectarian way that Northern Ireland was', according to the new Taoiseach. 'Our laws and our constitution, our practices and our attitude reflect those of the majority ethos and are not acceptable to Protestants in Northern Ireland.'

Before coming to power he had made no secret of his belief that the confessional approach adopted in Dublin was repugnant to Northern Protestants. 'If I were a Northern Protestant', he declared in 1979, 'I wouldn't be happy about unification with people who haven't shown themselves to be openminded. We need to shake people here out of their loyalty to the state to a wider loyalty to the Irish nation. This is so partitionist a state that Northern Protestants would be bloody fools to join it.'

As Taoiseach, therefore, FitzGerald called for a 'constitutional crusade' to change southern attitudes in order to break down some of the barriers that had kept the Catholic and Protestant communities divided. Having accepted that the Northern majority could not be coerced into a united Ireland, he suggested that Dublin give formal expression to this acceptance by removing Articles 2 and 3 from the Irish constitution. Article 2 was the provision which claimed sovereignty over 'the whole island of Ireland,' while Article 3 stipulated that the constitution would apply only to the Twenty-six Counties 'pending the re-integration' of the Six Counties. Those articles had prompted northern unionists to adopt 'their siege mentality', according to FitzGerald. He argued that their removal would placate the unionists 'and open up the possibility of easier dialogue between them and the nationalists in Northern Ireland'.

But Haughey dismissed the need for such a crusade out of hand. 'Our constitution,' he said in Ennis at the unveiling of a memorial to the late Eamon de Valera, 'enshrines in Articles 2 and 3 the clear assertion of the belief that this island should be one political unit — a belief stretching far back into history and asserted and reasserted time and again by the vast majority of our people North and South.'

Over the years de Valera himself had rejected the kind of approach now being advocated by FitzGerald on the grounds that the unionists would merely look on concessions as a sign of weakness. 'Is there anyone foolish enough to think that if we are going to sacrifice our aspirations that they are going to give up their cry of not an inch?' de Valera asked the Dáil. 'For every step we moved towards them, you know perfectly well they would regard it as a sign that we would move another, and they would not be satisfied, in my opinion, unless we went back and accepted the old United Kingdom, a common parliament for the two countries.'

There was undoubtedly a great deal of validity to what de Valera had said, but in dismissing FitzGerald's arguments, Haughey betrayed that quality of snide invectiveness that many people had found frightening over the years. He did not try to refute the Taoiseach's suggestions with reasoned arguments of his own; instead, he resorted to an emotional appeal impugning the patriotism of FitzGerald and those who agreed with him. The Fianna Fáil leader said, for example, that support for deleting Articles 2 and 3 came from 'the remnants of that colonial mentality that still lingers on in Irish life, a mentality that cannot come to terms with the concept of a separate, independent Irish Ireland'.

'Once again,' he continued, 'we are asked to accept a jaundiced view of ourselves. Once again we are being asked to look only at our faults and to believe that somewhere else things are ordered much better than they are here, and there exists a superior form of society which we must imitate.' There was no reason 'to apologise to anyone for being what we are or for holding the beliefs we do,' he said. 'We angrily reject accusations of either inferiority or sectarianism.'

In decrying the constitutional crusade, Haughey adopted the demogogic technique of introducing irrelevancies into the argument by endorsing patriotism and then renouncing an unpopular argument that he attributed to his opponent but which, in fact, his opponent had never made. FitzGerald did not say nor did he imply that the Irish people were inferior to anyone. He did criticise the sectarianism of the Irish system, and Haughey had basically acknowledged a need for reform as Taoiseach when he indicated his willingness to accept changes if the Northern Protestants would agree to unity. The main difference between the two leaders was a matter of timing — whether the changes should be made first as part of an effort to win over the Protestants in Northern Ireland, or made as a bargaining ploy at the last moment after the Northern majority had agreed to negotiate an end to partition.

Haughey was opposed to legislating with the aim of currying favour with the unionists. He told a party meeting on 17 October that any changes in the constitution 'should be undertaken on their merit, not with a view to impressing Northern unionists, the British, or anybody else.' Complaining that Fitz-Gerald's constitutional crusade was 'unnecessary, divisive and unhelpful', he added in an unscripted aside that it was 'the first time in history that a crusade was started by the infidels'.

Having already impugned the patriotism of those advocating constitutional change. Haughey's use of the word 'infidels' could be taken as a rather snide way of questioning the religious convictions of the same people, but in this instance the remark was probably more flippant than sinister. Still, his overall approach to the constitutional issue did little to endear him to people like George Colley, who had served on a constitutional committee which had advocated the same kind of changes back in the 1960s, and their findings had been endorsed by Haughey's idol, Seán Lemass.

Anglo-Irish relations had clearly taken a turn for the worse during the H-Block crisis, but things got back on track with a summit between FitzGerald and Thatcher in London on 6 November 1981. The two leaders afterwards issued a joint communiqué restating the fundamental position of each government. This reiterated that the goal of successive Irish governments was 'to secure the unity of Ireland by agreement and in peace', while the British reaffirmed that 'any change in the constitutional status of Northern Ireland would require the consent of a majority of the people of Northern Ireland'. The most significant aspect of the talks was an agreement to establish an Anglo-Irish Intergovernmental Council to give institutional expression to the 'unique character of the relationship between the two countries'. These meetings would first be held at ministerial and official levels but it was agreed that the respective governments would 'consider at the appropriate time whether there should be an Anglo-Irish body at parliamentary level whose members would be drawn from the British and Irish parliaments, the European parliament, and any elected assembly that might be established for Northern Ireland'. This proposal was a product of the joint studies arranged for at the Dublin Castle summit. The purpose of those studies had been so misunderstood that the two leaders now agreed to publish most of them in order to clear up the confusion.

Haughey lost no time in denouncing the latest talks. Quoting from the communiqué, he said that FitzGerald had given what amounted to *de jure* recognition to partition by agreeing 'that the consent of the majority would be required' to change the constitutional status of Northern Ireland. He admitted that he had earlier agreed that change 'would only come about' with the consent of that majority, but he contended this was only a recognition of the 'practical realities of the situation' and at worst a *de facto* recognition of partition.

Speaking in the Dáil four days later he dismissed the joint studies and the latest talks as a betrayal of 'the spirit and letter of the Dublin communiqué' of December 1980. He was contending that something much more far reaching had been envisaged at Dublin Castle, but this was not substantiated by the joint studies, which clearly showed that Haughey had been exaggerating the situation. Now he was skating on thin ice in criticising those studies because he had seen and approved of them before leaving office in July.

While theoreticians and academics might argue for hours about the importance — supposed or real — of a distinction between the *de jure* and *de facto* positions adopted by Haughey and FitzGerald, the issue was of little concern to the Irish electorate at large. Such constitutional arguments were a mere side issue to most people, who were much more interested in economic matters.

Haughey was also critical of the government's economic policies. 'Our approach is positive and theirs is negative,' he contended. 'We are development-investment minded, and they are committed to monetarism and deflation.' But his economic views were not shared by party colleagues like Colley, O'Donoghue, or O'Malley. It was Charlie McCreevy, one of his more ardent backbench supporters from 1979, who was the first to speak out publicly. In an interview with Geraldine Kennedy, the recently appointed political correspondent of the *Sunday Tribune*, McCreevy was particularly critical of Fianna Fáil's performance in opposition.

'We seem to be against everything and for nothing,' he said. When asked if he was disillusioned with the party leader, he pointedly refused to comment, thereby leaving little doubt about his own disenchantment with Haughey.

On 11 January 1982 McCreevy spoke out again in a similar vein as he complained that general elections were 'developing into an auction in promises' with scant regard for the national interest. 'We are so hell bent on assuming power that we are prepared to do anything for it,' he declared.

Bristling under the criticism, which he considered a challenge to his own leadership, Haughey asked the parliamentary party to expel McCreevy. The latter allowed things to go to the brink of a vote before intervening to announce that he would spare the meeting the necessity of a divisive vote by withdrawing from the whip voluntarily, though he nevertheless pledged his continued loyalty and support to the party.

Fine Gael were by no means immune from McCreevy's criticism. The party had made lavish promises during the June election campaign, but once in government FitzGerald pleaded an inability to implement the more expensive promises because the country's financial position was much worse than was believed before the election. The explanation was not entirely honest. Fine Gael knew when it made the promises that the country's finances were in bad shape.

Having come to power after promising to reduce taxation, the more honourable course would have been for FitzGerald to go back to the country and level with the people that it was not possible to implement his party's promises. As things turned out it would also have been the more expedient politically, but the Fine Gael leader lacked the political finesse to make the best of his situation, especially when Fianna Fáil were so obviously divided. Instead his government brought in a budget which not only failed to keep his promise to introduce certain tax reforms but actually violated a further promise by trying to put Value Added Tax on clothing and footwear. As a result the government, which was dependent on the support of two independent deputies, was defeated when all but one of them voted with the opposition. The Taoiseach was therefore compelled to seek a dissolution and ask for a general election under circumstances which were more unfavourable than if he had had the courage and integrity to seek a mandate for abandoning his party's campaign promises.

Following FitzGerald's announcement that he was going to seek a dissolution and ask the President to call a general election, Haughey made several efforts to contact President Hillery in an attempt to persuade him to exercise a constitutional right not to dissolve the Dáil. Article 13 of the constitution specifically states that 'the President may in his absolute discretion refuse to dissolve Dáil Éireann on the advice of a Taoiseach who has ceased to retain the support of a majority'.

FitzGerald had lost a vote on what amounted to a matter of confidence, so the President did not have to accede to his request for a dissolution. Haughey felt that, as Fianna Fáil leader, he should be given a chance to form a government. It was certainly worth a try. But Hillery was unwilling to take any telephone calls from him. Haughey therefore tried to attract the President's attention by issuing a statement to the media.

'It is a matter for the President to consider the situation which has arisen now that the Taoiseach has ceased to retain the support of the majority in Dáil Éireann,' he declared. 'I am available for consultation by the President should he so wish.'

If the President refused a dissolution, then the matter would be thrown back into the Dáil, where a Taoiseach would have to be elected in the same manner as after a general election. If Haughey then succeeded in forming a government, he would have been able to call for a dissolution and go to the country as Taoiseach with all the perks of office. Although something comparatively similar had occurred in Canada and more recently in Australia, President Hillery refused to exercise his constitutional prerogative in this instance. The Dáil was therefore dissolved and a general election called for 18 February 1982.

Haughey was in a buoyant mood when he met the media next morning. He wanted to make the rejected budget the central issue of the election campaign. He said that he placed a very high priority on the need to dispose of 'most of the provisions of yesterday's budget', but he was deliberately vague about his own plans. He then became irritated when journalists continuously pressed him for specific details of how he would handle the economy.

Faced with apparent contradiction in what Haughey was saying, reporters pressed him to reconcile those differences. He said, for instance, he was opposed to creating employment simply by adding people to the public payroll but, on the other hand, he blamed government policies for allowing 5,000 vacancies to develop in this sector. If elected, he said his government would have to decide whether to fill the vacancies or leave the people on the dole. The implications were unmistakable: he was intimating that he would fill the vacancies without actually committing himself to the course. He also adopted a somewhat similar approach to the question of food subsidies, which the coalition budget had sought to remove.

Previously Haughey had opposed food subsidies because they subsidised the wealthy as well as the needy. By abolishing them, he contended, the state would have more money to help the needy by increasing welfare payments. Now, however, he seemed to be engaged in some political gymnastics in order to exploit the unpopularity of the government's effort to abolish the subsidies. He intimated that it would be possible to retain them in a 'self-financing' manner by using them to keep down inflation and thus restricting wage claims. In that way, he argued, if might be possible to save more than the subsidies cost, but he emphasised that this was only a theory put forward by some economists, and he had 'a basic and inherent distrust of theoriticians'. Reporters pressed him to be more definite.

'I'm not here to be cross-examined!' he exclaimed angrily at one point.

'Mr Haughey, this is a press conference,' John Bowman of RTE reminded him. 'You *are* here to be cross-examined.'

'I've answered that question already!' he declared.

'You didn't answer it,' a reporter replied. But Haughey had answered it in as much detail as he was about to, and that was that.

Vincent Browne was insistent that politicans on all sides should 'be forced to state precisely' the cost of any scheme they proposed and to outline how they were going to pay for it. 'Already Fianna Fáil is ducking this one,' he wrote. 'Any politician who refused to state prescisely how any of his/her proposals is going to be paid for is either attempting to fool the electorate or is an idiot. Either way, they shouldn't be elected.'

Journalists were not the only people critical of Haughey's initial performance. Fianna Fáil's newly appointed spokesman on Finance, Martin O'Donoghue, was privately very critical. Before the introduction of the rejected budget the party's front bench had decided on a policy of accepting both the government's proposed spending and its projected deficit and would argue about the specific details.

Haughey obviously departed from the agreed course at his press conference. It was intimated strongly to him afterwards that if he continued to campaign as he had begun, then O'Donoghue, Colley and O'Malley would repudiate his policies. He therefore agreed to adopt the economic approach advocated by O'Donoghue, who was invited to prepare a speech for him. In it Haughey accepted the government's targeted deficit.

'We would stick to the same levels of borrowing and the current budget deficit,' he declared, 'because it would not be sensible, wise or prudent to depart too much.' But he contended some of the harsher aspects of the defeated budget could easily be eliminated.

If Haughey hoped that taking this line would unite the dissidents behind him, however, he must have been sorely disappointed. When interviewed on RTE Radio's 'This Week' programme next day, for instance, O'Donoghue beat around the proverbial bush rather than answer whether he thought Haughey was fit to be Taoiseach. Four times the interviewer asked the question, but each time O'Donoghue pointedly avoided answering it. In another RTE interveiw ten days later, Colley similarly refused to say that he hoped Haughey would be the next Taoiseach.

When Haughey tried to explain how the government's budget targets could be met without adopting the harsher measures proposed, he and his economic advisers were accused of 'creative accounting' because their figures simply did not add up. The shortfall was referred to as 'Fianna Fáil's funny money'. His credibility on such matters was further questioned at the height of the election campaign when *Magill* published a leaked Department of Finance document showing that Haughey's previous government had deliberately underestimated expenditure in the run up to the 1981 general election.

The Fianna Fáil leader's image had clearly become an electoral liability. The first IMS poll of the campaign indicated that only 31 per cent of the electorate preferred him for Taoiseach, whereas FitzGerald was the choice of 51 per cent. By the end of the campaign the Taoiseach gained a further 5 points against only 2 by Haughey. As a result the latter's photograph was dropped from some of his party's advertising.

Albert Reynolds, Fianna Fáil's National Director of Elections, accused Fine Gael of conducting a smear campaign against Haughey. Whether or not the opposition actually orchestrated the campaign is open to question, but there could be no doubt that Haughey received unfair treatment from the media, and this was acknowledged by some of his most outspoken critics.

'There was a lot of personal sniping against Charlie Haughey which was unfair,' Geraldine Kennedy candidly admitted. 'It could just as equally have been done on Garret FitzGerald, and it wasn't.' Nevertheless, she contended, the media had 'quite good reasons' for being biased against Haughey. 'The media was in a position to judge Charlie Haughey,' she explained. 'The media was in a position to appreciate the extent of the divisions within Fianna Fáil and to judge whether Fianna Fáil could implement a clear and consistent policy in government.'

She was apparently arguing that while the media had been unfair to Haughey, it was fair to be unfair to him which, of course, betrayed a kind of confused thinking.

'Any casual perusal of any cross-section of the Irish newspapers during the course of the campaign would reveal that people writing about politics were less than enamoured with Charles J. Haughey,' according to Seán Duignan, RTE's political correspondent. Fianna Fáil dissidents had been hinting that their leader was an unsuitable person to lead the country, and the media reflected this even though no specific evidence was cited to justify the unstated reservations about him. 'Because they were unstated and therefore unsubstantiated,' Duignan conceded, 'they were unfair.'

Haughey again fared well during a television encounter with FitzGerald on the second last day of the campaign. This time the format was more akin to a debate, without any panel of journalists. By general consensus the Fianna Fáil leader, who seemed relaxed and confident, was the winner. 'After all that had been written, said and implied about him,' two of his critics noted, 'Haughey probably appeared like an agreeable surprise, an ordinary, undramatic politician rather than a strange ogre.'

The election count was an extended affair with the final outcome remaining in doubt until quite late. Four staunch Haughey supporters lost their seats so there was a potential shift of power within the party with the election of eight new deputies. One of those being returned after a short absence from the Dáil was Jim Gibbons, who lost no time in raising the spectre of an impending challenge to Haughey's leadership.

'I expect the question of the leadership will be raised at the first meeting of the parliamentary party,' Gibbons told reporters following his victory. This was immediately interpreted as the first move in a bid to get rid of Haughey. As the count continued the *Evening Herald* went on sale quoting the remarks under a bold front page headline: 'Leadership Fight Facing Haughey'.

It was not until some hours later that the final votes were counted and it became apparent that Fianna Fáil were going to be three votes short of an overall majority in the Dáil. Disgruntled members of the party openly contended that Haughey's leadership had been a distinct electoral liability. The outgoing chairman of the parliamentary party, William

155

Kenneally, who had just lost his seat in Waterford, made no secret of his disillusionment. He told Geraldine Kennedy the party would have fared much better under a more popular leader, with the result that he 'would not be surprised' if the party's leadership became an issue in the very near future. As a result, she reported that 'a movement seemed to be brewing' within Fianna Fáil to overthrow the 'leader as he struggles to form the next government without an overall majority'.

Haughey was obviously stung by the story, which he described as 'rubbish' during an interview on RTE's lunchtime news programme. 'If I were in the *Sunday Tribune,*' he said, 'I would be inclined to look after my own future.'

Speculation about the leadership was certainly not helping Haughey's chance of regaining power. He needed the active support of at least two deputies from outside his own party and the abstention of another, in order to replace FitzGerald. This was likely to prove difficult when there was uncertainty about his own hold on the leadership of Fianna Fáil. He therefore had a meeting of the new parliamentary party called for Thursday, 25 February, with a view to selecting the party's nominee for Taoiseach.

If only to remove the uncertainty, his desire to have the issue resolved speedily was understandable. Of course, his opponents within the party felt he was simply trying to deny them time to organise properly. They therefore went into action and held a series of backroom meetings at which Colley threw his support to O'Malley, who then became the frontrunner among the potential challengers, though Dublin bookmakers were not impressed with his chances — at least, not at first. Haughey was quoted as an odds-on favourite to become Taoiseach with O'Malley at 4 to 1 behind even Garret FitzGerald.

To regain power Haughey's chance seemed to lie with securing the support of Independents, who included his Arms Crisis colleague Neil Blaney. John O'Connell, the sitting Ceann Comhairle, could be neutralised by being re-appointed, which meant that all Fianna Fáil needed was the support of the newly elected Dublin Independent, Tony Gregory, who seemed to share the Fianna Fáil leader's strong nationalist views on the partition problem. As far as Haughey was concerned, therefore, Gregory held the key to power.

'I have seventy-eight seats, plus Blaney, and O'Connell will be Ceann Comhairle,' Haughey told Gregory on Tuesday, 23 February. 'I need your vote to become Taoiseach. What do you want?'

Intermittent negotiations were conducted during the next two weeks. But this was not the only thing Haughey was working on. He also had approaches made to the Fine Gael deputy, Richard Burke, to see if he would be interested in being appointed Irish Commissioner to the EEC. This would necessitate his resignation from the Dáil and would mean that Fianna Fáil would need one vote less to gain power. But Burke killed the speculation with a statement emphasising that there was 'no possibility' that he would fail to vote for FitzGerald for Taoiseach when the Dáil reconvened on 9 March 1982.

Meanwhile O'Malley began canvassing support for a possible challenge to Haughey, and he was helped by Colley, Séamus Brennan, Martin O'Donoghue and others. Although many deputies had reservations about the timing of a challenge when there was a real chance of getting into power, O'Malley's people were encouraged by the response. In fact, at one point they were convinced they would have the support of a majority of deputies, and their optimistic predictions were reflected by the media. Based on his own soundings, Vincent Browne published a list of 30 Fianna Fáil deputies whom he believed would vote against Haughey, while he could only count 17 who would probably support him. A couple of days later, on the eve of the planned meeting, Bruce Arnold listed 36 against the leader with only 20 supporting him. In the circumstances it was not surprising that many betting people concluded that O'Malley was going to win. The odds on him were slashed all the way down to 2 to 1 on favourite, while Haughey drifted out to 7 to 4 against.

By this time Haughey's people were running scared. Ray MacSharry seemed to have venom in his voice as he warned on RTE Radio's *Day by Day* programme that Fianna Fáil would never forgive anyone who challenged for the leadership at such a crucial time. Throughout the day and into the early hours of the following morning they bombarded dissident and wavering deputies with telephone calls to support the leader. Nevertheless around midnight O'Malley announced he would be challenging Haughey for the party's nomination for Taoiseach.

There was therefore a great air of expectation about Leinster House in the morning as a crowd of reporters and interested spectators gathered. Photographers and a television camera were allowed into the meeting room beforehand, as Haughey stage-managed his entrance. His arrival was ceremoniously announced so that his supporters could greet him with a spontaneous burst of applause as the television cameras recorded the scene.

The meeting began with Haughey welcoming newly elected members. Then the first order of business was to choose a new parliamentary party chairman to replace Kenneally. After Seán Browne of Wexford was selected, the meeting turned to its main business.

Among those first to speak was Pádraig Faulkner, who said he had opposed Haughey in the past but was supporting him this time, and he urged O'Malley not to go through with the challenge because a contest would be too divisive and would rip the party asunder. Jim Tunney, Rory O'Hanlon, and Liam Lawlor, all of whom had been listed as anti-Haughey by both Vincent Browne and Bruce Arnold, spoke in similar vein. But it was Martin O'Donoghue who delivered the most devastating blow of all when he urged that there should be no contest. Suddenly it seemed that O'Malley's support had evaporated. He therefore announced that he would not allow his name to go forward, and Haughey was then chosen by acclamation. The whole meeting was over in little less than an hour.

On meeting the press afterwards Haughey emphasised *ad nauseam* that he had been selected unanimously and he complained repeatedly that media speculation about the O'Malley challenge had turned out to be just 'so much rubbish'. He clearly held the media responsible for the challenge, as he would do on the other two occasions when challenged during the next twelve months. The actual role played by the media in the various challenges will be examined in a separate chapter.

After seeing off O'Malley, Haughey was able to devote more attention to the task of winning the support of Gregory, who came up with specific demands in matters relating to employment, housing, health and education in Dublin, especially in the inner city area. Throughout the discussions, which were held at Gregory's headquarters, the Fianna Fáil leader seemed highly amenable. He personally agreed with most of the demands.

'You're pushing an open door,' was his stock response.

'It was clear he wasn't interested in the other Independents,' Gregory said afterwards. 'He believed I could accomodate him.'

FitzGerald also tried to win over Gregory with lavish promises but the Fine Gael leader was in a weaker position because, in addition, he needed to win the support of the Workers' Party and at least one other Independent, so he could not offer as much to Gregory. Thus Haughey won out on this auction for power by agreeing to have £4 million allocated to employ 500 extra men in the inner city, have 3,746 new jobs created in the same area within the next three years, have Industrial Development Authority (IDA) grants raised to attract new industries to the city, acquire a 27-acre port and docks site, provide government money to build 440 new houses in the inner city and another 1,600 in the rest of Dublin, have free medical cards provided for all pensioners, have the supplementary welfare system overhauled, increase the number of remedial teachers in the inner city, and to nationalise Clondalkin Paper Mills if no other option could be agreed upon within three months. Those were only some of the features outlined in the agreement, which both Haughey and Gregory signed as principals. The document was then witnessed by Michael Mullen, the General Secretary of the Irish Transport and General Workers' Union.

'As the Mafia say,' Haughey exclaimed on shaking hands with Gregory following the signing, 'it is a pleasure to do business with you.'

With this deal Haughey basically ensured his election as Taoiseach next day in the Dáil. For someone who expressed himself to be such a political admirer of his father-in-law, he seemed curiously oblivious to the example set by Seán Lemass under comparatively similar circumstances back in 1961. Fianna Fáil also lacked a majority then but Lemass refused to deal with anyone and was still re-elected Taoiseach. Had Haughey held out in a similar manner he would probably have been elected also because the three Workers' Party deputies voted for him. In all likelihood he never needed Gregory's vote.

12
The Year of the GUBU

Taoiseach Again
1982

"Mr Pym, tell President Galtieri if he wished to claim sovereignty over the island of
Ireland, we'd back him to the hilt"

Daily Express

AS Taoiseach Haughey's first task was to appoint a cabinet.
Colley had rejected his overtures for support during the run up
to the abortive O'Malley challenge so Haughey decided not to
appoint him Tánaiste or give him a veto over the appointments
of either the Ministers for Justice or Defence. He did offer him a
cabinet post but Colley declined it and returned to the party's
backbenches for the first time in almost twenty years.

The cabinet still consisted of a cross-section of the factions
within Fianna Fáil. O'Malley and O'Donoghue were included
from the dissident wing. Ray MacSharry was appointed
Tánaiste and both Seán Doherty and Albert Reynolds, two of
the three members of the gang of five in the Dáil, were given

cabinet posts. The other, Tom McEllistrim, was appointed a Minister of State. Patrick Connolly, who had been a counsel on Haughey's defence team during the Arms Trial, was appointed Attorney-General.

The appointment of Doherty as Minister for Justice raised most eyebrows. While serving as a member of the gárda's Special Branch, he had forged close ties with Haughey prior to the Arms Crisis and was a social as well as a political friend. He had served as Minister of State for Justice in the new Taoiseach's first government and his new appointment was viewed with uneasiness within the Department of Justice. He was the only former gárda ever to be appointed to the portfolio.

Haughey again announced that his first priority was to settle the partition problem and he set out for the United States, where he hoped to use the celebrations surrounding St Patrick's Day to enlist support for his own efforts to block an impending British effort to forge an internal settlement within Northern Ireland by establishing an elected assembly that would gradually be given devolutionary powers. As far as the new Taoiseach was concerned, Northern Ireland was a failed political entity so any attempt at achieving an internal settlement alone was doomed to failure. Even before the publication of James Prior's plan for 'rolling devolution', as it was called, the Taoiseach and John Hume, the leader of the SDLP, issued a joint statement denouncing the initiative of the Northern Secretary.

'The Prior initiative', Haughey complained on 23 May 1982, 'will be regarded in history as one of the most disastrous things that has ever happended in Anglo-Irish relations.' For one thing the establishment of the proposed Assembly would greatly weaken any chance the Taoiseach may have had of persuading Thatcher to move boldly on the partition question.

His relations with her were already strained as a result of his exaggeration of the Dublin Castle Summit of 1980, coupled with what the British believed were Haughey's efforts to exploit the partition issue in order to paper over his serious political difficulties at home. On the other hand, the Haughey government was annoyed at the extortionist tactics being employed by the British in vetoing new farm prices within the EEC in order to get Britain's budgetary contribution lowered. Things were further complicated as relations reached a new low during the international crisis over the Falkland Islands.

When the Argentines invaded the Falkland Islands — or Las Malvinas as they called them — on 2 April 1982, most Irish people did not even know where the islands were. Britain had seized the islands from Argentina in 1833 but now the overwhelming majority of inhabitants wished to remain British, so Britain protested against the seizure to the Security Council of the United Nations (UN), which passed Resolution 502 calling for an immediate Argentine withdrawal. Ireland was a member of the Security Council at the time, and the Irish representative supported the resolution, but Haughey's government indicated a reluctance to support a British request for an EEC embargo on trade with Argentina. He was personally 'very cool' towards the proposed sanctions, but his government eventually went along with the other EEC countries in unanimously implementing an embargo.

Irish trade with Argentina was comparatively small anyway. In fact, the total value of trade between the two countries in 1981 amounted to little over IR£15 millions. While the trade balance was in Ireland's favour, the Irish Meat Marketing Board predicted that the embargo would be even more advantageous to the country because Irish beef would be able to replace imports from Argentina on the British market.

For almost three weeks there was little hint of any real dissatisfaction with the position taken by the Haughey government until Síle de Valera issued a statement to the press on 22 April criticising the Irish government's handling of the crisis on the grounds that it eroded the country's supposed traditional policy of neutrality. She had lost her seat in the Dáil so her intervention was not all that significant, but Haughey had to take notice a couple of days later when Neil Blaney spoke out.

'We should support Argentina,' Blaney declared, 'for both political and economic reasons — politically because of the continued British occupation of the Six Counties of Northern Ireland, and economically because Argentina is one of the few countries with which we have a credit trade balance.'

As Blaney was one of the Independent deputies on whose support the Taoiseach was dependant, it was later argued that the Donegal deputy's remarks prompted Haughey to reverse his government's policy on the Falklands dispute, but this was probably an oversimplification. For one thing Haughey had already got some room for manoeuvre by appointing Dick Burke of Fine Gael as Irish Commissioner to the EEC. Having first refused the offer, Burke later changed his mind. This necessitated his resignation from the Dáil, with the result that the Fianna Fáil government needed one less vote to maintain its majority support. The Taoiseach also confidently expected that his party's position would be further enhanced by winning Burke's seat in a by-election because his wife's sister-in-law, Eileen Lemass, had narrowly missed winning the seat in the general election. Therefore, Haughey's policy change on the Falklands probably had more to do with his own preferences than with parliamentary pressures. After all, he had been reluctant to implement sanctions against Argentina in the first place.

Haughey's policy reversal followed the sinking of the Argentine battleship, *General Belgrano,* which went down with the loss of several hundred lives. This marked the real beginning of the Falklands war. The Irish government announced that it would be calling on the UN Security Council to bring about an immediate end to hostilities and would also be seeking the withdrawal of the EEC's economic sanctions against Argentina on the grounds that these were 'no longer appropriate'.

'We were never very enthusiastic about the imposition of sanctions,' he told a press conference on 6 May, 'but the argument was persuasive that they could be instrumental in applying pressure to achieve the implementation of Resolution 502 and so lead to a diplomatic solution.' While sanctions supporting the UN resolution were all right, he said that 'sanctions complementing military action are not acceptable to a neutral country'.

The Irish announcement was bitterly resented in Britain, where Haughey's attitude was seen as a blatant attempt to undermine her support within the Security Council and EEC. 'It appeared that he was going out of his way to make Britain's position difficult', according to Jim Prior.

The stand concerning EEC sanctions was largely symbolic, seeing that most Irish imports from Argentina were transhipped through Britain, so the decision was unlikely to have any practical effect in terms of trade. It was the Irish moves in the

Security Council which the British resented most because no reference was made to implementing Resolution 502. If the Irish proposal were accepted, Argentine forces would be able to remain on the Falkland Islands pending a diplomatic settlement. As a result of the invasion, which was in contravention of the UN Charter, Argentina would therefore enjoy an advantage that would not otherwise have existed.

Haughey was making no apologies for his government's behaviour. As an elected member of the Security Council, Ireland had a particular responsibility to do what the country could to secure a peaceful settlement. 'It would be easier to stay quiet and do nothing but that would be an abnegation of responsibility in this appalling situation,' he contended. 'Undoubtedly, when there is an emotional situation over the Falklands in Britain and elsewhere there will be misunderstanding. What we must do is keep our heads, act responsibly, act as a peace-loving nation.'

The Taoiseach deplored the escalation in the South Atlantic. 'In-built into any war is escalation of this sort,' he said. 'We went along with sanctions when they were in support of diplomatic political pressure. Once it became clear that they could be seen to support military activity, we had, as a neutral state, no alternative but to withdraw from the sanctions position and hope that our stand will be understood by the British government.'

What was not generally known at the time was that the British had sunk the *General Belgrano* even though it was well outside the exclusion zone proclaimed by Britain and had been moving further away for some hours. The sinking was obviously a deliberate attempt to provoke the actual war.

While the Irish media was generally supportive of the Dublin government's stance, it did report some strong criticism from abroad. The British Prime Minister was reportedly furious with Haughey. 'If he was to turn up tomorrow with a silver coffee pot,' one British government source was quoted as saying, 'she'd likely crown him with it.' Also in London, Gerry Fitt was outspoken in his condemnation of Haughey's government.

'The bellicose and belligerent statements emanating from the extremely anti-British government are not representative of the Irish people,' he said. British forces were already gaining the upper hand in the Falklands as the Irish representative was calling for a cease fire at the Security Council, so the Irish call was seen by the British as favourable to Argentina. 'It is not seen as humanitarian,' Fitt continued, 'but as an attempt to help the Argentines and stop the British now they are on the islands. Ireland is not seen as neutral but as having come down in favour of the Argentinians.'

In the midst of the chauvinistic fervour that swept Britain there was a considerable wave of anti-Irish sentiment and some virulent anti-Irish propaganda. 'It is tempting to yearn for a return of the Vikings to plunder Ireland's coastal area and rape her nuns so that we, too, can have an opportunity to declare high-minded neutrality and demand a diplomatic solution,' Auberon Waugh wrote in the *Sunday Telegraph*.

Irish goods suffered a decline in sales; British orders for Irish factories were cancelled, and a large number of British tourists planning to visit Ireland during the summer made alternative arrangements. What had promised to be a good Irish tourist season turned to a disaster as British travel agents cancelled bookings. For some people the ideological stand in pursuing peace justified the economic losses; others were more critical.

The Argentine regime, which was a military dictatorship that had seized power from a democratically elected government in the mid 1970s, had been particularly tyrannical and had shown scant regard for human rights, with the result that it had little international support. Garret FitzGerald charged Haughey with merely exploiting the international crisis in order to win radical nationalist votes in the impending by-election in Dick Burke's vacant Dublin West seat.

If this was the Taoiseach's aim, then he must have been sorely disappointed because a previously unheard of Fine Gael candidate won with a couple of thousand votes to spare. Within a month Haughey was faced with another and much more crucial by-election in Galway East following the death of Fianna Fáil's John Callanan. It was one of the safest Fianna Fáil seats in Ireland, but if Fine Gael could manage to snatch it then the government would need the support of the Workers' Party to survive.

Fine Gael pulled out all the stops. On 22 June the former Minister for Justice, Jim Mitchell, caused a sensation by disclosing that telephones which Haughey had installed in his own office shortly after his election as Taoiseach in December 1979 were capable of listening-in undetected on all telephones in Leinster House and Government Buildings. The implication of his charge was that the previous government had tapped the telephones of all members of the government, the Dáil and the Senate.

Within a week of becoming Taoiseach, Haughey had personally requested to have the Private Automatic Branch Exchange system, which he had used as Minister for Health and Social Welfare, installed in his new office. This contained a telephone console with a loud speaker and an executive over-ride button that could be used either by a secretary to listen into a call or by the minister to issue instructions to an aide over the telephone without terminating a call. While the over-ride was being used, however, there was supposed to be a bleep on the line every six seconds. But the consoles installed in Haughey's office and later in other offices were so programmed that a user could listen into a conversation undetected by using the over-ride with the loud speaker. Using the consoles someone could dial the number of any telephone served by the Leinster House exchange and if the number was engaged, listen into the conversation undetected by turning on the loudspeaker, replacing the telephone in its cradle, and then pressing the over-ride button.

Haughey described as 'absolutely ludicrous' and preposterous any suggestion that he had been aware of the over-ride's sinister capabilities. 'I never asked for an over-ride facility and I didn't even know the facility was there,' he explained. He said he only found out in late 1981 when FitzGerald informed him.

'I handed over these telephone consoles to the incoming Taoiseach, Dr FitzGerald, and I think that speaks for itself,' Haughey contended. In other words if there had been anything sinister, he would not have been so foolish as to leave the evidence behind him.

Fine Gael was not really in a strong position to exploit Haughey's expressed ignorance about the capabilities of the over-ride button, because two consoles — ordered while Fianna Fáil were still in power — were actually installed with FitzGerald's approval after he took over as Taoiseach in July 1981. Like Haughey, the Fine Gael leader stated that he was totally unaware of the significance of the equipment at the time.

No one doubted for a moment that FitzGerald was telling the truth, but some media people seemed to question Haughey's statement.

During August, while Doherty left the country on holidays, Haughey took over temporarily as Minister for Justice and soon found himself in the midst of one of the most sensational scandals in the country's history after a man being sought by the police in connection with two recent murders was arrested in the apartment of the Attorney-General, Patrick Connolly. The wanted man, Malcolm MacArthur, had been staying with Connolly for the past nine days during which he travelled in Connolly's state car and accompanied the Attorney-General to a hurling match at which he was introduced to the Gárda Commissioner and actually enquired about the investigation of 'that dreadful' murder he had himself committed.

Haughey, who came in for intense criticism as a result of some hamfisted efforts by the authorities to conceal the connection between MacArthur and the Attorney-General, excused his own initial dithering on the grounds that the whole affair was 'grotesque, unbelievable, bizarre, and unprecedented'. Those words prompted Conor Cruise O'Brien to coin the acronym GUBU.

Haughey's personal popularity and that of his government had been sliding steadily, a slide accentuated by the MacArthur Affair. In an MRBI poll published on 18 September only 36 per cent expressed satisfaction with the way he was doing his job, while 59 per cent expressed dissatisfaction, and the dissatisfaction with his government was even greater.

The MacArthur Affair was so extraordinary that credence was easily given to sensational rumours surrounding two other events which occurred within days of the publication of the latest poll. The first occurred when authorities sought to cover up the crash on 22 September near Ballyduff, Co. Kerry, of a state-owned escort car that had been assigned to protect Doherty, while the second incident five days later involved the dismissal under rather bizarre circumstances in Dowra, Co. Cavan, of an assault case against Seán Doherty's brother-in-law. Both incidents helped further to undermine confidence in the government and led to another heave to get rid of Haughey.

Late on Friday afternoon, 1 October 1982, Charlie McCreevy dropped a political bombshell by placing a motion of no confidence in Haughey's leadership on the agenda of the Fianna Fáil parliamentary party meeting to be held the following Wednesday. Haughey had tried to dismiss the February challenge by pretending the whole thing had been dreamed up by the media, but this time he met the trouble head on. Interviewed on RTE's 'This Week' programme on Sunday afternoon, he indicated he was going to demand a roll call vote on the issue so that the dissidents could be identified, because the party was fed up with 'the small section of deputies' who were continually sniping at him.

'The Fianna Fáil organisation wants to get back to a situation where we have the strength that derives from discipline,' Haughey said, 'and I will ensure that discipline will be enforced.' He added that he was going to begin by insisting that all members of his government should pledge their loyalty to him as the elected leader of Fianna Fáil. 'I will insist,' he declared, 'that the cabinet stand four square behind me with no shilly-shallying.' He had no doubt that he would be victorious. 'I am,' he said, 'absolutely confident of the outcome. As Seán MacEntee said: "go dance on somebody else's grave".'

Haughey also contended that, like the O'Malley heave, the McCreevy motion was a creation of the media. He later cited the fact that Geraldine Kennedy had been consulted in advance by the dissidents as conclusive proof that the media were involved in a conspiracy against him. This charge will be considered in the next chapter.

There was a certain amount of manoeuvring by both sides prior to the parliamentary party meeting. The Taoiseach secured the support of the party's national executive, while Colley announced that O'Malley and O'Donoghue would be resigning from the cabinet rather than support Haughey. The two men then waited until the morning of the meeting to submit their letters of resignation, thereby ensuring that the dissidents received positive publicity up to the last minute.

From early on it was clear that there would be a vital trial of strength between the two sides on whether the vote should be taken openly or in secret. Rule 83 of the Fianna Fáil *córú* (constitution) specifically stated that 'every ballot throughout the organisation should be held by secret ballot,' but the dissident position was really not all that strong, because the parliamentary party was traditionally free to make its own decisions without outside dictation from the party itself. Moreover, during the Arms Crisis Jack Lynch had demanded and secured an open vote of confidence. Now some of his supporters were demanding that his successor should agree to a secret vote, but they were being undermined by the precedent they had set themselves.

The parliamentary party meeting began at 11 a.m. on 6 October with 80 of the 81 Fianna Fáil TDs present, as well as 27 senators, and 5 members of the European parliament. Though the atmosphere was tense, the proceedings were orderly.

It was decided to discuss McCreevy's motion and the method of voting simultaneously. McCreevy explained he was objecting to Haughey's leadership because there had been a lowering of political standards and mishandling of the economy. He also cited the party's failure to secure a majority in the successive general elections. People wanted to be governed, not bought, he said, adding that it was time 'to get decency back into the party'.

Haughey was obviously nervous when he spoke. He paused frequently to choose the right words, or to rummage through notes. He defended himself and his government on the grounds that they had been facing unprecedented difficulties in the deepest recession since the 1930s. Having worked hard to prepare a new plan to tackle the economic situation, he said that they hould be given a chance to let it work. Under the circumstances he felt the motion was not only divisive but also badly timed.

This time the dissidents were determined there would be no repetition of the February debacle. They had arranged for people to speak in favour of the motion in order to prevent another precipitate collapse of their challenge. So the meeting dragged on throughout the day and into the night, with adjournments for lunch and tea. During the latter break, the dissidents seemed very pleased with themselves.

Some senior deputies like Pádraig Faulkner and Michael O'Kennedy had called for a secret ballot, so the dissidents were hopeful of winning this crucial test of strength. But again they had overestimated their support. When a roll call vote was taken on whether the vote on the actual motion should be by secret ballot, the voting was twenty-seven in favour with fifty-three against. The subsequent vote on the McCreevy motion was then defeated by fifty-eight votes to twenty-two.

Haughey had won and some of his supporters were anything but magnanimous in victory. 'These people have been flushed out now, once, finally and for all', was how one supporter put it. 'The situation after tonight is that they had better be ready to kiss Haughey's ass or get out of the party.'

The mood was so ugly that gárdaí tried to persuade McCreevy to leave Leinster House by a side entrance, but he refused. As he emerged by the front door, surrounded by six gárdaí, he was met by a jeering group of Haughey supporters, many of whom had been drinking throughout the day as they waited for the outcome of the meeting. When Gibbons left the building shortly afterwards he was not only jeered loudly but also jostled about by the unruly crowd. It was one of the ugliest scenes witnessed in Irish politics for many years. One of the hecklers tried to attack him and actually landed a glancing blow. These incidents, which were captured on television, were probably more damaging to the government than anything that happened during the day.

The next IMS poll, published on 23 October 1982, showed Haughey's popularity slumping ever further, and his party dropped to its lowest rating since the poll began in 1974. Only 23 per cent of those sampled were satisfied with the way his government was running the country, and his personal popularity had dropped another 4 points to 32 per cent.

As it was, his government was already in trouble as a result of the death on 18 October of Bill Loughnane, and the hospitalisation next day of Jim Gibbons following a heart attack.

The publication of Fianna Fáil's new economic programme, *The Way Forward*, virtually killed any chance of survival. Tony Gregory and the three Workers' Party deputies announced they would be voting against the new economic policies. When they did, Haughey was obliged to resign and ask the President to call a general election. Fianna Fáil's political prospects were bleak, if the polls were anything to go by.

Initially the campaign was a rather dull affair. It was the third general election in eighteen months and there was little public interest or enthusiasm, especially as there was little difference between the two main parties on the substantive issues. Both party leaders had, for instance, endorsed the recently published wording for a constitutional amendment to prohibit abortion. Haughey tried to exploit the issue by contending that FitzGerald was not sincere in supporting the proposed amendment. But the Fine Gael leader denied this and, to give strength to his denial, promised to ensure that the referendum would be held before the end of March 1983.

In the circumstances the media accepted FitzGerald's denial, but Haughey was right. Before endorsing the wording publicly FitzGerald told Dick Spring, the newly elected leader of the Labour Party, that he was personally opposed to the published wording but felt compelled to endorse it at the insistence of his party. Thus Haughey was outmanoeuvred on the issue.

The Fianna Fáil leader next accused FitzGerald of stealing official documents — in particular a financial document from which he quoted during their television debate in February, but the Fine Gael leader was Taoiseach at the time and he was therefore entitled to have the document. Few people took much notice of this charge, but Haughey was much more successful in the following days when he and his colleagues began playing 'the green card'.

Gerry Collins cited an address in the House of Lords in which the Duke of Norfolk said the Fine Gael leader had told him over lunch some months earlier that Britain's devolution plans for Northern Ireland were acceptable. This charge might well have died like the others but for a rather distorted report about remarks supposedly made by Jim Prior while visiting the United States.

FitzGerald had planned to make one policy statement on the Northern Ireland question and Prior was asked what policy he would like to see the Fine Gael leader adopt. While normal political prudence should have dictated that a government minister would not comment on policy matters in a foreign election campaign, the Northern Secretary replied that he would welcome a policy calling for an all-Ireland police force. FitzGerald had suggested the establishment of such a force in May during a televised lecture in which he went on to advocate an all-Ireland court structure. Prior emphasised that he did not know what policy FitzGerald was going to put forward.

'We will have to wait and see,' he said. But he was somehow mistakenly reported to have said that FitzGerald was actually going to advocate the establishment of an all-Ireland court and police force. This, of course, gave the impression the Fine Gael leader had either consulted or confided in the Northern Secretary beforehand.

Haughey immediately denounced the proposal and exploited the mistaken report of Prior's remarks. 'The fact that the Secretary of State for Northern Ireland knew in advance what Dr FitzGerald would say in his speech on Northern Ireland reveals now the degree of collusion that exists between the leader of Fine Gael and the British government', the Taoiseach contended. He went on to accuse the British of interfering in the Irish electoral process in trying to help FitzGerald 'in return for the support he had given British policy'. This, he said, represented 'one of the most serious threats to our political independence since the last war'.

These charges obviously struck a nerve, because FitzGerald responded with what the *Irish Independent* described as 'the most bitter personal attack of the election campaign'. He accused Haughey of adopting an attitude towards his proposals that was 'indistinguishable from Paisley.' The Fine Gael leader was obviously rattled, so Haughey exploited the issue by suggesting that the proposal would undermine Irish independence because it would mean the Royal Ulster Constabulary (RUC) would begin operating in the Twenty-six Counties and unarmed gárdaí would be sent into the North.

'What these foolish men are proposing to us', Haughey told a campaign gathering in Carlow, 'represents an insidious and dangerous threat to our future security because, up until now, we were able to administer our own security policies as an independent and sovereign nation.' If those proposals were implemented, he added, 'violence and bloodshed will be extended to our country as a whole without any benefit to anybody.' One Fianna Fáil speaker on the same platform actually accused FitzGerald of acting as a 'quisling'.

At a press conference on the last Saturday of the campaign Haughey charged that — in talking with the Duke of Norfolk, who had been head of intelligence at the British Ministry for Defence before retiring fifteen years earlier — FitzGerald either wittingly or unwittingly had 'discussions with what in fact is a trained British spy'. Of course, the Fine Gael leader rejected the sinister connotations being attached to his discussions with Norfolk. He said that he had met him simply as the senior Roman Catholic peer. As such the duke was recognised as the leader of Britain's Roman Catholic laity. FitzGerald certainly left himself open to the charge of overstepping his responsibilities.

'Dr FitzGerald, with no official standing, was over in London taking some action over the Prior initiative which was seen as promoting the proposal,' Haughey contended. 'That sort of initiative should be left to the Irish government of the day, rightly or wrongly.'

Haughey was right. When there were policy differences between the Dublin and London governments over which FitzGerald was not in agreement with his own government, he certainly left himself wide open to misrepresentation by engaging in discussions with a member of the British parliament — even if it was only with an obscure member of the House of Lords. Of course, Haughey's criticism would have sounded more sincere if he had not, under comparatively similar circumstances, met privately with Prior for over an hour in the latter's London apartment on 13 December 1981.

FitzGerald complained that Fianna Fáil were conducting a campaign of personal vilification, which Haughey dismissed as laughable in contrast to the 'cold, calculating and vilifying character assassination' of himself by members of Fine Gael in collusion with various journalists. In a rare demonstration of unanimity, all four national daily newspapers carried editorials rejecting the charges of collusion against FitzGerald. Yet there *was* a case for FitzGerald to answer.

On RTE's 'This Week' programme on the last Sunday of the campaign, the Taoiseach repeated his accusation that FitzGerald had met with a British spy by having lunch with the Duke of Norfolk. 'Now you can go from there and draw any conclusion you like,' he said. 'I have drawn my conclusions that he was, in fact, co-operating or collaborating or whatever word you like to use, with the British government.'

With Haughey again apparently impugning the patriotism of the Fine Gael leader, relations between the two men became even more strained. When they met for a televised debate towards the end of the campaign, the normally co-operative

FitzGerald refused either to be photographed or to shake hands with Haughey.

Whether 'the green card' actually made a difference to the outcome of the election may be open to question because there was a significant divergence in the findings of independent polls conducted by MRBI and by Research Surveys of Ireland (RSI). The latter actually detected a massive swing of ten per cent in favour of Fianna Fáil over Fine Gael following the introduction of the nationalist issue into the campaign. But, on the other hand, the MRBI polls conducted around the same time showed little movement at all. In fact, these had Fianna Fáil remaining static while both Fine Gael and Labour gained a percentage point each.

The election returns showed that the last MRBI poll slightly underestimated Fianna Fáil strength and overestimated that of Fine Gael, while the final RSI poll did the opposite in each case. All of the figures in both of those polls were within the standard 3 per cent margin of error, but the RSI poll was only out by 1 per cent and the MRBI poll by double that figure. Thus, if the previous RSI poll was accurate, it would appear that the 'green card' had come up trumps for Fianna Fáil.

Haughey again headed the poll in his own constituency, but his personal tally was down by around 1,500 votes. This was representative of a nationwide swing to Fine Gael and Labour: they won enough seats to form a majority coalition government.

The eventual outcome was therefore a foregone conclusion when the new Dáil convened on 14 December 1982. Haughey's name was put forward for Taoiseach but his nomination was defeated by 88 votes to 77. FitzGerald was then elected to succeed him.

13
The Man they Love to Hate

The Man and the Media, 1982

FIANNA FAIL
THE STABLE GOVERNMENT PARTY

COLLABORATION

COLLUSION

REFERENDUM CLAIM

APPARENTLY, THE BRITISH PREFER GARRET...
APPARENTLY, SO DO THE IRISH

POLLS

Irish Times, 19 November 1982

OVER the years Haughey had a mixed relationship with the media. 'If his relations with the press are anything to go by,' Olivia O'Leary wrote in December 1981, 'he is a suspicious man.' She thought he believed the media should act as it 'did in the sixties when reporters did not criticise, did not ask impertinent questions, and took gracefully whatever statement a government minister deigned to make to them.'

The press meekly allowed itself to be outmanoeuvred by his 'secret courts' in the early 1960s. As far as Haughey was concerned 'the secret courts' were his way of showing loyalty to a colleague in trouble. He was not worried that he was exploiting the known habits of the court reporters at their own expense. 'In any public challenge in the Dáil,' John Healy later explained, 'the reply would make the media look, at worst, as accomplices who might have taken a back hander to kill the case or, at best, people who were slovenly and lacked basic contacts in the building in which they worked for half a lifetime.'

'It was probably at this stage in his career and the affair of the secret courts which started the love-hate relationship between Haughey and the media', according to Healy. The press duly reported accusations made publicly against Haughey by his opponents, but little or no effort was made to investigate the murky insinuations. For instance, the press never followed up the case involving the forced resignation of the gárda who had arrested Donagh O'Malley for drunken driving.

Tim Pat Coogan, the future editor of the *Irish Press,* concluded in his book, *Ireland Since the Rising,* that those Fine Gael deputies who had been 'unsporting enough to enquire into the strange happenings that befell the policeman' were intimidated into silence by Haughey simply 'alluding to files in his office at the Department of Justice'. Those files were believed to contain damaging information about Fine Gael deputies. If those deputies were intimidated in this manner, it did not reflect favourably on their integrity, but it reflected even less on the courage of the media. Likewise, when questions were raised about the planning permission granted to Matt Gallagher to build houses on the Raheny property which he had bought from Haughey in the late 1960s, the media did not investigate them in any sort of sustained manner. Haughey had made a handsome profit on the sale, with which he bought Kinsealy.

Haughey was out of office when journalists began to adopt a more sceptical attitude towards statements issued by government ministers, but he was probably an indirect catalyst because the change occurred following the Arms Crisis. Initially most of the media seemed to accept Lynch's statement concerning the affair, with the notable exception of John Healy who wrote at that time that the crisis was just an effort 'to gut' Haughey politically.

In his early days as Taoiseach, Haughey enjoyed a good press as FitzGerald was roasted for his failure to substantiate the 'flawed pedigree' charge. People like Vincent Browne and Geraldine Kennedy were singing the new Taoiseach's praises, but they soon turned sour. In December 1980 a case against Haughey's brother Pádraig was postponed and reporters were refused information about the charges. Remembering how Haughey had facilitated his friends with 'the secret courts' in the 1960s, the media feared the postponement was a ploy to keep the case out of the newspapers, but the case went ahead in open court the following week. Pádraig Haughey was convicted of assault and driving after having had too much to drink. It was really the kind of case that would never have made the national newspapers except that the accused happened to be Charlie Haughey's brother. As such it was unfair to both men.

Prominent journalists admitted to being unfair to Haughey in covering the general election campaigns of June 1981 and February 1982, as has been pointed out in the previous chapter. But they rejected his subsequent accusations that the media conspired with his political opponents on two seperate occasions in 1982 to try and oust him from the leadership of Fianna Fáil.

At first Haughey publicly dismissed talk of a possible challenge in February 1982 as 'rubbish', but he took the precaution of having the parliamentary party meeting to select the nominee for Taoiseach brought forward. Although there was still no announced challenger the day before the meeting, Bruce Arnold reported in the *Irish Independent* that there was a groundswell of support for O'Malley to put his name forward. Arnold's article was strategically placed right across the top of the front page under the following headline: 'My score so far: Haughey 20, O'Malley 46, Unknowns 15'.

The headline was an example of sloppy proof reading, because Arnold had only referred to thirty-six deputies whom he listed as being prepared to support O'Malley — not forty-six as stated in the headline written by a sub-editor. However, the newspaper made no effort to correct the mistake, which was particularly significant because the figure cited would have amounted to a clear majority of Fianna Fáil deputies, whereas Arnold's own list was five short of the vital number.

Next morning, the day of the crucial parliamentary party meeting, the *Irish Independent* carried another front page article in which Raymond Smith repeated a dissident prediction that O'Malley had 'sufficient votes to oust Mr Haughey'. He also quoted one of the dissidents as saying that 'what's happening now is an exact carbon copy of how Mr Lynch was forced out of the Fianna Fáil leadership through a sequence of events'. The implications were unmistakeable: Haughey and his supporters had brought down Lynch and they were now receiving some of their own medicine.

But Lynch had not really been brought down; he had retired voluntarily. There had indeed been sniping against him in 1979 but it was Gibbons, one of Haughey's bitterest critics and the one who set the ball rolling in this latest challenge, who had been the first to break party discipline by refusing to support the government's contraception bill in April of that year. Moreover, it was two of Haughey's strongest opponents, Colley and O'Donoghue, who had persuaded Lynch to retire early in the belief that the time was opportune for Colley to win the leadership. It was unfair of Smith not to question the scenario of these events being painted by the dissidents, and it quickly became apparent that Haughey resented the article. At a press conference immediately after the collapse of the O'Malley challenge he pretended not to recognise Smith when the latter asked a question without first identifying himself.

'Who is this man?' Haughey asked, much to the embarrassment of the reporter.

'You can call me Mr Smith, or Raymond, or Ray, but you don't have to ask who I am.'

'To me', Haughey said contemptuously, 'you are just a face in the crowd. Now what is your question?'

It was a bad start to the press conference at which Haughey's annoyance at the *Irish Independent* would surface again and again. He interrupted in the middle of one question as Smith was saying that 'certain names have been mentioned in the papers as people who might vote against you —'

'I am *delighted* you mentioned that', Haughey interjected, 'because your particular newspaper published perhaps the falsest list of names in Irish journalism.' At another point he complained about 'rubbishy media speculation' and he went on to describe Arnold's list as 'utter rubbish'. Afterwards some Haughey supporters went looking for Arnold, who was advised by colleagues to leave Leinster House for his own safety.

The Fianna Fáil leader could feel justifiably aggrieved about some newspaper reports emanating from dissident sources. For instance, O'Malley was quoted next day as complaining that the parliamentary party meeting had been called at short notice in order to frustrate his challenge. In announcing what he called 'a three-day squeeze-job,' he seemed conveniently oblivious to the fact that neither he nor his dissident colleagues had objected in December 1979 when — with only two days notice — the party was called upon to select Lynch's successor. It was conveniently forgotten that Lynch had stepped down early and then rushed the meeting to select his successor purely in order to frustrate Haughey's chances.

Considerable space was afforded by the press to the views of dissidents, which was understandable because the impending challenge was a major news story. What the dissidents had to say was therefore newsworthy, even when inaccurate. But the inaccuracy of a charge like the accusation that Haughey had overthrown Lynch should have been identified. Instead, Smith reported it as it stood and the *Irish Independent* essentially endorsed it with an editorial charging that Haughey 'himself overthrew Mr Lynch.' This was absurd.

That Haughey was not given as much coverage as the dissidents in the run up to the abortive challenge, however, was his own fault, because he chose to pretend the challenge was only an illusion created by a hostile media. Yet both the *Irish Press* and *Irish Times* were editorially opposed to the O'Malley challenge, while the *Cork Examiner* was largely dismissive of it. It was therefore ridiculous to contend that the media as a whole was behind the move. It was the Fianna Fáil dissidents who were responsible, though many of them may well have become victims of their own propaganda about the desire for Haughey's removal after it was uncritically reported in the *Irish Independent*.

The latter, which accused Haughey of having an 'apparent persecution complex,' betrayed a bias not only in its uncritical reporting of accusations made by dissidents but also in the prominence it gave stories damaging to the Fianna Fáil leader. On the morning after O'Malley's challenge had fizzled out so pathetically, for instance, the newspaper actually had a lead story with the following headline running right across the top of the front page: 'Lynch endorses O'Malley and predicts he will lead F.F.'

The former Taoiseach had issued a statement in an apparent effort to console O'Malley. Jack Lynch was clearly partisan, as it

179

was his right to be, but the *Irish Independent* should have been impartial, and should not have left itself open to the charge of betraying the same kind of partisanship with the prominence it gave the statement.

John Healy later implied that the attitude adopted by the newspaper had something to do with the political ambitions of its principal shareholder, Tony O'Reilly, who supposedly harboured ambitions of becoming Taoiseach at the head of a Fianna Fáil government. If this were true O'Reilly would have had an interest in taking Haughey out of the political picture because there would never be enough room for the two of them at the top of the party. As O'Reilly remarked himself, 'the field is too small for two bulls'. He later explained that the remark was just a whimsical one made in jest.

On one occasion in the late 1960s Jack Lynch offered to appoint O'Reilly Minister for Agriculture without requiring him to stand for the Dáil. The Taoiseach would simply appoint him to the Senate, from where he could then be appointed to the government, but O'Reilly turned down the offer because, he emphasised, he had no political ambitions. Of course, some of the people working for him may well have believed, like Healy, that O'Reilly did want to be Taoiseach. It was quite common for supporters to tout the candidacy of an aspirant even before the individual concerned decided to run for a particular office. Just why the *Irish Independent* was so critical of Haughey must therefore remain open to question, but whatever the reason there can be little doubt that the newspaper did betray a bias against him.

In the months following the collapse of the O'Malley challenge the paper remained generally critical of Haughey as his government became embroiled in a series of controversies. Other newspapers adopted more varied attitudes. The *Irish Times* and *Irish Press* were editorially uncritical of the Gregory Deal, praised Burke's appointment to the EEC, supported the government's policy during the Falklands War, and were sceptical of Fine Gael motives in raising the telephone over-ride issue. Throughout this time the *Cork Examiner* adopted a rather bland, non-partisan editorial policy except following the announcement of Burke's appointment when it exploded with bitter criticism of Haughey's assertion that the appointment was made purely in the national interest. The *Sunday Tribune* enthusiastically endorsed Burke's appointment and supported Haughey's policy during the Falklands dispute, as did the *Sunday Independent*. But many eyebrows were raised when, in the aftermath of the Dublin West by-election setback, the *Sunday Press* denounced 'strokes and deals' and concluded that some of Haughey's advisers 'mistake razzmatazz for substance and action'. This signed editorial, in a newspaper that had traditionally been seen as a Fianna Fáil organ, may well have provided the impetus for Colley to make another thinly veiled attack on Haughey the following weekend.

The former Tánaiste denounced the 'new style of politics and politicians' who were spreading the idea 'that in politics success is all important no matter how achieved, that any deal or stroke or promise is justified if it results in the achievement of the retention of power.' His remarks were reminiscent of his famous reference to 'low standards in high places' fifteen years earlier. And, as on the previous occasion, he again denied he was referring to any member of the government, but to the whole political system.

There always were politicians ready to pay any price to get into office, he explained, but the big difference was that 'in the last three years there has been a tendency for this to be accepted at the top in politics'. By referring to the last three years and also specifically mentioning Burke's appointment, Colley left no doubt that, notwithstanding his own dishonest denial, he was indeed alluding to Haughey's conduct.

The government's position became precarious in early June following the death of a Fianna Fáil deputy. In fact it only managed to survive with the help of the casting vote of the Ceann Comhairle on a number of occasions before the summer recess. Colley or any one of his dissident colleagues could easily have brought Haughey down, but each time they dutifully followed him into the government lobby.

Even Geraldine Kennedy, whom the dissidents had been feeding with inside information for several months, had to acknowledge their inconsistency in criticising what was going on while at the same time propping up the government. Nevertheless she blamed Haughey for even their actions in putting party considerations before the national interest.

'They have become compromised by Mr Haughey's politics of power', she wrote. According to her, he had 'polluted' Irish politics and his opponents were making the mistake of trying to beat him at his own game. 'In playing politics the Machiavellian way,' she concluded, 'Charlie is *The Prince.*'

The over-ride controversy in late June was clearly an affair that Fine Gael exploited for electoral purposes during the Galway East by-election campaign. The telephones had already been re-programmed since the previous year, so the decision to publicise the matter at this time was obviously dictated by political considerations, as was widely recognised by the media. Even the *Irish Independent* warned that the over-ride affair had 'to be kept in perspective if we are not to get bogged down in a Watergate-style scenario'.

By mid-August, however, Haughey and his government were confronted with criticism from the entire media over their initial handling of information relating to the arrest of Malcolm MacArthur. The Gárda Press Office and Government Information Service at first refused to confirm that MacArthur had been arrested in the Attorney-General's apartment. As a result the press only reported that the arrest had taken place in the complex in which Connolly was living, rather than in his actual apartment. Nevertheless wild rumours began circulating almost immediately. The following day the *Evening Herald* reported that MacArthur was being investigated for the murder of Charles Self, an RTE producer who had been killed earlier in the year. That murder had received extensive publicity over the months because of protests of police harrassment from the homosexual community. It was widely believed that Self, who had been active in homosexual circles, had been killed by another homosexual.

The rumours were fuelled when the *Sunday Tribune* broke the news next day that MacArthur had actually been arrested in the Attorney-General's apartment. This gave rise to insinuations about a possible homosexual relationship between Connolly and MacArthur. Suddenly Dublin was awash with 'an endless stream of rumours, innuendoes, and lurid tales,' according to a report in the *Guardian*.

The media had to be very careful about reporting such rumours because of the danger of a libel action, but an official denial could easily have been used as the basis for a story about the rumours. In fact, the rumours were utterly without foundation. MacArthur was not involved in the murder of Self, and neither he nor Connolly were homosexual.

'We were dealing with a situation where an innocent man was being made the victim of some scurrilous rumours, and we felt any denials should come from him,' Frank Ryan, the deputy director of the Government Information Service, explained. 'We knew that any denials from us would be taken as giving greater weight to the rumours.' But this did not excuse the evasiveness about MacArthur's arrest in Connolly's apartment. 'Surely,' the *Irish Times* declared, 'nearly two days did not lapse before the Taoiseach or some other cabinet member woke up to the fact that rumour thrives when news concerning prominent people can be construed by the public as seeming to be played down.'

Following the Attorney-General's resignation the media spotlight was turned on Haughey, who gave a press conference at which he had to face some particularly thorny questions. He was obviously under intense pressure and the strain showed as he slipped up when asked why nobody had complimented the gárdaí on their handling of the investigation.

It was known that the police had set up a surveillance outside Connolly's apartment some days before the arrest; they might therefore have saved the Attorney-General and the government considerable embarrassment if they had arrested MacArthur outside the apartment. Thus, in asking why nobody had complimented the police, the reporter was really asking a loaded question.

'It was a very good piece of police work', Haughey replied as he praised the gárdaí for their painstaking efforts in 'putting the whole thing together and eventually finding the right man.'

By alluding to MacArthur as the 'right man', the Taoiseach was clearly prejudging his guilt, but the remark was unintentional. Faced with television lights, cameras, and the army of reporters, Haughey did not appreciate the implications of what he had said until told afterwards by an aide. Reporters were then asked to withhold the remark as it had been inadvertent.

Some segments of the British media — relishing Haughey's

embarrassment following what was seen as his unhelpful attitude during the Falklands war — took a keen pleasure in high-lighting the gaffe. Irish reporters had to be more circumspect because of the *sub judice* situation. They could not report what Haughey had said, but the fact that the Taoiseach had made a prejudicial comment was highlighted. The *Sunday Tribune* des-cribed the comment as 'a gaffe for which the greenest junior reporter would be sacked out of hand'.

This was unfair on a couple of counts. First of all it made the unspecified prejudicial comment seem much worse. And secondly, it should be noted that reporters write their stories and then have a chance of reading them over, while the politician answering questions at a press conference has no such oppor-tunity. In delicate circumstances politicians usually confine themselves to written statements. The Taoiseach, on the other hand, facilitated the journalists by answering their questions personally, and he could feel understandably aggrieved at the way in which his gaffe was highlighted.

In their book, *The Boss,* Peter Murtagh and Joe Joyce wrote that some people thought the Taoiseach had deliberately made his prejudicial remarks in order to undermine the state's case so that MacArthur would get off. Of course, some foolish people will believe just about anything, no matter how daft, but it was unfair of the two journalists to repeat the accusation without labelling it for what it was — arrant nonsense.

Much of the whole affair could be put down to bad luck in Haughey's case. After all, MacArthur had committed no crimes while staying with Connolly. And there was no question of any misconduct by the Attorney-General, yet he and the Taoiseach found themselves in the eye of an unprecedented political storm. 'If Charlie had ducks, they'd drown on him,' John Healy concluded.

The government seemed to learn very little from its inept handling of the MacArthur affair. In the following weeks there were two further incidents in which the failure of the authorities to explain some serious charges gave rise to considerable public speculation and further tarnished Haughey's own leadership image, because the cumulative impact of these matters brought his judgment in making appointments into question.

The first incident involved an attempt to cover up the crash of

Seán Doherty's Special Branch escort car just outside Ballyduff, Co. Kerry in the early hours of the morning of 22 September 1982. Had a proper statement been issued promptly after the accident the whole matter would probably have been cleared up without any wild rumours, but for the next four weeks the authorities pretended that nothing had happened.

Tom McEllistrim, who was with Doherty that night, told the press he had driven the minister back to his hotel around 2 o'clock in the morning and had actually seen him to his bedroom door, but the ministerial party had been seen entering the hotel around 4.30 a.m. If there was nothing to hide, people asked why was McEllistrim not telling the truth about the time?

Despite the fact that the crashed car had remained at the scene for some hours, the Gárda Press Office initially denied there had been any accident. The *Irish Times* managed to locate the car in a Dublin garage and it published a photograph of the garage owner frantically trying to pull across the garage door in a vain effort to conceal the car. It was only then, some four weeks after the crash, that the gardaí finally admitted there had been an accident. Because of the official deceit the whole affair was blown out of all proportions, and credence was given to unfounded rumours about Doherty driving the car and having a woman passenger. The fact is that the Special Branch driver was the only person in the vehicle at the time of the accident.

Tom McEllistrim later admitted that he had not been candid about the time of the group's return to the hotel because he had not wanted to admit that they had been in a pub until then. 'You mustn't say to the press that you were inside a pub until four o'clock in the morning', he explained with a laugh.

Meanwhile Doherty's name had already been dragged into another scandal when his brother-in-law, Garda Thomas Nangle, was acquitted on a charge of assaulting a Co. Fermanagh man after the latter failed to turn up for the court case in Dowra, Co. Cavan, on 27 September. The Fermanagh man had been detained for the day by the RUC for no disclosed reason. At his request the gardaí were informed of his detention, but the Dowra court was told only that he would not be attending and no reason was given for his absence, so the judge dismissed the case.

'OK, some fucking guard had some contact with a guy in the RUC or something like that', one of Doherty's colleagues told Geraldine Kennedy. 'We all know that something happened along the line.' But attempts by the media to investigate the matter further came up against the proverbial stone wall.

Although Haughey was not involved in the Ballyduff or Dowra incidents, both contributed towards further straining his already bad relations with the media. In both cases, and in the Connolly affair which preceded them, the media had a duty to investigate and report what had happened but were clearly frustrated by the authorities. At no stage was there any indication that the Taoiseach tried to discipline those who had deliberately sought to mislead the press in at least two of the affairs. By his inaction he effectively endorsed such behaviour.

With Haughey plummeting to a new low in the polls the time seemed right for the dissidents to make another bid to oust him — this time with the McCreevy motion.

Haughey immediately contended that the media was behind the latest move, and later cited Geraldine Kennedy's role as in support of his charge. Kennedy had been tipped off that something was brewing within Fianna Fáil. She made enquiries among the dissidents and learned of McCreevy's intentions. The dissidents, in turn, asked for her advice on media matters like deadlines, because they wanted to arrange it so that the whole affair would receive maximum publicity on the Sunday before the parliamentary party meeting.

A case can therefore be made for saying that Geraldine Kennedy was involved in the attempt to remove Haughey, but there is no evidence to substantiate his charge that the media as a whole was implicated. She was the only reporter who knew beforehand what was going to happen. Her colleagues were deliberately kept in the dark.

As of that Sunday, when Haughey first made his latest charge about the supposed media conspiracy, none of the national newspapers had time to formulate an editorial stand on the McCreevy motion, with the exception of the *Sunday Tribune* which, of course, had been forewarned by Kennedy. When the four national daily newspapers took editorial stands, the *Irish Times* and *Irish Press* were clearly opposed to the motion, the *Cork Examiner* was again largely dismissive as it confidently predicted Haughey's survival, while the *Irish Independent* merely implied that it was time for a change.

Three of the four political commentators who wrote about the motion in those newspapers were obviously critical of Haughey, but they actually split evenly on the question of his removal. This was because Conor Cruise O'Brien opposed the McCreevy motion in the hope that Haughey's survival would help to destroy Fianna Fáil at the next general election. Writing in the *Irish Times* John Healy predicted that the dissidents would be routed. They had shown themselves incapable of organising a proper challenge in the past, and he saw no reason to believe that they could do better this time. He concluded that Haughey was as 'blessed with his enemies as he is cursed with his friends'. This observation seemed all the more appropriate in the light of the disgraceful behaviour of his supporters towards Gibbons and McCreevy following the meeting, as well as the attempts to intimidate Geraldine Kennedy with threatening telephone calls in the middle of the night.

During the general election campaign of November 1982 Haughey's leadership again became the focus for much comment, but it was Garret FitzGerald who came in for the roughest ride as he found his patriotism being questioned by Fianna Fáil spokesmen. The Fine Gael leader complained about smear tactics being used against him, but as we have seen Haughey dismissed this as laughable in contrast to the 'cold, calculating and vilifying character assassination' of himself by members of Fine Gael in collusion with various journalists.

At one point during a press conference on the last Saturday of the campaign, Haughey looked pointedly at Bruce Arnold and reached for a file as if he were going to produce evidence of his accusation. He then seemed to change his mind, but the incident left a lasting impression on some of the journalists present. Joyce and Murtagh later referred to this in *The Boss,* but they did not mention that on that particular day the *Irish Independent* was carrying an article in which Arnold criticised the Fianna Fáil leader for saying there was a campaign of vilification against him when there was no evidence of it. On the other hand, Arnold continued, 'it would be hard to find a more text-book set of examples of vilification' than Haughey's own charges against FitzGerald of being untrustworthy on the pro-life amendment, of stealing secret documents, of collusion over the Northern assembly, and of collaboration with the British government.'

There could be little doubt that Haughey had been the victim of unfriendly reporting on occasions over the years and Arnold's latest article was an example of it, though the writer obviously considered his criticism justified. Arnold had previously sided with the dissidents in denouncing what he called 'the democratic travesty of a roll-call vote'. He not only ignored the fact that all votes in the Dáil are taken openly but also conveniently allowed the dissidents to forget that they had supported Lynch when he set a precedent by demanding a roll-call vote of the parliamentary party during the Arms Crisis. 'On sensitive issues like the confidence ballot provoked by Mr Charles McCreevy,' Arnold contended, the Taoiseach's 'behaviour has been so erratic, contradictory and perverse, as to represent a serious assault by Mr Haughey on himself.' It was not Haughey's behaviour which had been erratic but that of the dissidents.

It was also unfair of Arnold to dismiss all of Haughey's charges against FitzGerald so offhandedly and then classify them as examples of vilification without first analysing the bases for those charges. In some instances there *was* a case for FitzGerald to answer. He had not been completely honest on the pro-life issue, and his motives in discussing the Northern assembly with the Duke of Norfolk were left open to question, especially when Norfolk was later quoted as saying that the Fine Gael leader approved of the Prior initiative while the Dublin government was opposed to it. FitzGerald had no mandate to engage in diplomacy at the time, and he should at least have been more discerning in his choice of contacts abroad.

The media was impartial in its reporting of the full details of Haughey's criticism of FitzGerald, even though none of the editors of the four national daily newspapers took seriously his charge of sinister collusion. In a rare demonstration of unanimity, all four newspapers carried editorials rejecting the collusion charge with its quisling undertones.

The *Irish Press*, for instance, roundly denounced the Fine Gael leader's security proposals and accused him of starting the contest in vilification with the 'flawed pedigree' speech back in 1979, but it nevertheless dismissed the collusion accusation against FitzGerald. 'No one seriously believes that he is in active collusion with the British government in the North anymore than anyone sees the Duke of Norfolk as a British spymaster,' the *Irish Press* declared. Both the *Irish Independent* and *Cork Examiner* categorised the collusion charge as 'a red herring', and the *Irish Times* dismissed it as 'much ado about nothing.'

At one time or another each of the national newspapers was critical of Haughey. Some of the criticism was valid; some was not. Writers like Geraldine Kennedy and Bruce Arnold were hardly fair when they blamed him for the appalling behaviour of his supporters or contended that his treatment in the media amounted to a self-inflicted wound. Of course, some of Haughey's supporters behaved disgracefully to the two writers in question by trying to intimidate them (not to mention the taps on their telephones, which will be discussed in the next chapter). Having ignored their behaviour, Haughey must share some of the blame for the consequences. After all, physical threats or menacing telephone calls in the middle of the night are a poor way to make friends and influence people.

It should also be remembered that some political commentators were very sympathetic towards Haughey. Most notable were John Healy and Prionsias Mac Aonghusa. Over the years Healy complained with monotonous regularity about Fine Gael engaging in a campaign of character assassination against Haughey. He first made the charge as early as 1962. Years later he admitted that he heard about the 'secret court' which convicted Donogh O'Malley of drunken driving, but rather than expose the whole thing, he actually wrote in his 'Backbencher' column in the *Sunday Review* that the knives were out in Fine Gael to get Haughey. 'I cannot see the Minister with all his resourcefulness come out unscathed,' Healy wrote. Later he was probably the first senior journalist to question the motives behind the sacking of the two ministers during the Arms Crisis. 'The gutting of Charlie Haughey and Neil Blaney was something of a minor classic in the art of gut politics', Healy wrote before the week was out. In the aftermath of the Arms Trial, Mac Aonghusa was particularly bitter in his column in *Hibernia*. At one point he contended that Lynch was 'urgently in need of psychiatric treatment'. He also contended that the British were behind an effort to destroy Haughey because they could not control him whereas they supposedly regarded 'Lynch as a puppet to be manipulated at will'. Although *Hibernia* had ceased to publish before the decade was out, Mac Aonghusa continued to write in a comparatively similar vein in the *Sunday Press* under the pseudonym Gulliver.

There was certainly very little evidence to support Haughey's charge that the media conspired against him during the two challenges that were waged against his leadership of Fianna Fáil in 1982. Those challenges were mounted with so little notice that there was no practical way for any journal or even the Sunday newspapers to influence proceedings. Thus media influence was largely confined to the national newspapers and current affairs programmes on radio and television. On both occasions Haughey made use of the opportunity to give lengthy radio interviews to present his own case. On the other hand, the dissidents — mindful of McCreevy's temporary expulsion from the parliamentary party in January — had to be very careful about what they said publicly. Hence it fell to journalists to explain the dissident point of view, and this naturally lent credence to the suggestion that the media was involved in a conspiracy against Haughey.

For such a conspiracy to have existed would undoubtedly have required the collusion of the editors of at least some of the national newspapers. Yet on the two occasions that Haughey was challenged by the dissidents, the *Irish Times* and *Irish Press* supported him editorially, while the *Cork Examiner* remained aloof. Only the *Irish Independent* leaned towards the dissidents. Thus the bulk of the available evidence supports the conclusion that, while some elements of the media were unfair to Haughey, the media as a whole was not involved in a conspiracy to oust him.

14
In the Shadow of Watergate

The Tapping Scandal
1982-83

The Sunday Independent, 30 January 1982

THE new coalition government was in office barely a week when the public received the first indication of the coming political storm. Peter Murtagh, the security correspondent of the *Irish Times*, reported that the telephones of Bruce Arnold and Geraldine Kennedy had been tapped 'officially' with the full knowledge and approval of Seán Doherty, the last Minister for Justice.

Haughey quickly denied any involvement. 'I wouldn't countenance such action,' he declared during an RTE interview next day. He called for a judicial enquiry so that the charges could be investigated fully. 'The capacity to listen in to phone conversations is one which must be kept under the very closest, rigid scrutiny', he said.

Back in 1964 he had assured the Dáil that there were safeguards to ensure that telephone tapping could not be abused for political purposes. The request for a tap had to come from the Gárda Commissioner or a Deputy Commissioner, who had to be satisfied that the person to be tapped was involved with a subversive organisation or engaged in organised criminal activities. Moreover, an officer of the Department of Justice had then to advise the minister on the application. 'The Minister for Justice cannot initiate the procedure', Haughey said. 'He can act only when a written request comes from a responsible authority and when he is satisfied and when his departmental advisers are satisfied that the information concerned can be obtained in no other way.' Thus, he contended, 'the connivance of a whole group of people would have to be available before there could be the slightest possible abuse of power'.

'I don't think any politician himself should ever initiate because that would be an abuse,' Haughey explained when asked about the reported taps on the telephones of Arnold and Kennedy. 'There's a very limited number of reasons which justify the issue of warrants and it's to combat crime or subversion. Now I don't think either of the two journalists whose names have been mentioned would come within that category.'

Although he expressed concern about the allegations, he took his time in questioning Doherty about them. It was not until 21 December that he even approached him on the subject. Then, assured by Doherty that there was nothing to worry about, he did not bother to pursue the matter further.

Doherty had asked Deputy Commissioner Joe Ainsworth of the Gárda Síochána to have a tap placed on Arnold's telephone. Commissioner Patrick McLoughlin duly authorised this request on Ainsworth's recommendation. When the Department of Justice official charged with vetting the application asked for the reason for the desired tap, Ainsworth explained that Arnold was 'anti-national in outlook' and 'might be obtaining information from sources of a similar disposition'. There was no question of Arnold being involved with criminal or paramilitary organisations, so the official recommended that the tap should not be authorised. But Doherty ignored the advice and signed the necessary warrant. In the following weeks the tap produced nothing of value, so it was discontinued in the immediate aftermath of the over-ride controversy. By then Geraldine Kennedy had replaced Arnold as the greatest thorn in the side of the Taoiseach.

She had the confidence of someone privy to what was happening within the cabinet. On 11 July 1982, for instance, she quoted some cabinet exchanges and disclosed that the government had decided to reverse its economic policies and adopt an approach of fiscal rectitude. In another article she disclosed that Haughey had had secret talks in an effort to come to a political arrangement with the Labour Party, but any hope of this was killed when she broke the news of the discussions.

Haughey complained to Hugh McLoughlin, the then publisher of the *Sunday Tribune,* about Kennedy's articles. McLoughlin in turn told Conor Brady, the newspaper's editor, to keep a tighter control on Kennedy and to go easy on Haughey. He explained that the Taoiseach was 'desperately worried about the Kennedy woman' and wondered who in Fianna Fáil was talking to her. Of course, Brady naturally refused to divulge her sources.

A few days later Doherty asked for and then formally authorised a tap to be placed on Kennedy's telephone for reasons of 'national security'.

Haughey stated afterwards that he knew nothing about the tap. In fact, even the Gárda Commissioner who formally requested it was not aware that it applied to Geraldine Kennedy's telephone because the phone was actually in the name of a previous tenant of the apartment in which she was living.

The tap on Kennedy's telephone yielded more interesting material than that on Arnold's. Among the calls intercepted was a conversation in which she forwarned Peter Prendergast of the plan by Fianna Fáil dissidents to challenge Haughey with the McCreevy motion at the start of October. It was noteworthy that Doherty requested extra copies of these intercepts on the eve of the parliamentary party meeting which was due to discuss the McCreevy motion. Immediately after this meeting there was a curious incident when the Taoiseach's son, Ciarán, walked up to Geraldine Kennedy.

'I want to tell you one thing,' young Haughey said to her. 'You'll be hearing from us.'

She asked if this was a threat.

'You can take it as such,' he replied according to her.

She thought at the time he was annoyed at some remarks she had made on television the previous night. Of course, she did not know then that there was a tap on her telephone.

On Thursday, 20 January 1983 Michael Noonan, the new Minister for Justice, confirmed that the telephones of Arnold and Kennedy had indeed been tapped and that the procedures outlined by various Ministers for Justice had not been followed in either case. He also disclosed that Ray MacSharry had borrowed sophisticated gárda equipment and had secretly recorded a conversation he had had with Martin O'Donoghue on 21 October 1982. The tape was then transcribed by the gárdaí. In addition to these disclosures, Noonan announced that McLoughlin and Ainsworth would be retiring from the gárdaí in the immediate future.

When interviewed next day on RTE's lunchtime news Haughey accepted responsibility for what had happened but at the same time tried to distance himself from the abuses. 'Any head of government must take responsibility for anything that happens during his administration', he said. 'But I want to make it crystal clear that the government as such and I, as Taoiseach, knew absolutely nothing about any activities of this sort and would not countenance any such abuse.' He was particularly dismissive of the suggestion that the taps were connected with his own leadership problems within Fianna Fáil.

'I wouldn't need any such secret information from any such sources,' he contended. 'I know as a politician and leader of the party exactly what is going on in the party and who was saying what. The idea of resorting to telephone tapping or any other devices to get that sort of information is ludicrous.'

But if it was so ludicrous, why had he been so interested in learning Geraldine Kennedy's sources only days before the tap was placed on her telephone? In a front page article in the *Sunday Press*, where she had taken over as political correspondent following the collapse of the *Sunday Tribune*, she disclosed that Haughey had asked her publisher about her sources back in July. This story, which raised some serious questions, undoubtedly hurt Haughey politically.

Within Fianna Fáil Haughey appointed a four-man com-

194

mittee to investigate the whole affair. It was headed by Jim Tunney, the new chairman of the parliamentary party. From the very outset he discounted any suggestion that Haughey might have been responsible for any misconduct. 'All the evidence shows that Mr Haughey knew absolutely nothing about it,' he declared on the day the committee was set up.

In the following days the controversy escalated as both Doherty and MacSharry made hamfisted efforts at defending their own actions. MacSharry did not really use the gárda equipment for 'bugging' purposes. The term generally refers to eavesdropping electronically on the conversations of others. He simply recorded a conversation to which he was a party himself. Of course, if this was only 'a personal matter,' as he declared, then he should not have borrowed gárda equipment, even for the few hours, and he should not have wasted the time of the police who had to transcribe a private conversation.

This was only a trivial matter for which he should not have been pilloried in the press, though he was largely responsible for allowing the whole thing to be sensationalised out of all proportion by giving the impression that O'Donoghue had offered him money at this meeting to turn against Haughey. The impression was strengthened on Saturday, 22 January, when Tony Fitzpatrick, the Fianna Fáil press officer, indicated to reporters that Doherty was about to issue a statement which would not only confirm that O'Donoghue had offered £100,000 to MacSharry to withdraw his support of Haughey back in October, but also authoritatively divulge that previous governments had tapped journalist Vincent Browne, the headquarters of the Workers' Party, and even a foreign embassy in Dublin. Here was the making of an even bigger story than the political bombshell dropped by Noonan. Reporters were kept waiting for the story for eight hours and then Fitzpatrick denied there had ever been any question of issuing such a statement.

The whole thing was an apparent effort to exploit the early deadline for the Sunday newspapers in order to stampede the press into publishing rumours without taking responsibility for them. When this blatant piece of misinformation was discussed at a meeting of the Fianna Fáil parliamentary party next day, Haughey contended that the reported manipulation was just a Fine Gael propaganda ploy, notwithstanding the fact that the story had originated with the Fianna Fáil press officer.

Haughey was clearly on the defensive. Although he had already publicly stated that there was no justification for the taps, he now sought to justify Doherty's actions on the grounds that 'national security' had been endangered by 'cabinet leaks'.

'What leaks?' Pearse Wyse asked.

'The Fianna Fáil farm plan had appeared for instance in the *Farmers' Journal*,' replied Haughey to a chorus of incredulous laughter.

'Isn't it strange then that you would tap the telephones of journalists working in the *Tribune* and the *Independent*?' rejoined Wyse.

This use of the 'national security' cloak was the exact same one used by Nixon to defend the misdeeds of his people during the Watergate scandal in the United States almost a decade earlier. And this latest Irish scandal was rapidly beginning to look like a repetition of Watergate.

'The parallels to the Nixon White House are uncomfortably close and to the point,' thundered Vincent Jennings in a signed editorial in the *Sunday Press*. 'Wall-to-wall distrust and paranoia; anyone who disagrees with the leadership is an enemy, or worse — anti-national. Get them, the expletive deleted.'

There were some remarkable similarities between the Nixon presidency and what had happened to Haughey in recent months. For instance, there was the over-ride affair. Nixon had ordered the installation of emergency 'hot-lines' from the White House to the offices of all state governors. One governor who had his 'hot line' checked discovered that the line remained open to the White House even when the telephone was in its cradle. As a result the 'hot-line' amounted to an electronic bug capable of overhearing all conversations in the governor's office. When the telephones of other governors were checked some thirty were found to have the same 'fault', which was attributed to the telephone company. There was also a parallel with Haughey's prejudicial reference to MacArthur at the press conference following Connolly's resignation. During the murder trial of Charles Manson, Nixon had complained of the press glamourising 'a man who was guilty directly or indirectly of eight murders.'

Haughey and Nixon each contended that they were victims of

media conspiracies. Both the Watergate affair and what some called the 'Liffeygate' scandal began as a result of tampering with telephones, but there was no evidence that either leader was personally involved in the wrongdoings which initially led to the two crises. Nevertheless both leaders tried to defend the actions of their people on the grounds that 'national security' had been endangered.

There was one enormous difference, however. Watergate was the subject of a thorough, exhaustive investigation in which Congressional leaders were careful to avoid any taint of engaging in a political vendetta. The Democratic leadership went to great pains to ensure that their Republican counterparts in Congress were satisfied that the investigation was being conducted in an impartial manner. In the end Nixon was brought down, not because of any involvement in the initial crimes but because he impeded the investigation by engaging in a cover-up.

On the other hand, there was only a superficial investigation into the 'Liffeygate'. Some of the things which had happened while Haughey was Taoiseach could well have been more serious than anything involved in Watergate. For instance, the implications of the Dowra affair were enormous. There were charges that the police engaged in the most blatant form of obstructionism, with allegations that they were behind a virtual kidnapping in order to frustrate the judicial process. Were the gárdaí involved, and if so, why and at whose behest? Surely the investigation of the affair should not have been left only to the gárdaí themselves!

Serious questions were also left unanswered about the possible use of the over-ride facility. In late 1980, after a couple of telephone conversations with John Bruton at Leinster House, Peter Prendergast picked up his telephone to hear some people discussing the two conversations with an apparent view to making a report about what had been said. Who were those people? For whom were they preparing the report? How did they bug the conversations? Was the over-ride used in this instance and if so, was it used again during the seven months that Fianna Fáil remained in power?

Was it just a coincidence that Haughey was asking questions about Geraldine Kennedy's sources just before Doherty asked for the tap to be placed on her telephone? Was there any justification for basing the request for the tap on grounds of national security? Why did Doherty ask for copies of the transcripts of the tap intercepts on the eve of the crucial parliamentary party meeting in October? Did he show this material to anyone? Why did Ciarán Haughey single out Geraldine Kennedy after that meeting? Did he know the dissidents had taken her into their confidence? If so, how did he know? These are large questions, but none of them were properly examined in the cold light of day. No guilty men were punished; no innocent men had their names cleared.

Doherty contended that there was a sinister plot to bribe politicians. 'We had information,' he later stated, 'that large sums of money were on offer to sway politicians, that a foreign intelligence service was operating in the country and that information from within the cabinet was being made available in an unauthorised manner.'

'That was the security background to the 1982 situation', he explained. In the aftermath of the Falklands War, it was not beyond the bounds of possibility that Britain's MI6 would be prepared to pay a few hundred thousand pounds to oust Haughey. This would only be a drop in the proverbial bucket when compared with the money spent — not to mention the lives wasted — in the Falklands or Northern Ireland. 'I myself was offered £50,000 in cash to help oust C. J. Haughey as Taoiseach', Doherty continued. Even people within Fianna Fáil who were quite critical of Doherty and were convinced that he was the victim of an over-active imagination, have nevertheless accepted that he genuinely believed that there was a sinister plot against the government. If, for argument's sake, one were to accept that foreign money was being used as he has suggested, it would throw a new light on events. The matter should therefore have been investigated. Haughey called for a judicial enquiry, which was certainly warranted by all the unanswered questions.

In Irish society people are supposed to be presumed innocent until proven guilty, but in Haughey's case his opponents automatically assumed he was guilty. The coalition government was so intent on securing his removal that it decided against holding a judicial enquiry for fear that the delay involved in setting up the tribunal might afford him an opportunity to regroup his forces and hold on to the leadership of Fianna Fáil. In short, he might survive in spite of the guilt which they so readily assumed. Consequently the government left further investigation of the whole affair to the media, which was not equipped for the task.

The issues involved were much too serious to permit the suspicion that they were being exploited for political ends: in order to skewer selected politicians and roast them on the spit of inflamed public opinion. The media was stampeded by Noonan. No fair-minded person could honestly believe that it would be impartial in this case. Haughey was being railroaded. At least Nixon had been tried according to the rules.

Haughey was indeed responsible for appointing Doherty, who left himself wide open to the charge of having abused his powers by making representations to the police on behalf of his constituents, but it should be emphasised that initiating taps was not itself a violation of any law. Doherty merely ignored guidelines set by his predecessors, but if they had the power to set guidelines, then he had the power to change them. If the next government really believed his actions were so terrible, why did it not even try to change the law? One might also ask why McLoughlin and Ainsworth were forced to resign? Publicly they were only accused of carrying out instructions of the Minister for Justice. The courts had never ruled on the constitutionality of such instructions so the police were obliged to carry out the instructions. Surely it was not in the public interest that servants of the state should appear to be so unfairly treated? Yet there was no outcry in the media. Journalists were preoccupied with Haughey's political fate.

He certainly seemed to be in a precarious position. His party was dispirited and leaking like a proverbial sieve. Within a week Michael O'Kennedy had already begun canvassing openly for the party leadership, and he was quickly followed by O'Malley. There were rumours that Haughey had written a letter of resignation and would formally announce his decision at a meeting of the parliamentary party on Thursday, 27 January, by which time all four national daily newspapers had carried editorials depicting his position as party leader as untenable.

There was general agreement in the media that Haughey was all but finished politically that morning as the parliamentary party gathered for its weekly meeting. This was reflected both in the editorials and opinion columns as well as in news reports predicting his demise. But those predictions were made on the basis of incomplete calculations. Each of the newspapers published lists of deputies who were supposed to be opposed to Haughey, but when the names in all of those lists were compiled in one master list, they still did not add up to a majority of Fianna Fáil deputies. Most deputies were apparently keeping their views to themselves. The reporters simply jumped to the wrong conclusion. The *Irish Press* took the extraordinary step of publishing what amounted to a political obituary consisting of over two pages reviewing Haughey's whole career. The media was clearly writing him off, but he refused to be stampeded.

At the party meeting Ben Briscoe proposed that standing orders be suspended so that the leadership issue could be discussed. Although Haughey objected he was not able to prevent a debate, but he was adamant that he was not going to be driven out of office by a 'vindictive press'.

'I will take my own decision in my own time', he declared.

This was generally understood by those present to mean that he intended to step down within a few days. Even Mark Killilea, one of the original 'gang of five' who had spearheaded Haughey's drive for the leadership, admitted to the press that he believed the leader was indicating his intention of resigning. Eileen Lemass was actually reported as saying Haughey was finished and should recognise it.

Some people believed he would have been forced out at this meeting if the issue had been put to a vote, but there was widespread agreement within the party that the press had been unfair to him, so there was no desire to force the issue when he seemed prepared to step down. A number of deputies at the meeting were close to tears.

'I love you, Charlie Haughey', Briscoe blurted out at one point.

'I love you, too, Ben', Haughey replied.

'I hope the papers don't hear about this', someone was heard to groan at the back of the room.

But the confidentiality of the meeting was a shambles as reporters were given verbatim details of what had been said, including Haughey's charge that the media were conducting a vilification campaign against him. It all seemed so reminiscent of Nixon's final hours in the White House that one *Irish Times* columnist contacted Carl Bernstein, the famous Watergate reporter, for his views on the Irish situation.

While the *Irish Press* admitted that Haughey 'had certainly been targeted in some sections of the media', it refuted as 'simply untrue' his implied charge that the media had created the existing crisis. The national press as a whole agreed. 'The media did not tap telephones nor bug conversations,' the *Cork Examiner* declared. 'The media is entitled to question why this was done. The media did not mount a campaign against Mr Haughey; that came from within his own party and the media is fully entitled to report it. The media did not initiate moves for his removal from the leadership. Again these came from within Fianna Fáil — his own party and his own colleagues.'

Of course, Haughey still had some admirers in the press. Proinsias Mac Aonghusa contended in his *Sunday Press* column that 'no other Irish public figure has ever undergone such a sustained media campaign of vilification as Charles J. Haughey.' In the same newspaper Desmond Fennell criticised journalists in general for conducting a trial by media. 'With the *Times*-RTE-*Independent* axis in the forefront,' he wrote, 'virtually all of them decided to become prosecutors and hostile interrogators, magnifying forensically the charges against the accused.' Just because one of Haughey's appointees had 'been publicly embarrassed and another has been shown to have abused his power is no grounds for Mr Haughey to resign as leader of Fianna Fáil,' Fennell contended.

Whether Haughey ever intended to resign remains very much open to question. Some senior members of the party convinced O'Kennedy to throw his hat into the ring, and Haughey himself reportedly encouraged Brian Lenihan and Gerry Collins to run for the leadership. He was apparently encouraging people to run in order to confuse the contest before he began his fightback over the weekend.

A massive campaign was undertaken on his behalf at grassroots level with a large demonstration by supporters outside Fianna Fáil party headquarters in Dublin. He and his people frantically sought middle ground support to allow him to stay on for a few weeks until the ard fheis, at which he could enlist his greatest support within the party.

Those wishing to get rid of him, however, began to react to his survival efforts on Monday, 31 January. They made preparations to draw up a petition of deputies calling on him to stand down at the next parliamentary party meeting, which was due to be held on Wednesday, 2 February. Suddenly fate seemed to come to the leader's rescue.

Clem Coughlan, one of the deputies who had already called publicly for Haughey's resignation, was killed in a car accident on Tuesday morning. In the circumstances it would be inappropriate for the parliamentary party to discuss the leadership issue next day, seeing that it was normal for party meetings to be adjourned as a mark of respect. But the party's dissidents were determined that another meeting should be called for Friday, the day after Coughlan's funeral.

At the outset of the Wednesday meeting Haughey delivered a short tribute to the deceased deputy. Next the chairman, Jim Tunney, spoke of the tragic death and called for a minute's silence. Immediately afterwards, as Mary Harney was on her feet calling to be recognised, Tunney announced in Irish that the meeting was adjourned until the following week. He then bolted out the door.

'Dammit!' exclaimed one disgruntled deputy. 'He just ran out of the room.'

There was considerable resentment at Tunney's action. Forty-one deputies and seven senators had signed a petition calling for a parliamentary party meeting to be held on Friday, 4 February. They seemed determined that the leadership issue should be settled before the following Wednesday when the coalition government was due to bring in its first budget. This would be a golden opportunity for Fianna Fáil to score political points, especially as a harsh budget was expected. The chance would be lost, however, if the party was still embroiled in a leadership wrangle, because this would undoubtedly divert media attention from the budget. As a compromise it was agreed to hold the meeting on Monday, which would allow the leadership issue to be resolved before the budget and also afford the Tunney committee time to complete its report.

Some of the forty-one deputies who had signed the petition were supporters of Haughey who had done so in order to learn what the dissidents were planning but the media mistakenly assumed that all forty-one were likely to call for the leader's resignation. The press therefore concluded that he would definitely be toppled, as only thirty-seven were needed for an overall majority. He seemed to increase the tension himself late on Thursday afternoon when he issued a controversial statement.

'Despite everything that a largely hostile media and political opponents at home and abroad could do to damage not only me but the great party and traditions of Fianna Fáil', he contended that a large number of members and supporters had called on him 'to stay on' as leader. Consequently, he continued:

> Having calmly and objectively considered the situation in all its aspects I have decided that it is my duty in the best interest of the party to which I have devoted all my political life to stay and lead it forward out of these present difficulties. I am now, therefore, calling on all members of the party to rally behind me as their democratically elected leader and give me that total support that I need to restore unity and stability, to re-organise the party, to give it a new sense of purpose, to re-state our policies, to re-establish and implement the traditional code of party discipline, and to make it clear that those who bring the party into disrepute, cause dissension or refuse to accept decisions democratically arrived at can no longer remain in the party.

On the two previous occasions when Haughey's leadership had been challenged, his supporters contended that the dissidents did not have the right to remove him even with the support of a majority of the parliamentary party. Back in February 1982, when O'Malley was challenging for the leadership, the circumstances had been somewhat different but the argument was comparatively similar. On the eve of that parliamentary party meeting Brian Lenihan had emphasised on a 'Today Tonight' programme that the challenge was not for the leadership because Haughey was already the leader, but only for the party's nomination for Taoiseach. Haughey would remain as party leader regardless of the outcome, because even though he had initially been elected leader by the parliamentary party, his selection had subsequently been confirmed by the party's ard fheis, which was the supreme organ within the organisation. Thus, from a *de jure* standpoint he could be removed only by an ard fheis or by his own resignation. Likewise in October, after McCreevy introduced his motion of no confidence, it was noted that Haughey would remain on as Taoiseach regardless of the outcome of the vote. He been elected to the office by the Dáil so by law — irrespective of whether he had the majority support of his own party — he would remain as Taoiseach until replaced by the Dáil. Consequently many people believed that Haughey's statement in February was implying that the parliamentary party did not have the authority to remove him, although he did not specifically put forward this argument.

Briscoe was particularly critical of the statement. 'It was a most dreadful statement from a party leader', he declared during an RTE interview. 'If you examine it line by line you could only come to the conclusion that Mr Haughey no longer recognises the right of the parliamentary party which elected him to remove him from office.' Briscoe therefore decided to force the issue by formally tabling a motion for Monday's meeting calling for 'the resignation of Mr Charles J. Haughey as party leader now'.

The press lost little time denouncing Haughey's statement with editorials in three of the four national newspapers. The *Cork Examiner* took the unusual step of carrying an editorial condemnation on the front page. If recent events 'had happened in any other allegedly civilised country', the editorial declared, 'the leader of the day would have been long since gone.' Only the *Irish Press* avoided an editorial condemnation.

Amid all the furore Haughey was forced to issue a clarifying statement on Saturday, 4 February, emphasising he would accept the decision of the party meeting. 'I want it stated publicly and clearly,' he declared, 'that any decision of the parliamentary party will be fully accepted by me'.

Interviewed on the RTE lunchtime news next day, he stressed that his statement on Thursday had been misinterpreted. He would, he emphasised, 'with honour and dignity accept any decision of the parliamentary party'. Although personally confident of victory, he said that if somebody else should be elected to succeed him next day, that person would be accepted as president of the whole Fianna Fáil organisation. 'That's the way it's been done in the past,' he added; 'that's the way it will be done in the future.'

The overwhelming majority of political commentators had already written Haughey off, and very few dared to predict his survival. The idea that he might not be beaten was treated pretty much as a joke. 'We're going to miss Charlie all the same!' John Healy wrote the previous week, but by the morning of the crucial meeting he concluded that Haughey had a fighting chance of survival. He therefore included a spoof request in his column for someone who might have 'a job for a troupe of coffin-dancers who are free due to a last minute cancellation'.

The odds seemed very much against Haughey retaining the leadership. After initially excluding the possibility of his survival the bookmakers listed him only in joint fourth place with O'Kennedy behind Collins, O'Malley and John Wilson. Collins was being quoted as odds-on favourite with Haughey back at 4 to 1 and at a staggering 20 to 1 against being Taoiseach after the next general election. 'Even paying exaggerated respect to Mr Haughey's recuperative power and ability to survive,' the *Cork Examiner* declared, 'today should see the end of the Haughey era.'

The meeting, which lasted throughout the day and late into the night, began with skirmishes over whether to discuss the leadership issue or the report of the Tunney committee first. O'Malley's supporters wanted to discuss the leadership, but this was beaten on a vote. All of those present, including senators and members of the European parliament, were able to vote in this contest, so the outcome was not necessarily indicative of the feelings of Dáil deputies. Still, Haughey had clearly won the first round. He also won the next round by having his own proposal for the expulsion of Doherty and O'Donoghue from the parliamentary party deferred until the next meeting. Since the two of them were therefore entitled to remain with their voting privileges intact, the move clearly favoured Haughey. Doherty had already indicated his intention of supporting him. But O'Donoghue, who had lost his Dáil seat in the recent election, was only at the meeting in his capacity as a member of the Seanad, so he had no vote in the leadership contest. Haughey then got a further boost when the Tunney committee reported that there was no evidence to link the leader directly to the telephone tapping.

Following a four-and-a-half hour discussion on matters relating to the Tunney report, Briscoe formally proposed his motion calling for Haughey's resignation. But he had apparently done little to secure support for his motion, because he did not even have a seconder lined up! For a moment it looked as if the motion would fail for a lack of a seconder but McCreevy filled the void. Deputies then spoke for and against the motion.

Haughey's supporters depicted their man as having been crucified by a hostile media which, they said, should not be allowed to dictate how Fianna Fáil should be run. They stressed his willingness to expel Doherty and O'Donoghue, thereby distancing him from their deeds. His backers also exploited the idea that certain monied interests wanted to get rid of him, which they contended would be tantamount to admitting that Fianna Fáil was for sale.

Haughey's opponents, on the other hand, accused him of presiding over a succession of scandals which had done enormous damage to the party. He was depicted as a distinct electoral liability, and it was emphasised that he had failed to secure a majority in three consecutive elections. These people — and the media in general — conveniently forgot that Eamon de Valera had also failed to secure such a majority in his first three general elections as party leader.

Most of those at the parliamentary party meeting on 7 February 1983, on both sides of the argument, felt the media had been unfair to Haughey. His critics both inside and outside the party had never been seen to give his leadership a real chance, and in recent days they had been trying to get rid of him with almost indecent haste. Indeed at the meeting in question it was argued that they did not even want to wait for the Tunney report. All this helped Haughey to retain the support of many middle-ground deputies at this critical point. People love a fighter who battles against the odds, and he seemed to have been battling against enormous odds for the past several days. Even individuals who despised him were heard to express a begrudging admiration for his tenacity.

This time Haughey agreed to a secret vote. In all probability it was to his advantage because opponents who had found their own ambitions for the leadership thwarted for the present could now back him, as he was likely to be more vulnerable than a completely new leader. In addition, there were those who, according to one reporter, had been 'kissing Charlie on all four cheeks in October' but had recently found it necessary to express public reservations about him. Under the cloak of secrecy they were quietly able to return to his fold.

When the votes were counted Haughey survived by seven votes. He had, in fact, increased the majority by which he had first won the leadership over George Colley in the last secret vote in December 1979.

A group of stunned reporters heard the news outside. 'I saw at least two of my colleagues in the media turn visibly pale, total disbelief showing on their countenances', Raymond Smith wrote. 'We did not believe our ears.'

15
'Uno Duce, Una Voce'

Leader of the Opposition
1982-87

Irish Times 27 February 1985

FOLLOWING FitzGerald's election as Taoiseach on 14 December 1982, Haughey graciously accepted his successor's victory. 'We wish him well in this difficult assignment,' the Fianna Fáil leader said. 'For our party will go into opposition with, I hope, dignity and honour. We will endeavour in opposition to discharge our responsibilities as constructively as we can and with as great a sense of responsibility as we can, conscious of the fact that it will require not only the arduous efforts of the government but the full and constructive co-operation of the opposition in the Dáil to help the country meet the serious difficulties which confront us.'

With Haughey's third successive failure to lead Fianna Fáil to an overall majority in a general election, it was obvious that there would be another move to oust him from the party leadership, but the dissidents bided their time. They were in no great haste for the moment. He, on the other hand, was intent on strengthening his own base within the party. When O'Malley announced his own candidacy for one of the five vice-presidential positions in Fianna Fáil, Haughey asked him to withdraw because the move would be interpreted as a challenge to the leadership.

'That job is for old fuddy duddies', Haughey told him on 13 January.

O'Malley was unmoved. He noted that the description did not fit a decade earlier when Haughey began his political comeback following the Arms Crisis by running successfully for the office.

The bugging scandal broke the following week, so preparations for the party's ard fheis faded into the background. The dissidents decided that this was their chance to get a new leader. Haughey now renewed his call for the judicial enquiry which he had initially requested the previous month, so his latest call may be seen as something more than a desperate play for time until the ard fheis, as it was depicted by some.

From the outset O'Malley dismissed the idea of a judicial enquiry. 'The record of these enquiries is not very satisfactory,' he declared on a 'Today Tonight' interview on the night that Noonan formally confirmed the existence of the taps. O'Malley was obviously in sympathy with those who wished to railroad Haughey.

Then, when the crisis passed, Haughey's position as party leader was more solidly based than at any time since he was first elected. This was confirmed at the ard fheis later in the month when his supporters were almost in total control. The extent of this control became evident when O'Malley failed in his bid to win one of the vice-presidential positions.

There were only a few remaining pockets of resistance. In March 1983, there was a brief controversy when Paul W. Mackay, a former financial auditor of the party's books in Haughey's own Dublin North Central constituency, circulated a letter to all Fianna Fáil deputies stating that the party was 'financially bankrupt'. He complained of being dropped as auditor in June 1982 because he had persistently demanded full information about election expenditures during the two most recent general election campaigns.

'Traditionally,' he admitted, 'the financial affairs of the party have been shrouded in secrecy with the full financial facts only available to a handful of people. This situation may have been appropriate in the past but, in my view, this is not so at the present time.'

Mackay's letter really epitomised the weakness of the dissident position. Haughey's opponents posed as men of principle who were appalled at the way things were being done, yet when they had been in a position to do things differently themselves, they had behaved the same way. It was not a matter of principle; it was a question of power.

While consolidating his position as party leader, he also had to function as leader of the opposition. Despite his peroration on the election of the coalition, his and his party's approach to them was largely negative. Instead of bringing forward positive policies, he merely reacted on an *ad hoc* basis to what the government was doing.

Meanwhile the new Taoiseach operated with one eye constantly trained on Haughey. This was particularly apparent on the question of setting up the New Ireland Forum, the brainchild of John Hume. FitzGerald supported the idea of formulating a united nationalist position on the partition issue, but he was initially unable to persuade his cabinet colleagues. The cabinet voted by 12 to 3 against establishing a forum, but fearing that Haughey would endorse Hume's idea at the February ard fheis, FitzGerald privately persuaded a majority of his colleagues to go along with the idea. Just two days before Haughey's presidential address to the ard fheis, FitzGerald issued a statement calling for the establishment of the New Ireland Forum. In so doing he managed to take much of the wind out of Haughey's sails because, as anticipated, the Fianna Fáil leader duly endorsed Hume's proposal two days later.

This was not the first time that FitzGerald had outmanouvred Haughey. The previous November the latter had tried to embarrass the Fine Gael leader just before the general election by publishing the wording for a Pro-Life amendment to the constitution. But this ploy failed at the time because FitzGerald enthusiastically endorsed the proposal, despite his own better judgment. But FitzGerald soon found himself in an extremely embarrassing position as Taoiseach when the Protestant churches came out against the proposed amendment. He tried to introduce a new wording acceptable to Protestant leaders, but Haughey insisted that the promised referendum should go ahead on the published wording. When some dissident members of the governing parties indicated their readiness to stand with Fianna Fáil on the issue, FitzGerald was forced into a corner in which his own political ineptitude was mercilessly exposed. His government ended up bringing in the necessary legislation for a referendum on an amendment which he urged the electorate to reject. Its ultimate passage, against the wishes of the state's small Protestant minority, left the constitutional crusade in tatters.

Even before the voting FitzGerald admitted that it was necessary to put the constitutional crusade in cold storage until after the New Ireland Forum had completed its work. At its first session, which was held on 30 May 1983, Haughey emphasised that Northern Ireland was a political anachronism. He urged the Forum to formulate a nationalist position so that Northern unionists could be invited to a conference at which a new constitution could be drawn up for the whole island.

Notwithstanding his genuine desire for harmony with the unionists, Haughey was viewed with very deep suspicion on the other side of the border. When his daughter Eimear went to Northern Ireland for a gymkhana in the autumn, she was the victim of extensive abuse and returned home to Dublin in tears. In the following days the family was subjected to further pressure following the publication of *The Boss* by two journalists, Joe Joyce and Peter Murtagh. This book was a blistering indictment of his short-lived government in 1982. Serious questions were raised about the activities of some of his closest colleagues, and he could not escape responsibility in that it was he who appointed them in the first place. In a number of respects the book was unfair to him and his friends, but it was still a runaway bestseller.

It was against this backdrop that the Fianna Fáil leader broke down and wept openly at a meeting of the Forum after Dick Spring accused him of leaking some material to the press. Upon regaining his composure he vehemently denied that he would leak anything to the media, especially after the way he had been treated by journalists. At this point both FitzGerald and Spring felt genuinely sorry for Haughey, who had shown himself in a very human light in which neither had seen him before.

Nevertheless there was some further trouble early in the new year with the publication of a briefing document which had been circulated within Fianna Fáil circles by the party's acting press officer, Frank Ryan. In it he called on the party's local public relations officers to inform party headquarters without delay of any stories that 'might be incriminating to opposition deputies or councillors'. Coming so soon after the sensational disclosures made in *The Boss,* the affair proved particularly embarrasing.

Seán Doherty also began to make some noises off as he became restless for the restoration of the Fianna Fáil whip. At the time of its removal he thought that Haughey had no choice. A scapegoat was needed and he willingly allowed himself to be used as one. 'I was a very willing recipient,' he said. 'I carried the can for the party. I no longer feel that obligation.'

Despite the numerous questions about his conduct raised in *The Boss,* Doherty maintained that he had done nothing wrong and that he had been the victim of conspiracy. But he landed himself back in controversy in April 1984 when the *Tuam Herald* published an interview in which he advised Raymond Smith to 'keep in close touch with his doctor and not be alone in his own house because he might not be able to take care of himself'. Smith considered the remarks a threat; indeed, it is difficult to understand how he could have considered them otherwise.

Doherty had again become a liability to Fianna Fáil so he had to forget about rejoining the parliamentary party with the European elections coming up in June. The question of his readmission was quickly forgotten about anyway in the storm that followed the publication of the New Ireland Forum Report on 2 May 1984.

In outlining the nationalist desire for an end to partition, the Report emphasised that 'the particular structure of political unity which the Forum would wish to see established is a unitary state, achieved by agreement and consent, embracing the whole island of Ireland and providing irrevocable guarantees for the protection and preservation of both the unionist and nationalist identities.' The Report then went on to note that consideration had also been given 'in some detail' to other structural arrangements. In particular, the 'federal/confederal state and joint authority' were examined and outlined separately.

Following the publication FitzGerald, Spring and Hume gave the impression of being open-minded and willing to consider all of the structures outlined or any other proposals which might resolve the Northern problem. The Report specifically stated, for instance, that the Forum parties 'remain open to discuss other views which may contribute to political development'. But Haughey promptly contended that only a unitary state would be acceptable because none of the other models outlined in it 'would bring peace or stability to the North'. He was obviously dismissing federation or confederation, as well as joint Anglo-Irish authority, as possible solutions.

Suddenly the Report itself was overshadowed by this apparent dispute between the nationalist leaders. Haughey went on RTE's 'Day by Day' programme next morning to accuse the media of distorting his views in a way that was 'most unfortunate and totally uncalled for'.

'I did not dismiss anything in the Report at all', he contended. 'I said it spoke for itself. What anyone of us might or might not have preferred doesn't matter.' Instead of highlighting the slight differences that remained between himself and the other nationalist leaders, he argued everyone should 'concentrate on the fantastic amount of agreement'. For a short time it even looked as if he was backing down somewhat when he said it was unfortunate that politicians and journalists had been catapulted into instant comment. 'It would have been better,' he added, 'if we had all been able to sit back for two or three days, read the Report and then give our reaction.' But it soon became apparent that he had not changed his views about limiting a possible solution to a unitary state. On 11 May he stated it was 'dangerous and foolish to be putting a whole range of alternatives to the British government'.

Some people in Fianna Fáil were upset at the way in which Haughey was committing the entire party to a major policy without the parliamentary party so much as discussing the Report. Senator Eoin Ryan, who had been privately clamouring for a party meeting to consider the Report, publicly took issue with Haughey. He warned that the emphasis on the unitary state would frighten the British off discussions. It was two full weeks after the publication of the Report before the leader's critics had a chance to voice their concern within the parliamentary party because, as far as Haughey was concerned, any such discussion was going to have to wait on electoral considerations. The regular weekly meeting, due to be held on 9 May, was postponed so that Haughey could be in Cork when the party's candidates for the upcoming European elections submitted their nomination papers.

By the time the parliamentary party finally sat down to discuss the Report Haughey's colleagues were confronted with a *fait accompli* because he had firmly established a party line and any backtracking would undoubtedly have led to speculation about his leadership — this time in the midst of the European election campaign. He was ready to meet any possible challenge head on.

He moved a motion congratulating himself and Fianna Fáil's twelve other Forum delegates 'on their splendid contribution to the purpose of the Forum both in the work and the subsequent presentation of the Report. It re-affirms that party policy in relation to Northern Ireland will be enunciated by the party leader only, or by somebody designated by him.' Senator Ryan proposed an amendment stipulating that the leader should only enunciate policy 'after discussion with the parliamentary party', but this was rejected and the motion was then carried unanimously. By implication the rejection of Ryan's amendment amounted to a formal acknowledgment that henceforth the party leader would be entitled to announce policy on Northern Ireland without consulting his colleagues.

Following the three hour meeting Desmond O'Malley was openly critical of the way in which party debate on the Forum had effectively been stifled. With the campaign for the European elections already under way his remarks were widely resented in party circles. Seizing the opportunity, Haughey called for O'Malley's expulsion from the parliamentary party. The haste with which a meeting was held, with little more than twenty-four hours notice, was in stark contrast to the two weeks taken before the meeting to discuss the Forum Report. Haughey personally proposed the removal of the party whip, and his motion was carried by a sizeable majority of 56 to 16. Henceforth there could be little doubt about the extent of his control of the party.

'Uno duce, una voce!' P. J. Mara exclaimed afterwards in an aside to journalists. 'In other words,' he added, 'we are having no more nibbling at my leader's bum.' Mara was a long-time aide of Haughey's and had recently been appointed as party press secretary.

His extraordinary comment was made facetiously and was never intended for publication, but it was the kind of remark which was too good for a journalist to pass up. And it was to prove embarrassing for Haughey. The phrase, meaning 'one leader, one voice', was a slogan used by Italian fascists under Benito Mussolini. It was therefore exploited during the election campaign by opponents who tried to hurt Fianna Fáil candidates by depicting them as representatives of a neo-fascist party.

Fianna Fáil, on the other hand, turned the election into a referendum on the performance of the government at home. Although the combined vote of Fine Gael and Labour was marginally ahead of Fianna Fáil, the latter won eight of the fifteen seats to gain their first overall majority in any election since Haughey took over as leader.

Before the end of the year Haughey felt secure enough to permit the return of Doherty to the party fold. He had formally applied for readmission in January, but the application was not considered until eleven months later. And then it was not placed on the agenda; it was just brought up under correspondence at the start of a regular meeting on 5 December 1984. At the time there were only twenty-six deputies in attendance and the application was passed unanimously. Nine of the deputies present were believed to have voted against Haughey's leadership in February 1983; now, none of them dared object to Doherty's readmission.

By then Haughey's position *vis-à-vis* the government had been considerably enhanced following FitzGerald's disastrous summit with Margaret Thatcher in November. She was not only privately unreceptive to the ideas put forward in the Forum Report, but at a press conference afterwards she seemed to go out of her way to be dismissive of the different structures outlined in the document. 'That is out . . . That is out . . . That is out', she declared, referring in turn to a possible unitary state, federation or confederation, and joint authority. When FitzGerald gave a televised press conference immediately afterwards, he was not aware of her comments, which had already been televised live in Ireland. As a result his demeanour — as he behaved with diplomatic decorum in blissful ignorance of what he later described as her 'gratuitously offensive' display — left him looking particularly weak and ineffective. From a public relations standpoint the summit and its pathetic aftermath were disastrous.

The Taoiseach afterwards tried to blame Haughey for the government's difficulties with Thatcher. She obviously had little sympathy for the aspirations of Irish nationalists, which should not have been too surprising. Only weeks earlier she narrowly escaped an attempt on her life when a bomb went off in the Brighton hotel at which she was staying for the Conservative Party conference. Nevertheless FitzGerald attributed her attitude to suspicions roused by Haughey's conduct following the Dublin Castle summit of 1980.

'We witnessed a disastrous process when the Irish leader, for his own short-term political advantage, in anticipation of an early election, exaggerated beyond any reality a so-called "historic breakthrough" with Mrs Thatcher', the Taoiseach emphasised during the adjournment debate winding up the autumn session of the Dáil on 14 December 1984. 'The boasts of that occasion created some ephemeral approval on the part of his own party. But, tragically, the very process of exaggeration immediately destroyed any prospect of developing a real dialogue with the British about doing something for the people of Northern Ireland.' He went on to accuse the Fianna Fáil leader of exploiting 'the misery of the people of Northern Ireland' for short-term electoral gain.

Haughey was indignant. He promptly protested and accused FitzGerald of lying in accusing him of exploiting the misery of the northern people. The Fianna Fáil leader was ordered to withdraw the unparliamentary charge of lying or leave the chamber. In the circumstances he chose to walk out in protest.

Early in the new year the government was confronted with an internal crisis over its attempts to amend Haughey's family planning act to permit the sale of non-medical contraceptives like condoms without a doctor's prescription. Some members of the Roman Catholic hierarchy vociferously opposed the new bill and a number of Fine Gael and Labour deputies threatened to vote against the measure. In the circumstances there was a real chance that the government would be defeated, but Fianna Fáil hopes suffered a serious setback when O'Malley spoke out strongly in support of the bill. Although no longer in the Fianna Fáil parliamentary party, he was still a member of the organisation. And in view of that membership he did not take the logical step of actually voting for the bill. Instead, he just absented himself from the Dáil while the vote was being taken. Nevertheless some people believed his comments had weakened the resolve of dissidents within Fine Gael and Labour and thus helped to save the government from considerable embarrassment. O'Malley suddenly became the scapegoat for the opposition's failure to bring down the government.

A special meeting of the Fianna Fáil national executive was convened to discuss a motion calling for O'Malley's expulsion from the organisation 'for conduct unbecoming a member'. Haughey left nobody in any doubt that he was in favour of expulsion. In the run up to the meeting he told a number of people who tried to intercede on O'Malley's behalf: 'It's him or me.'

O'Malley, who was permitted to address the meeting, requested that the vote on his expulsion should be by secret ballot. Haughey, on the other hand, asked for a unanimous decision. 'I want it to be unanimous for the good of the party and the organisation,' he emphasised three different times. When it became apparent that this was out of the question, he demanded a roll call vote. Whatever about the parliamentary party being free to establish its own procedure, the national executive was bound by the party's *Corú*, which stipulated that all votes should be secret. Yet none of the eighty-two members present dared to challenge Haughey's ruling. A roll call vote was taken and the motion to expel O'Malley was approved by 73 votes to 9.

Interviewed on RTE radio the following morning O'Malley admitted that his difficulties with Haughey went back to the time of the Arms Crisis. 'I came to know in some detail about those events and all the details surrounding them and I inevitably began to form certain opinions then and quite honestly those opinions have never left me,' the Limerick deputy explained. The implication of this was that, as a result of his special access to information while serving as Minister for Justice, he came to know something about Haughey which was even more damning that anything yet revealed. This seemed like another version of the 'flawed pedigree' approach in which a sweeping accusation was being made without any specific effort to substantiate it. The interviewer did not pursue the matter at the time but many months later, on the 'Late Late Show', Gay Byrne challenged O'Malley to 'put up or shut up — stop saying these things, or else say what you mean.' But O'Malley, like so many before him, refused to clarify the matter.

Three members of the party's committee of fifteen, which is elected annually at the ard fheis, voted against O'Malley's expulsion, and it was noteworthy that two of them were defeated when they stood for re-election. One of them admitted that Haughey probably had not orchestrated their defeat; he did not have to. They had not voted as he wished, so in the spirit prevailing within the party they were considered disloyal and politically eliminated. One of their replacements was Captain James J. Kelly of Arms Crisis fame.

Haughey's critics within the parliamentary party had effectively been silenced and he had the satisfaction of seeing Fianna Fáil improve its standing within the country. In the local elections of June 1985 the party's first preference vote was more than 11 per cent ahead of the two governing parties *combined*. By October Fianna Fáil had stretched its lead to a staggering 19 per cent, and Haughey was 14 percentage points ahead of Fitz-Gerald in a public opinion poll conducted by RSI.

The Taoiseach desperately needed something to boost his own flagging leadership and his government's weakening position. For some time he and a number of his cabinet colleagues had been preoccupied with secret talks with the British concerning Northern Ireland. Now his best hope seemed to be in gaining some kind of significant concessions from them.

With the government obviously preparing for a propaganda campaign to secure popular support for an impending agreement with Britain, Haughey voiced grave misgivings and warned of the danger of 'a sell out'. In a speech on 5 October he complained about 'a well-orchestrated media campaign which is under way at present, not just here, but among Ireland's friends abroad, to condition public opinion and prepare the ground for some as yet unspecified development.'

'This is a time for great vigilance', he continued. 'There is a great deal at stake. The Irish people must not again have a treaty imposed or be asked to accept some dubious settlement entered into in response to the short-term political needs of those involved.' Ignoring his own complaints about FitzGerald's contacts with Prior and Norfolk in 1982, he now sent his deputy leader, Brian Lenihan, to the United States in an effort to ensure that prominent Americans would not be stampeded into supporting the forthcoming Anglo-Irish agreement, which was signed at Hillsborough Castle near Belfast on 15 November 1985.

One senior member of the British government described the agreement as 'very modest', according to *Time* magazine. 'If it were any more modest,' he added, 'we could scarcely call it an agreement.' From a tangible standpoint there was not very much in the agreement, other than a decision to establish an Inter-governmental Conference, comprising representatives of the Dublin and London governments, to consider a wide range of matters relating to the administration of Northern Ireland. FitzGerald described this as 'almost joint authority'. The conference was to have its own secretariat based in Belfast, but there was no derogation of Britain's actual sovereignty over Northern Ireland. On any matter on which the representatives of the two governments could not agree at the Inter-governmental Conference, the British would ultimately have the final say. But the whole arrangement amounted to a recognition by the British that the Dublin government had a right to be consulted on matters relating to the internal affairs of Northern Ireland.

Haughey dismissed this aspect as insignificant because, he contended, the Irish government had always had a right to make its views known. 'This arrangement gives them nothing more on that score', he added. 'Perhaps it gives them a formal way of doing so, but it doesn't change the right or the status of the government in doing it.'

In the past, however, Irish leaders who tried to intercede with the British on behalf of Northern nationalists were often told, in effect, to mind their own business. It should be remembered, for instance, that as late as the eve of Haughey's first formal meeting with Thatcher, the latter told the House of Commons that the affairs of Northern Ireland were a matter for the people of Northern Ireland, her government, the Westminster parliament 'and no one else.' In short, she was indicating that Northern Ireland was none of Dublin's business. Thus the establishment of the Inter-governmental Conference was at least a symbolic step away from the old entrenched position adopted by Thatcher and her predecessors.

Another important aspect of the agreement was a formal declaration by the two governments 'that, if in the future a majority of the people of Northern Ireland clearly wish for and formally consent to the establishment of a united Ireland, they will introduce and support in the respective parliaments legislation to give effect to that wish.'

Again Haughey tried to dismiss the significance of this aspect of the agreement by contending that it contained 'nothing new'. He argued that this had always been the position because it was 'unthinkable' that the British government would stand in the way of Irish unity if the majority wished it. 'The alternative would be nonsense', he contended, 'so thanks for nothing is what I say to that.' In trying to belittle this aspect of the agreement Haughey's stand screamed in the face of history. If the British had been willing to accept the wishes of the majority back in 1920 or 1921 there would have been no partition in the first place. Moreover, the British state papers for the late 1940s contain numerous references to Britain's need to retain a physical presence in Northern Ireland for strategic purposes. Indeed, one of Haughey's staunch admirers had already pointed out that a 1949 cabinet memorandum emphasised that Britain could not allow the area to withdraw from the United Kingdom 'even if the people of Northern Ireland desired it.'

Haughey voiced his strongest objections against what he contended were the constitutional implications of the agreement. He vehemently denounced the very first article of the accord affirming 'that any change in the status of Northern Ireland would only come about with the consent of a majority of the people of Northern Ireland'. The Fianna Fáil leader complained that this provision was 'in total conflict with the constitution and in particular Article 2 of the constitution', which claimed sovereignty over the whole island.

'For the first time ever,' he emphasised, 'the legitimacy of partition, which is contrary to unification, has been recognised by an Irish government in an international agreement.' He added that the agreement was also 'totally against the principles enshrined in the New Ireland Forum Report.'

'From our point of view it gives everything away,' he said. 'It confirmed the status of Northern Ireland as an integral part of the United Kingdom and it confirmed that there would be no change in that status without the consent of the Northern Unionists.'

Haughey's constitutional arguments ignored Article 2 (b) of the agreement which clearly stated that 'there is no derogation from the sovereignty of either the Irish government or the United Kingdom government'. While that clause may well have been inserted as a sop to Northern unionists, it also guaranteed the Republic's constitutional position because it meant that there was no derogation of the Republic's *de jure* claim to sovereignty over the Six Counties. Admittedly the agreement contained a recognition of the fact that the area was under foreign rule, but Article 3 of the Republic's constitution already recognised that fact.

FitzGerald had astutely anticipated Haughey's criticism regarding the constitutionality of the agreement and had carefully prepared a trap. The clause to which the Fianna Fáil leader took such extreme exception was taken practically verbatim from the communiqué which Haughey and Thatcher had issued following their first summit meeting back in May 1980. When the Taoiseach disclosed this, Haughey suddenly found himself at pains to explain why the very words he had used five and a half years earlier should now mean something different. If agreeing to those words constituted a sell-out, then it was he who was guilty of a sell-out in May 1980.

In an effort to depict the Hillsborough agreement in the best light possible, the government orchestrated a very successful public relations effort by ensuring that international support was lined up and then publicised almost simultaneously at home. The SDLP came out strongly in favour of the agreement.

221

The party's deputy leader, Seamus Mallon, who had previously been seen as an admirer of Haughey, was particularly enthusiastic. On top of this, the hysterical reaction of Paisley and his supporters undoubtedly enhanced the agreement in the eyes of nationalists on both sides of the border. Anything Paisley hated that much couldn't be all bad! The authorities in Dublin did not claim that an end to partition was in sight, à la Haughey and Lenihan in December 1980, but Paisley might just as well have said as much in his demagogic rantings. He described the agreement as the 'process of rolling Irish unification'.

Haughey was not impressed. 'The agreement', he said, 'is either worthy of support or it is not, and no snow job or public relations job can change that.' He had clearly been outmanoeuvred in the short term, at any rate, because the agreement was greeted with considerable approval throughout the Republic. The next IMS poll saw a dramatic drop in Fianna Fáil support and, for the first time in sixteen months, FitzGerald squeezed ahead of Haughey as the popular choice for Taoiseach.

O'Malley seized this opportunity to launch the Progressive Democratic Party along with Mary Harney, another disillusioned Fianna Fáil TD. The new party flourished initially, drawing its main support from frustrated voters who had supported Fine Gael in November 1982, but who were fed up with the inability of the coalition to tackle the issues they had promised to tackle. There was little comfort for Haughey in this, however, because satisfaction with his performance dropped to the lowest point since the black days of 1983 and he actually trailed both FitzGerald and O'Malley as the people's choice for Taoiseach in an IMS poll published on 18 January 1986.

There were two further defections from Fianna Fáil the following week when Pearse Wyse and Bobby Molloy joined the Progressive Democrats. Of the twenty-two deputies who had voted against Haughey's leadership in October 1982 only nine were still in the Fianna Fáil parliamentary party little over three years later. The most vocal of those critics were all outside the party with the exception of Charlie McCreevy, whose vulnerability was dramatically exposed in the run up to the local elections in 1985 when he was denied a party nomination to run for the Kildare County Council. Any vague doubts which may

222

have remained about Haughey's grip on the party leadership were well and truly laid to rest.

Meanwhile Fine Gael was confronted with a massive defection of those liberal voters who had been attracted to the party by FitzGerald's promise of a New Ireland that would be pluralist and non-sectarian. In an attempt to woo them back, the Taoiseach introduced legislation for a referendum to end the constitutional proscription against divorce.

Fianna Fáil officially remained aloof during the ensuing referendum campaign. Nevertheless, Haughey later admitted that most members of the parliamentary privately campaigned against the proposed amendment. He consistently predicted it would be rejected by the electorate, but he admitted at being surprised by the magnitude of its defeat. FitzGerald's constitutional crusade, already mortally wounded by the success of the Pro-Life amendment, was effectively buried by the rejection of his Divorce amendment.

In the wake of this rejection the government was noticeably divided and demoralised. Probably the most cohesive factor keeping its various elements together was the desire to keep Haughey out of office. The Taoiseach and his people therefore exploited the 'Haughey Factor'. They attacked him at every opportunity.

They blamed him for the country's economic ills, and there were howls of Fine Gael indignation after he told a Bodenstown gathering on 12 October 1986 that the position of Northern nationalists had 'seriously worsened' in the eleven months since the signing of the Hillsborough agreement. Haughey was accused of pandering to republican sympathisers in order to woo their political support.

Haughey's opponents seemed to scrape the bottom of the proverbial barrel when they raised a furore after the Libyan leader, Colonel Gaddafi, described Haughey as 'my very dear friend' during an RTE television interview. The Minister for Industry and Commerce, Michael Noonan, disingenuously contended that this would damage IDA efforts to attract American industry to Ireland. He conveniently ignored the fact that his own complaints and those of his colleagues did more to publicise Gaddafi's remarks than anything else.

The coalition government obviously tried to hold on to

power by exploiting doubts about Haughey's suitability for office because of the shadows which have marred his political career. People may well question the benefits of his accomplishments or the legacies of his failures, but there can be no doubt that — love him or loathe him — he possesses a style and a presence which no one has matched since de Valera retired from active politics in 1959.

Only one prize had eluded him: an overall majority as leader of Fianna Fáil. His fourth chance came on 17 February 1987, the day for which FitzGerald had called a general election after the Labour Party had pulled out of his government.

During the election campaign, Fine Gael effectively had the same dual strategy as in 1982. It tried to make a virtue of its own economic candour while exploiting public doubts about Haughey's suitability for office on account of the shadows surrounding his political career. Those shadows had loomed all the larger following a High Court decision on 12 January 1987 to award Geraldine Kennedy and Bruce and Mavis Arnold monetary compensation for the violation of their constitutional rights by Haughey's last government.

In the event, however, it was not so much the memory of the GUBU government as the intervention of Desmond O'Malley's new Progressive Democrat party which denied Haughey an overall majority yet again. At least half the 14 seats they won would normally have gone to Fianna Fáil, who ended up with 81 seats, three short of a majority.

It was disappointing, but at least Fianna Fáil was overwhelmingly the largest party in the new Dáil and the only one capable of forming a government. Once again, the Taoiseach's office awaited the arrival of Charles J. Haughey.

Notes

The sources for all quoted material are given in these notes. The reference numbers refer to pages and paragraphs ending on the various pages. Thus 44/1 refers to the material quoted in the first paragraph ending on page 44. In this specific instance the quoted material actually appears in the unfinished paragraph at the end of page 43. Dáil Éireann, *Parliamentary Debates* are abbreviated throughout as *DEPD*.

Chapter 1 (pp. 1-15)
2/3 T. Ryle Dwyer, *De Valera's Darkest Hour* (Cork, 1982), 147.
2/4 *Ibid.*
3/4 *Dáil Éireann, Private Sessions of Second Dáil*, 153.
4/1 T. Ryle Dwyer, *Michael Collins and the Treaty* (Cork, 1981), 152.
4/2 Kenneth Griffith and Timothy E. O'Grady, *Curious Journey* (London, 1982), 275.
5/2 CJH interviewed by John Waters, *Hot Press*, 14 Dec. 1984.
5/4 *Ibid.*
6/1 *Ibid.*
7/1 CJH to Editor, *Irish Times*, 11 May 1962.
9/2 John Healy, 'Haughey in the Coming Times', *Irish Times*, 5 Dec. 1984.
9/3 *Ibid.;* Conor Cruise O'Brien, *States of Ireland* (London, 1974), 180.
9/4 CJH interviewed, *Hot Press,* 14 Dec. 1984.
9/5 *Ibid.*
10/1-2 *Ibid.*
10/4 *Ibid.*
10/5 Cruise O'Brien, *States of Ireland,* 179-80.
11/2 Anne Harris, 'Charlie's Other Island,' *Sunday Independent*, 9 Nov. 1986; 'Charlie, the Acceptable Face of Fantasy,' *Ibid.*, 8 Sept. 1985.
11/3 *Ibid.*, 8 Sept. 1985.
11/4 Ann Ruth Wilner, *The Spellbinders* (London, 1984), 8.
12/2 CJH interviewed by Deaglán de Bréadún, *Irish Times*, 28 Mar. 1984.

12/3 *Ibid.*

12/4 *Irish Times,* 9 July 1969.

13/1 CJH, 'My Ireland', RTE TV, 11 May 1986.

13/2 CJH interviewed by de Bréadún, *Irish Times,* 29 Mar. 1984.

13/3 *Irish Independent,* 8 Sept. 1985.

14/2-3 CJH interviewed, *Hot Press,* 14 Dec. 1984.

14/4 *Irish Independent,* 8 Sept. 1985.

15/2 *Ibid.*

15/3 *Irish Times,* 28 Mar. 1984.

Chapter 2 (pp. 16-25)

17/2 *DEPD,* 161:1194

17/3 *Ibid.,* 166: 155; 176:365-6.

18/1 *Ibid.,* 162:946-7.

18/2 *Ibid.,* 168:784; 164:879.

19/3 *Ibid.,* 162:910.

19/6-10 *Ibid.,* 174:736-9.

20/1 *Ibid.*

20/3 *Ibid.,* 176:189.

21/2 CJH interviewed by June Levine, *Sunday Tribune,* 6 Oct. 1985.

21/3-5 CJH interviewed by de Bréadún, *Irish Times,* 28 Mar. 1984.

21/6 Vincent Browne, ed., 'The Peter Berry Papers,' *Magill,* June 1980.

21/7 *Ibid.*

22/3 *Ibid.*

23/2 *DEPD,* 188:1652; 185:926.

23/3 *Ibid.,* 184:1228.

24/2 *Ibid.,* 188:1593-4.

24/3-5 *Ibid.,* 184: 608.

25/1 *Ibid.,* 191:2371.

Chapter 3 (pp. 26-41)

27/1 *DEPD,* 192:34.

27/3 *Ibid.,* 111.

28/2 *Irish Times,* 10 Nov. 1961.

28/3 *Ibid.,* 14 Nov. 1961.

29/1 Conor Brady, *Guardians of the Peace* (Dublin, 1974), 242.

29/3 Peter Berry, 'The Peter Berry Papers,' *Magill,* June 1980.

30/1 J. Bowyer Bell, *The Secret Army* (London, 1970), 392.

30/5 *DEPD,* 198:83.

31/2 *Ibid.*

32/1 John Healy, 'Down to Our Last Hero,' *In Dublin,* 30 Oct. 1986, 15-17.

32/3 *DEPD,* 196:2348, 2353.

32/4 *Ibid.*, 2353.
33/1 *DEPD*, 203:1222-3; Conor Brady, *Gurardians of the Peace*, 241.
33/2 *DEPD*, 198:126.
33/3 Kavanagh interviewed by Liam Mac Gabhann, *This Week*, 19 June 1970.
33/4 Berry, 'The Peter Berry Papers,' *Magill*, June 1980.
34/1 see facsimile examples, Dáil Éireann, Committee of Public Accounts, *Interim Report*, 19 (Part I):373-6.
34/2 CJH interviewed by de Bréadún, *Irish Times*, 28 Mar. 1984.
34/4 Berry, 'The Peter Berry Papers', *Magill*, June 1980.
35/1 *Ibid.*
35/5 *Ibid.*
36/2 *DEPD*, 207:552
36/3 CJH interviewed by de Bréadún, *Irish Times*, 28 Mar. 1984.
37/2 *DEPD*, 197:461.
37/3 *Ibid.*, 194:690.
37/4 CJH interviewed by de Bréadún, *Irish Times*, 28 Mar. 1984.
38/2 *Ibid.*, 194:779-80.
38/3 *Ibid.*, 193:255.
39/2 *DEPD*, 203:1572.
39/3 *Ibid., 196:372.*
39/4 *Time,* 12 July 1963; *DEPD,* 204:880.
40/1 *Sunday Independent,* 9 Aug. 1964.
40/5 CJH interviewed by de Bréadún, *Irish Times*, 29 Mar. 1984.
41/2 *Irish Times,* 9 Oct. 1964.

Chapter 4: (pp. 42-55)
43/2 *DEPD*, 231:45.
43/3 *Ibid.*, 214:820.
44/1 *Ibid.*, 200:1026.
44/2 *Ibid.*, 215:406.
44/5 *Ibid.*, 222:1499.
45/1 *Ibid.*, 219:1286.
45/2 *Ibid.*, 1300, 1310.
45/3 *Ibid.*, 1313.
46/3 Haughey to Feely, 14 Apr. 1966, q. *Ibid.*, 222:1005-6.
47/1 *Ibid.*, 1506.
47/2 *Ibid.*, 1498.
47/3 *Ibid.*, 2403.
49/3 *Ibid.*, 1499.
50/1 CJH speech, Limerick, *Irish Times*, 3 Oct. 1966.
50/2 *DEPD*, 224:1084.
50/3 NFA Statement, *Irish Times*, 4 Oct. 1966.
51/3 *Ibid.*, 8 Oct. 1966.

52/1 Fergal Tobin, *The Best of Decades* (Dublin, 1984), 176-7.
52/3 *Irish Times,* 10 Oct. 1966.
52/5-6 *Ibid.,* 26 Oct. 1966.
53/1 *DEPD,* 224:1980.
53/4 Tim Pat Coogan, *Ireland Since the Rising* (London, 1966), 110.
54/4 *DEPD,* 225:902.
54/6 *Ibid.*

Chapter 5 (pp 56-71)
57/1 *DEPD,* 225:714.
57/2 *Ibid.,* 816, 888.
57/3-4 *Ibid.,* 226:113.
58/1 *Hibernia,* 18 Oct. 1968.
58/2 *DEPD,* 227:1255.
58/3 *Ibid.,* 228:486.
58/4 *Ibid.,* 240:664.
59/1 *Ibid.,* 227:1269.
59/3 *Ibid.,* 227:1493.
59/4 *Ibid.,*228:502; 227:1559-60.
59/5 *Ibid.,* 1560, 1567.
60/1 *Ibid.,* 1700-1.
60/2 *Ibid.,* 1701; 228:385-6.
60/3 *Ibid.,* 228:1370.
61/1 *Ibid.,* 234:57.
61/2 *Ibid.,* 231:59.
62/2 *Ibid.,* 230:1115.
62/3 *Ibid.,* 1116.
63/1 *Ibid.,* 115, 1104.
63/3 D. J. Maher, *The Tortuous Path: the Course of Ireland's Entry into the EEC, 1948-73* (Dublin, 1966), 222.
64/1 *Sunday Independent,* 19 Nov. 1967.
64/2 *DEPD,* 231:834.
64/3 *Ibid.,* 1295.
65/2 *Hibernia,* 29 Nov. 1968.
65/3 *DEPD,* 240:633, 642.
66/2 *Ibid.,* 240:671.
66/4 *Ibid.,* 949.
66/6 *Ibid.,* 1464.
67/3 Conor Brady, 'The Party', *Irish Times,* 19 July 1978.
67/5 Kevin Boland, *The Rise and Decline of Fianna Fáil* (Cork, 1982), 101.
68/1 Brady, 'The Party', *Irish Times,* 19 July 1979; Haughey interviewed by de Bréadún, *Ibid.,* 29 Mar. 1984.
68/2 *Irish Times,* 11 May 1967.

68/5 *Irish Times,* 4 June 1969.

69/1 *Evening Herald,* 17 June 1969.

70/1 *DEPD,* 243:1849-54.

70/2 *Ibid.,* 245:1720.

70/3 *Ibid.,* 1722.

70/4 *Ibid.,* 1747.

70/5 *Evening Herald,* 22 Apr. 1970.

71/1 *DEPD,* 245:1679.

71/2 'The Peter Berry Papers', *Magill,* June 1980.

71/3 *Ibid.*

Chapter 6 (pp. 72-86)

72/1 Lynch, statement, 6 May 1970.

73/1 *DEPD,* 246:642-3

73/4 Lynch, Address, RTE TV, 13 Aug. 1970.

74/1 Kevin Boland, *Up Dev* (Dublin, 1977), 42.

74/4 John Kelly's unsworn statement at Arms Trial, 14 Oct. 1970.

75/1 CJH's testimony before Committee of Public Accounts, 2 Mar. 1971, Oireachtas Éireann, *Reports from Committees,* 19 (Part 2): 697, 686. (Hereafter this source is cited simply as 'CPA Minutes'.)

75/2 *Ibid.,* 687.

75/3 Murray's testimony, 7 Jan. 1971, *Ibid.,* 8.

75/4 CJH's testimony at Arms Trial, 19 Oct. 1970.

75/6 Boland, *Up Dev,* 44.

76/1 'The Peter Berry Papers', *Magill,* June 1980.

76/2 *Ibid.*

76/3 Haughey's testimony, 2 May 1971, CPA Minutes, 309.

77/1 Hefferon's testimony, 27 Jan. 1971, *Ibid.,* 329.

77/2-3 Capt. Kelly's report, q. Browne, 'The Arms Crisis 1970', *Magill,* May 1980.

77/3 Seamus Brady, *Arms and the Men* (Dublin, 1971), 90.

77/4 *Ibid.*

78/1 Hefferon's testimony, 27 Jan. 1971, CPA Minutes, 309.

78/2 Capt. Kelly's testimony, 3 Feb. 1972, *Ibid.,* 371.

78/5 'The Peter Berry Papers', *Magill,* June 1980.

79/2 CJH's testimony, 2 Mar. 1971, CPA Minutes, 684.

80/1-3 Fagan's testimony, 26 Jan. 1971, *Ibid.,* 213.

80/4 *Ibid.,* 220

80/5 'The Peter Berry Papers', *Magill,* June 1980.

80/8 *Ibid.*

81/1-5 *Ibid.*

81/6 Boland, *Up Dev,* 45, 72.

82/1 CJH's testimony, 2 Mar. 1971, CPA Minutes, 704.

83/5 'The Peter Berry Papers', *Magill,* June 1980.

83/6 *Ibid.*   84/1 *Ibid.*
84/4 *DEPD*, 246:642.
84/5-6 'The Peter Berry Papers', *Magill,* June 1980.
84/8 *DEPD,* 246:642.
84/10-11 'The Peter Berry Papers', *Magill,* June 1980.
85/1 Boland, *Up Dev,* 73.
85/4 *DEPD*, 246:643.
85/6 James Kelly, *Orders for the Captain?* (Dublin, 1971), 53.
86/1 'The Peter Berry Papers', *Magill,* June 1980.
86/2 CJH, statements, 8 and 25 May 1970.
86/3 *Ibid.,* 25 May 1970.

Chapter 7 (pp. 87-100)
89/1 *Sunday Press,* 26 July 1970.
89/6 Browne, 'The O'Malley-Haughey meeting', *Magill,* Dec. 1980.
90/1 O'Malley interviewed by Gay Byrne, 'Late Late Show', RTE 1
    TV, 9 May 1986.
90/2 Tom MacIntyre, *Through the Bridewell Gate* (London, 1971), 17.
90/5-6 Gibbons' testimony, 25 Sept. 1970.
91/3-10 Berry's testimony, 29 Sept. 1970.
91/14 Gibbons's testimony, 25 Sept. 1970.
92/1 *Ibid.*
92/6 Hefferon's testimony, 29 Sept. 1970.
93/1-4 *Ibid.*
93/6 MacIntyre, *Through the Bridewell Gate,* 65.
93/7 Kelly, *Orders for the Captain?,* 125.
93/8 *Private Eye,* 9 Oct. 1970, q. in *Ibid.*
94/1 Kevin Boland, *We Won't Stand (Idly) By* (Dublin, 1974), 92.
94/5 Cruise O'Brien, *States of Ireland,* 234.
95/2-6 CJH's testimony, 19 Oct. 1970.
96/2-5 *Ibid.*   96/7 *Ibid.*   97/1-9 *Ibid.*   98/1 *Ibid.*
98/2 MacIntrye, *Through the Bridewell Gate,* 172-182.
98/3 Niall McCarthy's address to the jury, 20 Oct. 1970.
98/4 McKenna's address to the jury, 22 Oct. 1970.
99/1-2 *Ibid.*
99/3-4 Henchy's instructions to the jury, 23 Oct. 1970.
100/1 *Ibid.*
100/2 Boland, *'We Won't Stand (Idly) By',* 92.
100/4 Kelly, *Orders for the Captain?,* 221.
100/5 *Irish Times,* 24 Oct. 1970.
100/6 *Ibid.*

Chapter 8 (pp. 101-114)
101/1-3 *Irish Times, 24 Oct. 1970.*

102/1 Boland, *Up Dev*, 89.

102/2 *Irish Times*, 24 Oct. 1970.

102/3 Boland, *Up Dev*, 89.

102/4 Tadhg Kennedy, *Charles J. Haughey: Kinsaley* (Dublin, 1986), 24.

103/1-6 Fleming's testimony, 9 Feb. 1970, CPA 'Minutes', 417-20.

103/7-8 CJH to P. Hogan, q. in Dáil Éireann, Committee of Public Accounts, *Interim and Final Reports*, 262.

104/1 CJH's testimony, 2 Mar. 1971, CPA 'Minutes', 494, 685, 682.

104/3 *Ibid.*, 697.

104/5 *Ibid.*, 688-9.

105/3 *Ibid.*, 704.

105/4 Brady's testimony, 16 Feb. 1971, *Ibid.*, 567.

105/5 *Ibid.*

106/1-3 Fagan's testimony, 27 Jan. 1971, *Ibid.*, 295.

106/4 Capt. Kelly's testimony, 10 Feb. 1971, *Ibid.*, 508; Fagan's testimony, 21 Jan. 1971, *Ibid.*, 212.

106/5 CJH's testimony, 2 Mar. 1971, *Ibid.*, 693, 697.

106/6 *Ibid.*, 699.

106/7 *Ibid.*, 693.

107/1-2 *Ibid.*, 693.

107/3 Pádraig Haughey's testimony, 17 Feb. 1971, *Ibid.*, 593-4.

107/4 CPA, *Interim and Final Reports*, 27.

107/5 CPA *Final Report*, 65.

108/2 *DEPD*, 246:838.

108/4 *Hibernia*, 19 Nov. 1971.

108/5 Kevin Boland interviewed by Michael O'Reagan, *Irish Times*, 13 Mar. 1983.

109/1 John N. Young, *Erskine H. Childers* (London, 1985), 157-8.

109/2 *Sunday Press*, 3 July 1983.

109/4 James Downey, *Them & Us* (Dublin, 1983), 164.

110/1 Conor Cruise O'Brien, 'Shades of Republicans', *Irish Times*, 27 Mar. 1975.

110/2 Rita Childers to Seán Browne, *Irish Times*, 4 Feb. 1975.

111/1 *DEPD*, 281:72-3.

111/2 *Ibid.*, 278:928, 933.

111/4 *Ibid.*, 929.

112/1 *Ibid.*, 294:1249.

112/4 *Irish Times*, 1 June 1977.

113/1 *Ibid.*, 2 June 1977.

113/2 *Ibid*, 1 June 1977.

114/2 Lynch interviewed on 'Today Tonight Special,' RTE TV 1, 29 May 1986.

Chapter 9 (pp. 115-128)

117/2 *Irish Times,* 6 Dec. 1979.

117/3 *DEPD,* 300:248.

117/4 *Ibid.,* 304:942.

118/1 *Ibid.,* 303:1191.

118/3 *Irish Medical Times,* 'The Haughey Performance', q. *Hibernia,* 22 Nov. 1979.

118/4 *Ibid.*

119/2 *DEPD,* 308:649-50.

119/3 *Ibid.,* 1941.

121/2 *Hibernia,* 30 Nov. 1978.

121/4 *Ibid.,* 21 Dec. 1978.

122/1 *DEPD,* 320:320-35.

122/3 *Hibernia,* 12 Apr. 1979.

123/5 Vincent Browne, 'The Making of a Taoiseach,' *Magill,* Jan. 1980.

125/1 Dick Walsh, *The Party* (Dublin, 1986), 141.

125/3 *Irish Independent,* 7 Dec. 1979.

125/4 *Cork Examiner,* 6 Dec. 1979.

126/4 *Irish Press,* 8 Dec. 1979.

126/5 *The Economist,* 15 Dec. 1979.

127/2-5 *Irish Times,* 8 Dec. 1979.

127/7 *DEPD,* 317:1323-36.

128/1 *Ibid.*

128/2 *Irish Times,* 12 Dec. 1979.

Chapter 10 (pp. 129-144)

130/1 Dermot Scott, 'Adapting the Machinery of Central Government', in David Coombes, ed., *Ireland and the European Communities* (Dublin, 1983), 79.

130/3 *Irish Times,* 21 Dec. 1979.

131/4 Vincent Browne, 'The Misconduct of the Arms Trial', *Magill,* July 1980.

132/1 *Ibid.*

132/4 Gibbons interviewed on 'This Week', RTE Radio 1, 27 July 1980.

133/2 Address, RTE TV 1, 10 Jan. 1980, Charles J. Haughey, *The Spirit of the Nation* (Cork, 1987), 324.

133/3 *Kerry's Eye,* 22 May 1981.

134/1 Haughey, *Spirit of the Nation,* 325-6.

134/2 *Hibernia,* 22 May 1980; Barry White, *John Hume* (Belfast, 1984), 215.

134/3 *Irish Times,* 22 May 1980.

135/2 *Ibid.,* 4 Nov. 1980.

136/1 *Ibid.,* 10 Nov. 1980.

137/1 *Ibid.,* 9 Dec. 1980.

137/2 Haughey, *The Spirit of the Nation,* 407; Bruce Arnold, *What Kind of Country?* (London, 1984), 155.

137/3 Ed Moloney and Andy Pollak, *Paisley* (Dublin, 1986), 340, 382-3.

138/2 Arnold, *What Kind of Country?,* 157.

138/3 *DEPD,*330:1599, 1588.

139/1 Joe Carroll, 'End of Term Report on the Neutrality Debate', *Sunday Tribune,* 3 Jan. 1982.

139/2 T. Ryle Dwyer, *De Valera's Finest Hour* (Cork, 1982), 111-44.

139/3 *DEPD,* 330:1599; Deirdre McMahon, *Republicans and Imperialists: Anglo-Irish Relations in the 1930s* (New Haven, 1984), 81.

140/1 *Irish Times,* 11 Apr. 1981.

140/3 Tom Collins, *The Irish Hunger Strike* (Dublin, 1986), 248-9.

141/5 Gene Kerrigan, 'Charlie and The Press Gang', *Magill,* Feb. 1983.

142/1 Olivia O'Leary, 'The Daddy and the Boyo', *Magill,* 14 June 1981; Vincent Browne, 'Twisting Slowly, Slowly in the Wind,' *Ibid.*

142/2 Arnold, *What Kind of Country?* 207.

142/3 Bruce Arnold, Vincent Browne, Paul Tansey, and Michael Mills, 'How We Bored the Nation', *Magill,* 14 June 1981.

143/1 *Ibid.*

143/3 *Irish Times,* 25 May 1981.

Chapter 11 (pp. 145-159)

146/3 FitzGerald interviewed on 'This Week', RTE Radio 1, 27 Sept. 1981.

146/4 *Irish Times,* 13 Feb. 1978.

147/1 FitzGerald interviewed on 'This Week', RTE Radio 1, 27 Sept. 1981.

147/2 Haughey, *The Spirit of the Nation,* 523.

147/3 Boland, *Up Dev,* 144.

147/4 Speech in Ennis, 11 Oct. 1981; Haughey, *The Spirit of the Nation,* 524.

148/1 *Ibid.*

148/2 Speech in Dundalk, 17 Oct. 1981, *Ibid.,* 531; Pádraig O'Malley, *Uncivil Wars* (Belfast, 1983), 34.

149/1 *Irish Times,* 7 Nov. 1981.

149/2 CJH at Burlington Hotel, 7 Nov., *Ibid.,* 9 Nov. 1981.

149/3 *DEPD,* 330:1580-1602.

150/2 *Ibid.*

150/3 McCreevy interviewed by Geraldine Kennedy, *Sunday Tribune,* 27 Dec. 1981.

150/4 Vincent Browne, 'Charlie McCreevy', *Magill,* Jan. 1982.

151/5 CJH, statement, 27 Jan. 1982, *Irish Times,* 28 Jan. 1982.

152/2 CJH at press conference, 28 Jan. 1982.

153/1-5 *Ibid.;* Gene Kerrigan, 'Campaign Notebook', *Magill,* Feb. 1982.

153/6 Vincent Browne, 'Editorial', *Magill,* Feb. 1982.

153/9 CJH interviewed on 'This Week', RTE Radio l, 31 Jan. 1982.

154/2 Vincent Browne, 'Learning to Cook at O'Donoghue's Ball', *Magill,* 14 Feb. 1982.

155/1-2 'Magill Debate', *Magill,* Mar. 1982.

155/3 Joe Joyce and Peter Murtagh, *The Boss* (Dublin, 1983), 25.

155/5 *Evening Herald,* 19 Feb. 1982.

156/1 *Sunday Tribune,* 21 Feb. 1982.

156/2 CJH interviewed on 'This Week', RTE Radio l, 21 Feb. 1982.

157/1 Marie Crowe, Philip Molloy and Ken Whelan, 'The Making and Breaking of a Government,' Part 5, *Irish Press,* 14 May 1982.

158/4 Extensive exerpts from CJH's press conference on 'Today Tonight', RTE TV 1, 25 Feb. 1982.

159/2 Gene Kerrigan, 'Pushing on the Open Door', *Magill,* Mar. 1982.

159/3 Crowe, Molloy and Whelan, *Irish Press,* 14 May 1982.

159/5 *Ibid.*

Chapter 12 (pp. 160-174)

161/4 CJH interviewed on 'This Week', RTE Radio l, 23 May 1982.

162/2 *Irish Times,* 9 Apr. 1982.

162/5 *Ibid.,* 24 Apr. 1982.

163/2-3 *Ibid.,* 7 May 1982.

163/4 Jim Prior, *A Balance of Power* (London, 1986), 236.

164/2-3 CJH interviewed on 'This Week', RTE Radio 1, 23 May 1982.

164/5 *Irish Times,* 18 May 1982.

165/1 *Irish Press,* 25 May 1982.

165/2 Liz Curtis, *Nothing But the Same Old Story* (London, n.d.), 80.

166/3-4 *Irish Times,* 23 June 1982.

167/2 *Ibid.,* 13 Jan. 1982.

168/1-2 CJH interviewed on 'This Week', RTE Radio l, 3 Oct. 1982.

169/1 *Evening Herald,* 2 Oct. 1982.

169/3 *Sunday Independent,* 10 Oct. 1982.

170/2 *Irish Press,* 7 Oct. 1984.

172/1 *Ibid.,* 20 Nov. 1982.

172/2 *Ibid.,* 18 Nov. 1982; *Irish Times,* 18 Nov. 1982.

172/3 *Irish Independent,* 19 Nov. 1982.

172/4 *Irish Times,* 19 Nov. 1982.

173/1-2 *Sunday Press,* 21 Nov. 1982.
173/4 *Ibid.*
173/5 CJH interviewed on 'This Week', RTE Radio 1, 21 Nov. 1982.

Chapter 13 (pp. 175-190)
175/1 *Magill,* Dec. 1981.
176/1-2 Healy, 'Down to Our Last Hero', *In Dublin,* 30 Oct. 1986.
176/3 Coogan, *Ireland Since the Rising* (London, 1966), 110.
176/4 *Irish Times,* 9 May 1970.
177/3 CJH interviewed, 'This Week', RTE Radio 1, 21 Feb. 1982; *Irish Independent,* 24 Feb. 1982.
178/1 *Irish Independent,* 25 Feb. 1982.
178/3-5 *Irish Times,* 26 Feb. 1982.
178/6-7 'Today Tonight', RTE TV 1, 25 Feb. 1982.
179/1 *Irish Press,* 26 Feb. 1982.
179/2 *Irish Independent,* 26 Feb. 1982.
179/4 *Ibid.*
180/2 Healy, 'Down to Our Last Hero', *In Dublin,* 28 Oct. 1986.
181/1 *Sunday Press,* 30 May 1982.
181/2 *Sunday Independent,* 6 June 1982; *Irish Times,* 11 May 1967.
181/3 Colley interviewed by Geraldine Kennedy, *Sunday Tribune,* 6 June 1982.
182/1 *Ibid.,* 4 July 1982.
182/2 *Irish Independent,* 23 June 1982.
182/4 *The Guardian,* 20 Aug. 1982.
183/2 *Irish Times,* 18 Aug. 1982, 16 Aug. 1982.
183/5 Joyce and Murtagh, *The Boss,* 234.
184/1 *Sunday Tribune,* 20 Aug. 1982.
184/4 *Irish Times,* 17 Aug. 1982.
185/5 Inverviewed by Pat Kenny, RTE Radio 1, 8 July 1983.
186/1 Transcript of Kennedy's telephone conversation, q. *Sunday Press,* 18 Mar. 1984.
187/2 *Irish Times,* 4 Oct. 1982.
187/3 *Sunday Press,* 21 Nov. 1982.
188/1 *Irish Independent,* 20 Nov. 1982.
188/2 *Ibid.*
189/1 *Irish Press* and *Cork Examiner,* 22 Nov. 1982; *Irish Independent* and *Irish Times,* 18 Nov. 1982.
190/1 Healy, 'Down to Our Last Hero', *In Dublin,* 30 Oct. 1986; Sunday Review, 1 July 1962; *Irish Times,* 9 May 1970; *Hibernia,* 18 Dec. 1970, 19 Feb. 1971.

Chapter 14 (pp. 191-207)
191/1 *Irish Times,* 18 Dec. 1982.

191/2 CJH interviewed on RTE, q. *Irish Times,* 20 Dec. 1982.

192/1 *DEPD,* 209:450-1.

192/2 CJH interviewed on RTE, q. *Irish Times,* 20 Dec. 1982.

193/1 Noonan's statement, q. *Irish Times,* 21 January 1983.

193/3 *Sunday Press,* 23 Jan. 1983.

193/4 Noonan's statement, q. *Irish Times,* 21 Jan. 1983.

193/7 Transcript of telephone conversation between G. Kennedy and Bruce Arnold, 7 Oct. 1982, *Sunday Press.* 18 Mar. 1984.

194/2 *Ibid.*

194/5-6 CJH interviewed on 'News at One-Thirty', RTE Radio 1, 21 Jan. 1983.

195/1 *Irish Times,* 22 Jan. 1983.

195/2 *Ibid.*

196/2-5 *Irish Times,* 25 Jan. 1983.

196/7 *Sunday Press,* 23 Jan. 1983.

196/8 *Sunday Independent,* 22 Aug. 1982; Vincent Bugliosi, *Helter Skelter* (New York, 1974), 439.

197/1 Raymond Smith, *Charles J. Haughey: The Survivor* (Dublin, 1983), 107ff; Smith, *Haughey and O'Malley,* 67ff.

198/3 *Sunday Independent,* 7 Dec. 1986.

200/2-3 *Irish Times,* 28 Jan. 1983.

200/6-7 *Irish Press,* 28 Jan. 1983.

200/8 Smith, *Charles J. Haughey,* 33.

201/2 *Irish Press* and *Cork Examiner,* both 28 Jan. 1983.

201/3 *Sunday Press,* 30 Jan. 1983. Reprinted in Desmond Fennell, *Nice People and Rednecks: Ireland in the 1980s* (Dublin, 1986), 72, 73.

202/4 *Irish Times,* 4 Feb. 1983.

203/2 CJH, statement, 3 Feb. 1983.

204/2 Briscoe interviewed on RTE, q. *Irish Times,* 5 Feb. 1983.

204/3 *Cork Examiner,* 4 Feb. 1983.

204/4 CJH, statement, q. *Sunday Independent,* 6 Feb. 1983.

205/1 CJH interviewed on 'This Week,' RTE Radio 1, 6 Feb. 1983.

205/2 *Irish Times,* 29 Jan., 7 Feb. 1983.

205/3 *Cork Examiner,* 7 Feb. 1983.

207/1 Gene Kerrigan, 'Charlie and the Press Gang', *Magill,* Feb. 1983.

207/3 Smith, *Charles J. Haughey,* 1.

Chapter 15 (pp. 208-224)

208/1 *DEPD,* 339:31.

209/2 *Sunday Press,* 23 Jan. 1983.

209/5 'Today Tonight,' RTE TV 1, 20 Jan. 1983.

210/1-2 Facsimile, Mackay memo, 23 Mar. 1983, *Sunday Tribune,* 12 May 1983.

210/5 Stephen O'Byrnes, *Hiding Behind A Face: Fine Gael Under FitzGerald* (Dublin, 1986), 304-5.

212/2 *Sunday Press*, 15 Jan. 1984.

212/3 Olivia O'Leary, 'Seán Doherty's Pot of Gold', *Magill*, Apr. 1984.

212/4 Smith to Frank Wall, 10 Apr. 1984, *Sunday Press*, 15 Apr. 1984.

213/1 New Ireland Forum, *Report*, 5.7; 5.9.

213/2 *Ibid.*, 5.10; *Irish Times*, 3 May 1984.

213/3-4 CJH interviewed by John Bowman, 'Day by Day', RTE Radio 1, 3 May 1984.

214/3 Geraldine Kennedy, 'The Discussion that Never Was', *Sunday Press*, 20 May 1984.

215/1 Gerald Barry, "Il Duce's Voce', *Sunday Tribune*, 4 Jan. 1987; Walsh, *The Party*, 147.

216/1 Smith, *Garret*, 417.

216/3 *Irish Times*, 15 Dec. 1984.

217/2 O'Malley interviewed by David Hanly, *Morning Ireland*, RTE Radio 1, 27 Feb. 1984.

217/3 Geraldine Kennedy, 'The Meeting — Who Said What', *Sunday Press*, 3 Mar. 1985.

218/1 O'Malley interviewed by Gay Byrne, 'Late Late Show', RTE 1 TV, 9 May 1970.

219/1 Haughey, *The Spirit of the Nation*, 992.

219/2 *Ibid.*, 993.

219/3 *Time*, 25 Nov. 1985.

219/4 CJH press briefing, *Irish Times*, 16 Nov. 1985.

220/1 see page 134.

220/2 Article 1 (c) of Anglo-Irish Agreement, 1985.

220/3 CJH press briefing, *Irish Times,* 16 Nov. 1985; Feehan, *Operation Brogue*, 17.

221/1-2 CJH press briefing, *Irish Times*, 16 Nov. 1985.

222/1 Paisley, interview, RTE Radio 1, 15 Nov. 1985.

222/2 CJH press briefing, *Irish Times,* 16 Nov. 1985.

223/5 Haughey, *The Spirit of the Nation*, 1159.

223/6 Gerald Barry, 'The Kiss of Death', *Sunday Tribune*, 2 Nov. 1986.

Bibliography

BOOKS

Arnold, Bruce. *What Kind of Country: Modern Irish Politics, 1968-1983.* London: Jonathan Cape, 1984.

Bell, J. Bowyer. *The Secret Army: A History of the IRA.* London: Anthony Blond Ltd, 1970.

Bloch, Jonathan and Fitzgerald, Patrick. *British Intelligence and Covert Action: Africa, Middle East and Europe since 1945.* Dingle: Brandon Press, 1983.

Boland, Kevin. *The Rise and Decline of Fianna Fáil.* Cork: Mercier Press, 1982.

Boland, Kevin. *Up Dev!* Dublin: Private, 1977.

Boland, Kevin. *'We Won't Stand (Idly) By.'* Dublin: Private, 1974.

Bowman, John. *De Valera and the Ulster Question, 1917-1973.* Oxford: Clarendon Press, 1982.

Brady, Conor. *Guardians of the Peace.* Dublin: Gill & Macmillan, 1974.

Brady, Seamus. *Arms and the Men: Ireland in Turmoil.* Dublin: Private, 1971.

Bugliosi, Vincent, with Gentry, Curt. *Helter Skelter: The True Story of the Manson Murders.* New York: Bantam Books, 1974.

Collins, Tom. *The Irish Hunger Strike.* Dublin: White Island Book Co., 1986.

Coogan, Tim Pat. *Ireland Since the Rising.* London: Pall Mall, 1966.

Coombes, David. ed. *Ireland and the European Communities: Ten Years of Membership.* Dublin: Gill & Macmillan, 1983.

Cruise O'Brien, Conor. *States of Ireland.* London: Hutchinson & Co., 1972.

Curtis, Liz. *Nothing But the Same Old Story: The Roots of Anti-Irish Racism.* London: Private, n.d.

Downey, James. *Them & Us: Britain Ireland and the Northern Question, 1969-82.* Dublin: Ward River Press, 1983.

Dwyer, T. Ryle. *De Valera's Darkest Hour: In Search of National Independence.* Cork: Mercier Press, 1982.

Dwyer, T. Ryle. *De Valera's Finest Hour: In Search of National Independence, 1932-1959*. Cork: Mercier Press, 1982.

Dwyer, T. Ryle. *Michael Collins and the Treaty: His Differences with de Valera*. Cork: Mercier Press, 1981.

Edmonds, Seán. *The Gun, the Law and the Irish People: From 1912 to the Aftermath of the Arms Trial 1970*. Tralee: Anvil Books, 1971.

Feehan, John M. *Operation Brogue: A Study of the Vilification of Charles J. Haughey Code-named 'Operation Brogue' by the British Secret Service*. Cork: Mercier Press, 1984.

Feehan, John M. *The Statesman: A Study of the Role of Charles J. Haughey in the Ireland of the Future*. Cork: Mercier Press, 1985.

Fennell, Desmond, *Nice People and Rednecks: Ireland in the 1980s*. Dublin: Gill & Macmillan 1986.

Griffith, Kenneth and O'Grady, Timothy E. *Curious Journey: An Oral History of Ireland's Unfinished Revolution*. London: Hutchinson & Co., 1982.

Haughey, Charles J. *The Spirit of the Nation: The Speeches of Charles J. Haughey*, ed. Martin Mansergh. Cork: Mercier Press, 1986.

Joyce, Joe and Murtagh, Peter. *The Boss: Charles J. Haughey in Government*. Dublin: Poolbeg Press, 1983.

Kelly, James. *Orders for the Captain?* Dublin: Private, 1971.

Kennedy, Kieran A. and Dowling Brendan R. *Economic Growth in Ireland: The Experience since 1947*. Dublin: Gill & Macmillan, 1975.

Kennedy, Tadhg. *Charles J. Haughey: Kinsaley*. Dublin: Atlantic Press, 1986.

MacIntyre, Tom. *Through the Bridewell Gate: A Diary of the Dublin Arms Trial*. London: Faber and Faber, 1971.

McMahon, Deirdre. *Republicans and Imperialists: Anglo-Irish Relations in the 1930s*. New Haven: Yale University Press, 1984.

Maher, D. J. *The Tortuous Path: The Course of Ireland's Entry into the EEC, 1948-73*. Dublin: Institute of Public Administration, 1986.

Maloney, Ed and Pollak, Andy. *Paisley*. Dublin: Poolbeg Press, 1986.

O'Byrnes, Stephen. *Hiding Behind A Face: Fine Gael under FitzGerald*. Dublin: Gill & Macmillan, 1986.

O'Malley, Padraig. *Uncivil Wars: Ireland Today*. Belfast: Blackstaff Press, 1983.

Prior, Jim. *Balance of Power*. London: Hamish Hamilton, 1986.

Smith, Raymond. *Charles J. Haughey: The Survivor*. Dublin: Aherlow Publishers, 1983.

Smith, Raymond. *Garret: The Enigma. Dr Garret FitzGerald*. Dublin: Aherlow Publishers, 1985.

Smith, Raymond. *Haughey and O'Malley: The Quest for Power*. Dublin: Aherlow Publishers, 1986.

Sunday Times Insight Team, The. *Ulster*. Harmondsworth, England: Penguin Books, 1972.

Tobin, Fergal. *The Best of Decades: Ireland in the 1960s*. Dublin: Gill & Macmillan, 1984.

Walsh, Dick. *The Party: Inside Fianna Fáil*. Dublin: Gill & Macmillan, 1986.

Watts, David. *The Constitution of Northern Ireland: Prospects and Problems*. London: Heinemann, 1981.

White, Barry. *John Hume: Statesman of the Troubles*. Belfast, Blackstaff Press, 1984.

Whyte, J.H. *Church and State in Modern Ireland, 1923-1979*. Dublin: Gill & Macmillan, 1980.

Wilner, Ann Ruth. *The Spellbinders: Charismatic Political Leadership*. New Haven and London: Yale University Press, 1984.

Young, John N. *Erskine Childers: President of Ireland*. Gerrard's Cross: Colin Smythe, 1985.

NEWSPAPERS, PERIODICALS, ETC.

Cork Examiner

Crane Bag

The Economist

Evening Herald

Evening Mail

Evening Press

The Guardian

Hibernia

Hot Press

In Dublin

Irish Independent

Irish Press

Irish Times

Magill

Sunday Independent

Sunday Press

Sunday Tribune

This Week

Index

244